Defoe's Britain

Other Books of Interest from St. Augustine's Press

Jeremy Black, *Smollett's Britain*

Jeremy Black, *The Importance of Being Poirot*

Jeremy Black, *The Age of Nightmare*

Jeremy Black, *In Fielding's Wake*

Michael Davis, *Electras: Aeschylus, Sophocles, and Euripides*

David Ramsay Steele, *The Conquistador with His Pants Down: David Ramsay Steele's Legendary Lost Lectures*

Rémi Brague, *Moderately Modern*

Marvin R. O'Connell, *Telling Stories that Matter: Memoirs and Essays*

Thomas F. Powers, *American Multiculturalism and the Anti-Discrimination Regime: The Challenge to Liberal Pluralism*

John von Heyking, *Comprehensive Judgment and Absolute Selflessness: Winston Churchill on Politics as Friendship*

Peter Fraser, *Twelve Films about Love and Heaven*

Gene Fendt, *Camus' Plague: Myth for Our World*

Jean-Luc Marion, *Descartes's Grey Ontology: Cartesian Science and Aristotelian Thought in the Regulae*

Will Morrisey, *Herman Melville's Ship of State*

Frederic Raphael and Joseph Epstein: *Where Were We?: The Conversation Continues*

Paul Murray, O.P., *Moling in Meditation: A Psalter for an Early Irish Monk*

Roger Scruton, *The Politics of Culture and Other Essays*

Roger Scruton, *The Meaning of Conservatism: Revised 3rd Edition*

Roger Scruton, *On Hunting*

Gabriel Marcel, *The Invisible Threshold: Two Plays by Gabriel Marcel*

Stanley Rosen, *The Language of Love: An Interpretation of Plato's Phaedrus*

Winston Churchill, *Savrola*

Winston Churchill, *The River War*

Defoe's Britain

JEREMY BLACK

THE WEIGHT OF WORDS SERIES

ST. AUGUSTINE'S PRESS
South Bend, Indiana

Manufactured in the United States of America.

1 2 3 4 5 6 29 28 27 26 25 24

Library of Congress Control Number:

Paperback ISBN: 978-1-58731-205-2
Hardback ISBN: 978-1-58731-206-9
Ebook ISBN: 978-1-58731-207-6

∞ The paper used in this publication meets the minimum requirements of the American National Standard for Information Sciences – Permanence of Paper for Printed Materials, ANSI Z39.48-1984.

St. Augustine's Press
www.staugustine.net

For
Katie Godfrey and Benjamin Fingerhut
With thanks for their support.

Table of Contents

Preface

> "He told us, that he had given Mrs [Elizabeth] Montagu a catalogue of all Daniel Defoe's works of imagination; most, if not all of which, as well as of his other works, he now enumerated, allowing a considerable share of merit to a man, who, bred a tradesman, had written so variously and so well. Indeed, his Robinson Crusoe is enough of itself to establish his reputation."
> Samuel (Dr) Johnson, 10 April 1778[1]

The Pursuit of the Future was a unifying theme in the life of Daniel Defoe (1660–1731), a future of individual redemption, social improvement, and political outcomes. This pursuit was inspired in part by Defoe's position as an outsider to the present. A Dissenter (Protestant Nonconformist) who took his stance as far as joining a rebellion and thus taking part in treason in 1685, Defoe was by his background and fortunes an individual who had only an episodic and precarious stance in the Establishment and, more commonly, was perforce aware of an outsider status, or at best, one highly dependent on the vagaries of political fortune, polemical and literary success, and business and legal chance. This ensures an edge to his career and, when added to demographic risk, to his life.

This study is not a biography, in whole or part, of Defoe. There are excellent studies available, and they should be pursued for the relevant details, although there is of course none of the conveniences of technology such as photography. Offering a reward of £50 for helping secure his arrest for *The Shortest Way*, the *London Gazette* of 14 January 1703 describes:

> a middle sized spare man, about 40 years old, of a brown complexion, and dark brown coloured hair, but wears a wig, a

1 R.W. Chapman (ed.), James Boswell, *Life of Johnson* (Oxford, 1980 ed.), p. 928.

> hooked nose, a sharp chin, grey eyes, and a large mole near his mouth.

This is the longest physical description of Defoe. Instead of biography, we have here a study of Britain in the Age of Defoe, a work intended to throw light on his life and to benefit from a close reading of his works, but also to stand on its own and as separate to an engagement with the author himself.

The range of Defoe's interest and the extent of his writings would make the latter a different task, as indeed would be any attempt to offer an easy coherence to personality, career and works. Yet, Defoe can be approached as a traveller, both literally so, and in his interests and imagination. These travels could take him from the English town of Colchester where the fictional Moll Flanders grows up, to the tropical Atlantic island where the fictional Robinson Crusoe is shipwrecked. There are also the travels of challenge and redemption that Defoe pursues himself and through his characters, expanding on the approach of John Bunyan in *the Pilgrim's Progress* (1678), but giving it novelistic particularity that Bunyan somewhat lacked in his writing. The journey of the evil to an earthly perdition and a hellish end was extensively rehearsed by commentators, both the explicitly religious and the 'secular.' In his range of interests, vigorous engagement with life and issues, often polemical content and style, and willingness to engage with low life, Defoe prefigures Tobias Smollett—another writer covered in this series—and, to a lesser extent, Henry Fielding, who can be more 'polite.' Defoe was an outsider, as Smollett was to be, but Fielding certainly was not.

"One whose business is observation," Defoe's description of himself in his *Tour thro' the Whole Island of Great Britain* (1724–6), captured, however, a pose as well as a reality, for he had values aplenty to offer. As a writer, Defoe brought together a reality usually presented as—and endorsed by—history, with the imaginative focus of storytelling, and the direction of, variously, propaganda, analysis, and the exemplary tale. He was an inventive as well as prolific writer.[2]

2 M.E. Novak, *Realism, Myth, and History in Defoe's Fiction* (Lincoln, NE, 1983).

The subterfuges of politeness as a social pose are those that Defoe, Smollett, and Fielding not just avoid but also scorn, and this gives their writings a particular flavor, although Defoe characterizes his work more with the Dissenter engagement with redemption. Thus, *Robinson Crusoe* (1719), a book more complex than the actual narrative, is a religious study, an account of a soul in danger, and shows how Crusoe demonstrates resilience and not despair. Here and more generally, the themes of guilt, repentance, and mercy were not some simple trade-off of human sin and divine grace, but rather deeply felt by Defoe, as narrator but also through the characters he presented. The role and work of divine Providence in the natural world were much to the fore, not least because they linked the national to the individual, Defoe's public history to the histories of fictional individuals he wrote about.

Indeed, this urgent need for redemption reflects the theme of salvation that is front and center in Defoe. It draws on his religiosity, his sense of existential political threats from the Stuarts, and even his socio-economic vision, for work is presented as crucial to prosperity. Work, and more generally appropriate behavior, is a matter of earning salvation through employment and forgiveness. This links human to divine, as well as individual to collective.

As a result, despite tensions and inconsistencies, there is a fundamental harmony between the different themes of Defoe's life, notably his Dissenter education, his work as a merchant, his employment as a journalist and government agent, his publications on socio-economic matters, and the books of his later years, the last of which account for his subsequent and current reputation. Furthermore, although his consistency might be in question from critics, a characteristic he shared with such contemporaries as Isaac Newton,[3] Defoe sought clarity in his style of writing.

For the biographer, which I am not here,[4] there is of course the need to study all stages of the life, all aspects of the career, and the entirety of

3 J. Henry, "'Pray do not ascribe that notion to me': God and Newton's Gravity," in J.E. Force and R.H. Popkin (eds), *The Books of Nature and Scripture* (Dordrecht, 1994), p. 142.

4 See most recently, N. Seager (ed.), *The Cambridge Edition of the Correspondence of Daniel Defoe* (Cambridge, 2022).

the writings. That is valuable but only engages with part of the focus of present public interest in Defoe. As with Charles Dickens or George Bernard Shaw, it is instructive to consider Defoe as a journalist, but that is not an explanation of why his non-journalistic works appear in popular imprints. The novels make the greatest impact today, and yet can be seen in part as an instance of Defoe's wider and impressive ability to write well in and across genres. His sense of genres as overlapping was captured not only in presenting novels as histories, but also in the *Review* on 24 November 1705 when he refers to "a double capacity, as a speech, and as a pamphlet." Exactly the same could be said of sermons. In the *Consolidator* of that year, Defoe further shows his range as a writer when he offers a satirical account of humanity from the perspective of a lunar commentator.

This book fits into a sequence of books I have written in which writers are used to throw light on their times, and vice versa, a sequence beginning with Fleming, Shakespeare and Austen, and continuing with Dickens, Christie, Doyle, Fielding, Smollett, and the Gothic novelists. I have found the approach a fascinating one, not least in leading me to re-read much from earlier years. With Defoe, I return in part to the years I spent on my doctorate. I recall with great pleasure those individuals who have inspired and helped me. For this book, I have benefited greatly from the comments of Laura Alexander, Jonathan Barry, Grayson Ditchfield, Alan Downie, Perry Gauci, William Gibson, Jonathan Oates, and Pat Rogers on all or part of earlier drafts. They do not necessarily agree with my argument, but all advice has been most welcome. I know how much time it takes. I am happy to dedicate this book to Katie Godfrey and Benjamin Fingerhut with thanks for their support, which is much appreciated.

Abbreviations

Add.	Additional Manuscripts
AE	Paris, Ministère des Affaires Etrangères
AM	Archives de la Marine
AN	Paris, Archives Nationales
Ang	Angleterre
Beinecke	New Haven, Connecticut, Beinecke Library
BL	London, British Library, Department of Manuscripts
Bod.	Oxford, Bodleian Library, Department of Manuscripts
Chewton	Chewton House, Chewton Mendip, papers of 1st Earl Waldegrave
CP	Correspondance Politique
HL	Huntington Library, San Marino, California
HMC	Historical Manuscript Commission reports
LO	Loudoun papers
NA	London, National Archives
NAS	Edinburgh, National Archives of Scotland
SP	State Papers

1. Defoe and Modernity

Taking an active role in rebellion in 1685 was the most dramatic event in Defoe's life. It could have cost him his life, either in battle or in the subsequent judicial retribution associated with Judge Jefferies and his "Bloody Assizes." Defoe's role could also have led to his being spared but, as a punishment transported—as were some of those about whom he wrote—to the colonies as cheap labor, and certainly kept there until the overthrow of James II's political control in the colonies provided a fresh shake of the dice. Luckily, Defoe escaped capture and punishment.

This role was a young man's action, but also one that reflected necessity for an active Dissenter (Protestant Nonconformist). Indeed, Monmouth's rebellion in 1685 was in part a penultimate sequel to the bitter civil conflict, including civil wars, of 1639–60, as well as the efforts for the creation of a Dissenter future. In the *Review* on 22 December 1705, Defoe was to provide a bleak account of the anxieties of his youth. Referring to the fears of Dissenters in 1678–88, he wrote of the "terrible apprehensions we had of the growth of Popery, and its introduction in this kingdom, hand in hand with slavery." Defoe referred in this article to writing out some of the Bible because he feared that English translations would be banned in a return to Catholic Latinity, and also to his belief at the time in the Popish Plot of 1678, the false notion of a Catholic conspiracy. Indeed, it is possible to trace the influence of Thomas Hobbes, author of *Leviathan* (1651) and not the most optimistic of thinkers, in Defoe's work,[1] while John Bunyan, alongside Richard Baxter, the greatest Dissenter writer of the generation before Defoe, spent much time in prison.[2] This was in marked contrast to

1 C. Kay, *Political Constructions: Defoe, Richardson, and Sterne in Relation to Hobbes, Home, and Burke* (Ithaca, 1988).

2 C. Hill, *A Turbulent, Seditious, and Factious People: John Bunyan and His Church, 1628–1688* (London, 1988).

John Dryden's very different ability to turn his praise from Oliver Cromwell to support for Charles II and later to produce pro-Catholic works under James II.

Throughout Defoe's life there was a fear of Catholic plots and, as Defoe lay dying in 1731, French invasion preparations indeed were rumored as the Anglo-French alliance collapsed. Many of the fears were lurid. In 1715, Edmund Gibson, then Archdeacon of Surrey, noted the belief that there was to have been a massacre in London of Protestants as part of the Jacobite uprising.[3]

Monmouth's throw of the dice was not to achieve its goal. However, James II (VII of Scotland; r.1685–8), the target of the rebellion, was to be overthrown in what became to its supporters the "Glorious Revolution" of 1688–9. In practice, that transformation, however, was largely achieved in England, as later in Ireland, by invading Dutch, Danish and other troops under William III of Orange (r. 1689–1702). They provided the muscle for an opposition that could not otherwise overthrow James and that wanted William to come to their rescue.

Defoe praised the "Glorious Revolution," but he had risked his life in 1685; as he did not really do three years later, although events then might have worked out differently. There was a novelistic character to the Monmouth rebellion in the adventure story of a young hero. However, aside from being totally unsuccessful, it was far from easy for those who took part but escaped, and it left long shadows. Indeed, Defoe referred to the defeat at Sedgemoor in his *Tour*, as did Henry Fielding in *Tom Jones* (1749) with the "Man on the Hill," who also had escaped Sedgemoor occurring in action set in 1745.[4] When Defoe was an infant there had been unsuccessful attempts to overthrow the newly acceded Charles II (r. 1660–85), but these conspiracies did not have the traction of that mounted in 1685 against his brother James by one of Charles' illegitimate sons, John the Duke of Monmouth. Sailing from his exile in the United Provinces (Netherlands), the rash Monmouth landed unopposed, with eighty-two companions and a supply of arms, at Lyme Regis. Such invasions had

3 Gibson to William Nicolson, Bishop of Carlisle, 1 Oct. 1715, Bod., Add. A. 269 f. 40.

4 H. Fielding, *Tom Jones* (London, 1749), VIII, 14.

become almost a norm, often successful, onward from 1399 to the overthrow of Richard III by Henry Tudor, later Henry VII, in 1485. Two centuries later, although the Dorset militia at Bridport resisted an attack, another militia force at Axminster collapsed. Recruits came in rapidly to Monmouth, in what was an area with many Dissenters. In his *Tour*, Defoe was to comment on the large number of sheep in the area, but that also contributed to political radicalism, with smaller tenants gradually ousted from their lands in favor of large entrepreneurs. Cloth workers moreover were easily radicalized.[5]

Having been proclaimed king at Taunton on 19 June, Monmouth had eight thousand men by the time he marched on Bristol. However, the strength of the resistance deterred him from attacking the city, and Bath also did not surrender. Losing the initiative, Monmouth fell back into Somerset where, on 6 July, he attempted a night attack on the recently-advanced royal army. Defoe suggested that this came close to success, only for the surprise to be lost. This was a fate that was to wreck a similar attempt by Monmouth's (legitimate) distant relation, James' grandson, Charles Edward Stuart (Bonnie Prince Charlie) shortly before he was crushed at Culloden in 1746.

In both battles, as also with Charles II's defeat by Cromwell at Worcester in 1651—to which Defoe referred in his *Tour*—the poorly-organized rebel army was totally defeated by its experienced opponents' superior firepower. Unlike Charles II and Bonnie Prince Charlie, each of whom had novelistic escapes, the fleeing Monmouth was captured while hiding in a ditch. The bungling executioner required five blows with the axe to dispatch him. A simultaneous Scottish rising by Archibald, 9th Earl of Argyll, rapidly failed and Argyll was likewise executed.

By 1685, Defoe was a merchant and figure in London Dissenter society. Born in London, the son of James Foe, a tailor-chandler, he had initially prepared for the Presbyterian ministry, most particularly by attending Charles Morton's Dissenting Academy at Newington Green with Samuel Wesley. As with his previous schooling at Dorking, Defoe was under the influence of significant Dissenter figures, and this would have been a major

5 J.H. Bettey, "South Dorset: economic pressures and village desertions," in *Notes and Queries for Somerset and Dorset*, 33, 333 (March 1991), pp. 3–6.

pedigree for a minister. However, in the early 1680s, Defoe had a major change of direction, becoming not a cleric but, instead, a hosiery merchant in London, and marrying and receiving a useful dowry. Yet, far from accommodating to the politico-religious ascendancy, he remained a Dissenter and was to be buried in Bunhill Fields, the major London cemetery for Dissenters.

Defoe's role in 1685 throws some light on what might appear the clear signs of modernity in his work, notably the embrace of trade and industry in his *Tour*, and the more general association, by both Whigs and later commentators, of Whiggism with progress. Indeed, that is very much the approach adopted by Pat Rogers in his important study of the *Tour*.[6] A positive treatment of an optimistic account, this is a confident discussion that fruitfully approaches the context, conception, and contents of this work from a number of angles, notably those of form and function, time and place. The key theme is that of an epic by Defoe greeting modernization, that of the "Glorious Revolution" of 1688–9, and a series of eighteenth-century iterations—notably the Agricultural, Industrial, and Transport—the last a topic that greatly fascinates Rogers and to which he attaches considerable attention.

Optimistic accounts of revolutions, as in "Agricultural Revolution," "Financial Revolution," and others, however, can underplay the extent to which contemporaries generally lacked such happy confidence and frequently sought to understand more troubling experiences. Thus, in 1725, during an international crisis, Thomas the Duke of Newcastle, then Secretary of State for the Southern Department, was concerned about "the fall of public credit," which was attributed by a source in the General Post Office to the interaction of rumor and a lack of confidence:

> it proceeds from the management of a broker or brokers who have the character of being employed by men of figure in the government. They sold and continue to sell such large sums that the rest naturally conclude cannot be for people of small figure, several stories are invented and industriously handed

6 P. Rogers, *Defoe's* Tour *and Early Modern Britain: Panorama of the Nation* (Cambridge, 2021).

> about that abundance of honest timorous people are drawn into sell.[7]

In his contemporary *Complete English Tradesman* (1725–7), Defoe notes concerns about financial failure.[8] As in the *Tour*, Defoe's interest in transport and travel suggests a ready ability to reach places, but the reality for contemporaries—and, ironically, the "truth" of his fiction—was very different. To a degree, the latter challenges the idea that "mapping" is the analytical device best suited to approach Defoe's work,[9] as—alongside his wish to overcome space through understanding it—there is for his fictional characters unsteadiness in the comparable process.

Furthermore, the concepts, for example of particular revolutions, deserve scrutiny. Thus, while the concept of the public sphere, one in which Defoe has been readily located by modern commentators, has attracted scholarly attention—and indeed become fashionable—doubts regarding its scale, coherence, and impact direct attention to the need to handle this established concept with care,[10] and especially given its secularizing agenda. Care is also needed with the fashionable idea of "politeness" in society.

Defoe was scarcely alone in emphasizing the value of trade. In his *Magnae Britanniae Notitia: or, The Present State of Great Britain* (1726), a work far less accessible than Defoe's *Tour*, John Chamberlayne trumpets:

> Great Britain may be justly counted the principal nation for trade in the whole world, and indeed the most proper for trade, being an island which hath many commodious ports and havens, natural products, considerable manufactures, great en-

7 J. Bell to Newcastle, 29 Sept. 1725, NA. SP. 35/58 f. 96.

8 Defoe, *The Complete English Tradesman* (2 vols, 1725–7), I, vi.

9 See the very interesting, K. Ellison, K. Kincade and H.F. Nelson (eds.), *Topographies of the Imagination: New Approaches to Daniel Defoe* (New York, 2014).

10 J.A. Downie, "How Useful to Eighteenth-Century English Studies is the Paradigm of the 'Bourgeois Public Sphere'?" in *Literature Compass*, 1 (2003), pp. 1–18, and "Public and Private: The Myth of the Bourgeois Public Sphere," in C. Wall (ed.), *A Concise Companion to the Restoration and Eighteenth Century* (Oxford, 2005), pp. 58–79. See also J. Black, *Why the Industrial Revolution happened in Britain* (Stroud, 2023).

> couragement from the state for the sake of customs and duties paid, the breeding of seamen, and the increase of shipping, freedom in religion, the pleasure and healthfulness of our clime, the ease and security of our government; all conducing to the encouragement of maritime trade.

Alongside similarities, however, Defoe was very concerned to emphasize contrasts between his work and that of other writers,[11] and in the case of the *Tour* in particular differentiated himself from historians.

The focus on trade in the *Tour* and its later discussion might lead to an underestimation of the intensely political character of the 1720s, the period of the South Sea Bubble, the Atterbury Plot, the general election of 1722, and a new Whig Split from 1725. In addition, Britain was close to war in 1725–7; while, separately, there was a serious agricultural depression and problems in the major industry, that of woollen cloth production. Not only was the Whiggism Defoe espoused unstable in these years, as it had markedly been already so with the Whig Split of 1717–20 and the still potent divisions of the early 1720s; but, in addition, there were Tory views as well as the Jacobitism that was attractive to foreign powers opposed to the British Crown—such as Sweden, of which Charles, 2nd Viscount Stanhope, a Secretary of State, confidentially warned in 1716—in an account straight out of conspiracy commentary, both fictional and factual, and one that also referred to the success of the Dutch raid on the naval anchorage in the Medway River in 1667:

> 10 or 12 men of war from the port of Gothenburg might … come up the river [Thames], destroy our docks and naval stores, and land forces in the very heart of the kingdom without our being in a condition to hinder them.[12]

Assumptions about change that were different from those of a benign modernization can be approached from the Tory writers of the period, such

11 *Tour*, 9.

12 Townshend to fellow Secretary of State, William Stanhope, 15 Sept. 1716, Maidstone, Kent Archive Office, 0145/30.

as their leading journalist under George I, Nathaniel Mist, whose weekly newspaper Defoe infiltrated on behalf of the government. The same is true regarding the need to engage with mainstream Church of England writers of the period, as well as their later scholarly commentators. Their perspectives can be very different from the axiomatic Whig ones.

Texts, indeed, should be clearly placed in the multiple contexts in which they would have been read. In this case, it is the inherently contentious and multifaceted character of modernization, as well as debates at the time about it—debates conducted with a lack of agreement about past, present, and future—that are striking. Attempts today to present only one view therefore face problems. Rogers argues that there is an epic quality to the *Tour*:

> … it seeks to portray the greatness of the newly united Britain as a great adventure, fit for panegyrical treatment in spite of the many challenges that the nation confessedly faces.... Along with many contemporaries, Defoe thought that he was recounting the story of Britain at the moment when she had just reached the point where she could live up to an epic.[13]

Just so, but many contemporaries did not take this view. Moreover, underlining the range of reference and resonance, but also the sometimes ambiguity of Defoe, there is in the *Tour* not only Defoe as an anticipator, but also a retrospective account of his earlier journeys, notably in the 1700s, but also before. Separately, as with other travelogues, on the continuum from real to imaginary, there was a stay-at-home delight for the reader. Yet, for the works of the period—literary and otherwise— there was a forcing-house of the immediate, through which these were perceived in different perspectives. Defoe was obviously a man of his time as well as whatever it means to be a citizen of the modern world, but both had a range of meanings and should be seen in that light. Defoe, his *Tour* and his period are at once too protean and complex to be readily summarized. Thus, in his *Defoe's Politics: Parliament, Power, Kingship and* Robinson Crusoe (1991), Manuel Schonhorn challenges the view that Defoe should be seen as a "modern."

13 Rogers, *Defoe's Tour*, p. 84.

Instead, Schonhorn emphasizes Defoe's traditionalism in the portrayal of William III as a guardian-king maintaining order by the use of the power of the sword.

Defoe's very biography offered him different experiences as well as varied perspectives through which to shape them. As a successful merchant, Defoe, who wrote against James, had supported William's seizure of power. This, however, was to be followed by an enforced change of direction, one due to Defoe's over-extension in business projects, notably marine insurance, which was rendered more risky by the fiscal and economic turmoil and warfare of the early 1690s. He went bankrupt, for £17,000, a formidable sum in 1692. In his search for expedients, Defoe fortunately found patronage that took him into public office—albeit at a minor level—but in anticipation of Henry Fielding benefiting from the same. Alongside continued business roles, this officeholding was followed by further work for the government that helped in his political identification by others as well as himself. The latter led to his writing important works, beginning with *The True-Born Englishman* (1701), an attack on Tory chauvinism, followed by *The Shortest Way with the Dissenters* (1702), a similar attack on religious intolerance, but one in which the irony he could generally handle so well provides his opponents with an opportunity to have him imprisoned.

Robert Harley, a moderate Tory minister, was instrumental in helping Defoe reinvent himself as a government agent with a link to the top, largely through providing Harley with information and also in writing *The Review*. This enabled Defoe to survive renewed economic failure. With a Presbyterian and Country Whig background, Harley had a complex passage to becoming a moderate Tory.

The fall of Harley in 1714 brought Defoe fresh problems, including a renewed experience of prison. In 1715, he settled with the new Whig ministry that had gained power the previous year and wrote on its behalf. Defoe eventually moved in a new direction with a series of successful novels in 1719–24, from which his fame derives. These novels were presented as factual, as in the preface of *Moll Flanders* (1722), which begins:

> The world is so taken up of late with novels and romances, that it will be hard for a private history to be taken for genuine,

> where the names and other circumstances of the person are concealed.

In that for *Roxana* (1724):

> … this story differs from most of the modern performances of this kind … the foundation of this is laid in truth of fact; and so the work is not a Story, but a History.

In his novels, Defoe captured the realities of English society rather than fantasies of politeness that interested other writers.

He followed these by differently factual works, most famously *A Tour thro' the Whole Island of Great Britain* (1724–6), but also others including *The Complete English Tradesman* (1725–7), and *An Essay on the History and Reality of Apparitions* (1727). Health and legal problems, however, bedevilled his last years, and Defoe went into seclusion as a result, dying in 1731.

The scale, range, and often immediacy of Defoe's writings offered a variety of views, notably on high politics, but there were also key themes. An essential conservatism, at least as far as social image is concerned, is suggested by Defoe's portrayal in the *Tour* of Wilton House, "the seat of that ornament of nobility and learning, the Earl of Pembroke," Thomas the 8th Earl, who was a great collector of sculptures, rare books, and jewels, earning criticism from Pope for his taste. Defoe hitherto had largely praised newly-established stately homes, such as Wanstead House, the palatial seat of the Child family, bankers who had only reached the peerage in 1718, or the "fine houses of the citizens of London," near Carshalton "some of which are built with such a profusion of expense, that they look rather like seats of the nobility, than the country houses of citizens and merchants."[14] In the case of Wilton, an encomium on the building and its grounds, Defoe offered praise for longevity, for the new palace was that of a long-established family:

> that yet more glorious sight, of a noble princely palace, constantly fitted with its noble and proper inhabitants; vis. the lord

14 *Tour*, 2.

> and proprietor, who is indeed a true patriarchal monarch, reigns here with an authority agreeable to all his subjects (family); and his reign is made agreeable, by his first practising the most exquisite government of himself, and then guiding all under him by the rules of honour and virtue; being also himself perfectly master of all the needful arts of family government.... [T]he family like a well governed city appears happy, flourishing, and regular, groaning under no grievance, pleased with what they enjoy, and enjoying everything which they ought to be pleased with.[15]

Although Defoe's commercial ethic could apparently be challenged by the presentation of an older, nobler society in Jacobite literature,[16] it is not only there. In practice, as this example shows, Defoe could also draw on the latter stance. This range, more generally, reflects the variety of circumstances, but also the eclectic nature of Defoe's sources and the speed of his composition. The last gave the *Tour* and other writings a somewhat improvised character, rather than a smoothness of polish, or, in this case, revision in the cause of consistency.

Establishing Defoe's views is made particularly complex because of major debates over the attribution of works to him, debates that became more pronounced onward from the 1980s. Attribution is directly linked to issues of Defoe's consistency and, thus, integrity and personality.[17] Charges of inconsistency and mercenary considerations were frequent in the partisan debates of the period, and Defoe was no exception, although he also earned particular obloquy,[18] as with Charles Gildon's attack in *The*

15 *Tour*, 3.

16 M. Pittock, "Jacobite literature: love, death and violence," in P. Dukes and J. Dunkley (eds.), *Culture and Revolution* (London, 1990), p. 39.

17 W.R. Owens and P.N. Furbank, "Defoe and the Dutch Alliance: Some Attributions Examined," in *British Journal for Eighteenth-Century Studies*, 9 (1986), pp. 169–81, esp. p. 181; and *The Canonisation of Daniel Defoe* (New Haven, 1988). For recent works see, for example, N. Seager, "Literary Evaluation and Authorship Attribution, or Defoe's Politics at the Hanoverian Succession," in *Huntington Library Quarterly*, 80 (2017), pp. 47–69.

18 Anon., *A Letter from a Tory Freeholder* (London, 1712), p. 12.

Life and Strange and Surprising Adventures of Mr D—De F—(1719). At the same time, few found consistency easy in the rapidly-changing politics of the three decades after the Glorious Revolution. Defoe's inconsistencies might be considered alongside the more general and repeated remarks that the national character was changeable, passing from optimism and menaces to panicky terrors.[19]

So also it is with the issue then, and now, of attribution. This was scarcely unique to Defoe, not least due to a general lack of original manuscripts, but the situation has ensured a lack of certainty in the Defoe canon that amounts to instability. Moreover, there were to be such claims about later writers as well, including Fielding.

From another direction, let us note the multiple contingencies involved in the "Glorious Revolution," notably James' mental collapse in 1688, and the extent to which the future—the modern world—could well have been Stuart and absolutist. This outcome would have set Britain on a pattern similar to that of most European states. Defoe himself was well aware of contingencies, as read in his far-from-short discussion in the *Tour* of the failed French-backed Jacobite invasion attempt of Scotland in 1708. Contingencies helped undermine consistency, and this occurs in foreign policy as much as domestic politics. *Mist's Weekly Journal* of 12 September 1719 provides an apt discussion of the interplay between long-term antipathies and short-term transience:

> we think princes should never covet to rivet in the minds of their own and the neighbouring nations, strong national aversions to, or antipathies against, one another; for as there are hardly two neighbouring nations to be found in the world, but what have alternately been both friends and enemies, sometimes such national antipathies have been a great obstacle to their uniting, when at the same time their interests have summoned them to show the strictest friendship, and to exert acts, even of mutual kindness and affection.

19 Iberville, French envoy, to Huxelles, French Foreign Minister, 6 Jan. 1716, AE. CP. Ang. 288 f. 22.

Also significant is the sense that the presentation of Defoe as "modern" underplays the extent to which Dissenters had their own chronology of history and redemption. In the *Tour* Defoe very much offered a Protestant account, and one not of an establishment Protestantism but from a Dissenter background. Thus, he used his visit to St. Andrews to write of the murder near there in 1679 of James Sharp, the Archbishop:

> This murder is matter of history, but is so foolishly, or so partially, or so imperfectly related by all that have yet written of it, that posterity will lose both the fact and the cause of it in a few years more.... [T]he archbishop had been a furious and merciless persecutor, and, indeed, murderer of many of the innocent people, merely for their keeping up their field-meetings.... [T]hey saw the bishop coming towards them in his coach, when one of them says to the other, we have not found the person we looked for; but lo, God has delivered our enemy, and the murderer of our brethren into our hands, against whom we cannot obtain justice by the law, which is perverted. But remember the words of the text, If ye let him go, thy life shall be required for his life.

Defoe continued by noting that "however Providence ordered it ... none of the murderers ever fell into the hands of justice," whereas another individual, who had not actually wielded a knife, was executed. This was contextualized by the next historical episode, that of the battle of Sheriffmuir (1715), in which, according to Defoe, "the good Protector of Great Britain ... gave that important victory to King George's troops," as opposed to their Jacobite opponents. This was somewhat misleading, being true for the aftermath rather than for the battle itself. Again, for the battle of Killiecrankie (1689): "Providence had better things in store for Great Britain."[20] On a frequent pattern, that of being on the side of the observer, Providence was clearly linked in this case to the present order.

Defoe referred to conquests in Scotland by Agricola, Edward I, and Cromwell—adding of the last two, "our English Caesars have outgone the

20 *Tour*, 13.

Romans"—before explaining why he preferred the Hanoverians, in the shape of George I, to Cromwell whom he described as ruling "with a rod of iron":

> just now we find King George's forces marching to the remotest corners, nay, ferrying over into the western, and north-western islands; but then this is not as a foreigner and conqueror, but as a sovereign, a lawful governor, and father of the country, to deliver from, not entangle her in the chains of tyranny and usurpation.[21]

This, of course, was not how northern and eastern Scotland regarded the imposition of the power of George I and, later, George II.

Religious factors can be seen more generally in Defoe's work as in his discussion in *Roxana* (1724) of marriage, which is presented as "decreed by Heaven." The centrality of the self in Defoe's novels, notably *Roxana*, might make Defoe appear modern,[22] but much of this centrality is in terms of established issues such as repentance.

More generally, the religious dimension does not sit conveniently with the standard terms and content of debates about modernity. Partly as a result, but also due to the extent to which modernity itself is really a categorization of thought and experience—and an often rhetorical one at that—there is need for care when labelling Defoe in these terms. Aside from his strong religiosity, he was interested in aspects of magic. Indeed, there are similarities to Isaac Newton (1642–1727), who also sought to apply reason to the world of nature, but, moreover, had alchemical interests.

It is better to think of Defoe as an individual who drew on a range of intellectual concepts from political economy as a way to understand society, and more significantly to reason as a duty for the devout in order to understand God's purpose. In particular, this understanding offered the possibility of moving beyond clerical attempts to obfuscate to the profit of the Church and the misleading of humanity. For Defoe, his Dissenter convic-

21 *Tour*, 13.

22 P. Backscheider, *A Being More Intense: A Study of the Prose Works of Bunyan, Swift, and Defoe* (New York, 1984).

tions therefore led him to scrutinize creation, not in order to bring in a secular future prefiguring of Adam Smith's *Wealth of Nations* (1776) and a liberalism of economic rationale, but rather to understand and further God's purposes by bringing the potential of creation, both individual and collective, to a fruition that set Providence and humanity together as one.

2. Life and Death

"One whose business is observation, as mine was."
Defoe on Kirkcudbright, *Tour*, 12

Defoe's bluntest book was his account of the Great Plague in 1665. Commercial advantage played a role in the choice of topic because Marseille was affected by plague in 1720–1 and it was by no means clear that this would not spread to Britain. If the Black Death of the 1340s could spread rapidly to Britain, then it was by no means certain why there should not be the same in the 1720s. Thus, Defoe's book—purportedly an account by a contemporary of the Great Plague in 1665—was at once a guide to the present, a commercial profit from current concerns, a story of great interest, and an attempt to understand divine purpose. The last was more at the heart of the book than a reading in terms of disease-prevention would suggest. Indeed, the reprinting of the work and discussion of it during the Covid pandemic of 2020–22 were characterized by just such an ahistoricism as it neglected Defoe's religious theme. Simultaneously, like his journalism of the time and his other more overt guides to how to deal with plague, Defoe was contributing to a large-scale medical and political debate about the causes and proper responses to plague, including the parliamentary acts.

Defoe captured the Great Plague through individual stories as well as focusing on the pandemic as a whole. With the skill of a novelist, he also manages to offer a sense of suspense to what was a well-known tale, and to discuss the multiple differences between contemporary views and predictions, and present assessments.

Destroying hopes that bubonic plague was in decline, the brutal and rapidly-spread Great Plague of 1665 had fewer deaths as a percentage of London's population than some earlier plagues, while some other places in 1665 had more than in London, but more people died there than elsewhere, and therefore it was in percent that the plague hit London hardest. The 1636 epidemic had killed over 60,000 people, but 1665 was to see even more lost. As deaths mounted, helped by a long, hot summer, red crosses were painted on the doors of the infected houses in a fruitless attempt at isolation.

Civil society did not break down during the Great Plague. Indeed, Defoe praised the ability of the City authorities to provide security and sustenance, and, by comparison, criticized the Crown. Yet there was an inability to keep records as accurate as is suggested by Defoe's thoughtful use of the Bills of Mortality in order to discuss the course of the epidemic. Although not all deaths would have been from plague, City records indicate that some 68,596 people died during the epidemic, although the actual number of deaths is suspected to have exceeded 100,000 out of a total population estimated at 460,000. The authorities could not keep up as deaths mounted in the long, hot summer, while the diarist Samuel Pepys was told by his parish clerk, "There died nine this week though I have returned but six." Moreover, the recording did not work well for Quakers or poor transients. Dead paupers were thrown into large burial pits such as one at Tottenham Court.

Many fled London, including the Court, the wealthy, most doctors, and a large number of the parochial clergy. This exodus helped ensure the spread of the plague outside London, both in the South-East and more broadly, a process covered by Defoe and which hit hard places linked to London such as Newcastle.

The flight of clergy was a serious issue as, in response to the crisis, many of the churches in London were thronged. In a classic instance of his partisanship, Defoe made much of this flight, contrasting it with the determination of Dissenting clergy to stay and continue to minister to all, not only their flock but also the members of the Established Church. After the epidemic, there was no let-up in measures against the Dissenters.

For Defoe, this episode was still of great weight over a half-century later. This reflected the turmoil of his early years, although that was a turmoil heard of in retrospect rather than one that he could have grasped readily at the time. The Act of Uniformity of 1662 had led to the ejection of Presbyterian clergy from their parishes, and, under the Conventicle Act, worship with five or more people was forbidden unless it was in accordance with Anglican rites. The Five Mile Act of 1665 prohibited Dissenting ministers from living within five miles of any corporate town or place in which they had served prior to the act. They also had to take an oath of non-resistance to royal authority before they could teach. As manifested in the Great Plague, however, God's Providential purpose to Dissenters made a mockery of such legislation.

Beginning in April 1665, the Great Plague did not abate until the November frosts. It saw London's economy ruined, a topic discussed by Defoe. Public places, moreover, were closed, sports banned, a 9:00 pm curfew imposed, and fairs prohibited.

This brutal visitation was to be the last major outbreak, and indeed Scotland had had its last in 1649. However, the end to such epidemics could not be foreseen. For Defoe in the *Journal*, the explanation was that of God:

> Nothing but the immediate finger of God, nothing but omnipotent power, could have done it. The contagion despised all medicine … it pleased God, with a most agreeable surprise, to cause the fury of it to abate.

In the event, mutations in the rat and flea populations were probably more important in preventing a recurrence of plague than clumsy and erratic public health measures, or alterations in human habitat thanks to construction in brick, stone, and tile that would in large part come about due to the Great Fire of London in 1666, though the plague hit worst those parts of London not affected by the Fire or by rebuilding after it, possibly because many of the city's inhabitants were able to leave town. Quarantine had a role in preventing the spread of plague, and that linked concern about the practicalities of the Marseille plague with the effectiveness of measures taken in 1665.

Although not linked to plague, Defoe was to comment extensively on building material in his *Tour*. There was a pronounced social dimension in building materials, John Evelyn (not the famous diarist, but an office-holding relative) reporting in 1702: "Truro a very pretty neat town built of stone and covered with slate as most of the houses in this county [Cornwall] are, excepting those which belong to the poor sort which generally consist of mud walls covered with thatch."[1] Soon after, Evelyn added: "John Evelyn of Nuffield, a proper handsome young gentleman very promising in all respects and member of Parliament for Bletchingley in Surrey was taken ill of the smallpox … he died … in the 24th year." This was followed by a Latin tag from Horace that translates as "Why should our grief for a man so loved know any shame or limit."[2]

The frequency of the death of the young, a frequency that Defoe offered his fictional creations, did not prevent grief for them. There were many to mourn. Thirty-eight percent of the children born in the town of Penrith between 1650 and 1700 died before reaching the age of six.[3] Defoe visited Penrith in his *Travels*, but there was no reason to comment on such commonplace statistics. Roxana loses a daughter "at about six weeks old." Defoe also had lost a daughter.

The eighteenth century was to see significant population growth, but that was not the case during Defoe's lifetime. Indeed, after the growth of 1500–1650, Britain's population did not rise greatly for a century. In England, it fell between 1660 and 1690, probably due to enteric diseases, gastric diseases, and declining fertility. Disease was particularly serious because Poor Law relief helped to limit the demographic consequences of poor harvests. There was much discrepancy in population changes regionally, and not least in migration. London's growth from 1650 to 1750—from about 400,000 to about 675,000—was such that it absorbed about half the surplus of births over deaths from the rest of England. In Ireland and Scotland the population fell in the 1690s, and Scotland's population in 1745 was roughly the same as a century earlier. There was no official census until 1801, but the population of England and Wales probably rose from 5.07 million in 1666 to 5.59 in 1731, with the widespread death crises of 1696–9, 1727–30 and 1741–2 wiping out the growth of the intervening years in many areas. In Warwickshire in 1727–20, twenty-one percent of the population died in the town of Alcester and 30–35 percent in Stratford and

1 BL. Evelyn papers, vol. 49 f. 29.

2 *Ibid.* f. 33.

3 S. Scott and C.J. Duncan, "Smallpox epidemics at Penrith in the 17th and 18th centuries," in *Transactions of the Cumberland and Westmorland Antiquarian and Archaeological Societies*, 93 (1993): p. 159.

Bidford.[4] England dominated Britain demographically, although much less so than today. In 1689, the English population was about 4.9 million, compared to about 2 million for Ireland, about 1.2 million for Scotland and about 0.3 million for Wales.

The demographic regime was a composite and interaction of millions of events, many unplanned, and these existed in a dynamic situation, with epidemics, marriages, and migration particularly variable. As a result, the aggregate family structure of the age was unstable, albeit differently unstable from today. There were some comparisons that may surprise, but the context was generally different. For example, marriages were generally late. At the end of the seventeenth century, English men married at about 28 and women at about 27, but because, unlike today, most childbearing was within marriage, having children was thus postponed until an average of more than ten years past puberty, which itself occurred later than in modern Britain. The average age at marriage did not fall markedly until the 1730s, and this was a product of improved work opportunities at that time. Earlier, Defoe had supported an expansion of the population in order to provide more workers; "while there is a foot of land in England unimproved, we cannot have too many people."[5]

Meanwhile, diseases continued to be virulent and fatal. Immunity to smallpox, which replaced the plague as the most feared disease, was low, not least because a virulent strain began to have an impact in the second half of the seventeenth century.

Everyone was at risk. The stately homes of the period offered scant defence then and little guide now to the frequent harshness of life, a harshness that affected all ranks of society. Queen Mary died of smallpox in 1694, and none of Queen Anne's children survived her, which brought Stuart rule to an end. The details for individual families reflect a general harshness. Sir Hugh Acland (1637–1713), the owner of Killerton in Devon, survived his son John and was succeeded by his grandson, another Hugh, who lived from early 1696 till 1724. Edward Phelips IV (1678–1734) of Montacute

4 A. Gooder, "The population crisis of 1727–1730 in Warwickshire," in *Midland History* 1(1972): pp. 1–22.

5 *Review*, 23, 30 June 1709; P. Earle, *The World of Defoe* (London, 1970): 146–9.

in Somerset married his cousin Ann (1687–1707), only for her to die after the birth of her second daughter. Other Windsor [sic], 3rd Earl of Plymouth, married Elizabeth Lewis in 1730, only for him to die aged 25, his wife to follow a year later, and the estates to be inherited by the 4th Earl, aged only 18 months. Caleb Fleming (1698–1779), a Dissenter minister, had ten children of whom only one survived him and unsurprisingly defended infant baptism.

Aside from fatal illnesses, there were chronic conditions that doomed sufferers to pain, discomfort and difficulties. Thus, in New Year greetings, Stephen Poyntz could wish "you many years free from gout."[6]

It was difficult to cope with disease, not least because medical knowledge was limited. Towns had quite a lot of physicians and if other medical practitioners were included, there were plenty. However, aside from a lack of appropriate treatments, there were also the issues created by living conditions, not least among these poor sanitation, crowded residences, and a shortage of sufficient food. Infection was a particular problem in the winter because, as James Thomson's *Winter* (1726) made clear, that was a season of indoor life that contrasted with the varied outdoor activities of the other periods described in *The Seasons* (1730). The same animal rhythm was true of other activities, as agrarian life helped determine marriage and thus affected courtship. Indeed, Thomson's *Spring* referred to "the passion of the groves." Although he meant the courtship of birds, the parallels between animal and human loves were frequently noted, both being seen as desirable. Many pastorals appeared in the 1710s, with John Gay's *The Shepherd's Week* (1714) more realistic about hard toil than Ambrose Philips' *Pastorals* (1709). Mrs. Sullen in George Farquhar's play, *The Beaux' Strategem* (1707), also expressed doubts about the standard poetic description of the countryside.

Concepts of health and safety were somewhat different from those today. Thus, Defoe noted of Stilton, that the cheese:

> is brought to table with the mites, or maggots round it, so thick, that they bring a spoon with them for you to eat the mites with, as you do the cheese. (*Tour*, 7)

6 Poyntz to Charles Delafaye, 1 Jan. 1730, NA. SP. 78/194 f. 3.

All of these contributed to poor resistance to disease. There could also be an issue with a lethargy that Defoe noted in some of the places he visited. Very differently, a sense of environmental damage was captured by Defoe's description of Aberystwyth:

> This town is enriched by the coals and lead which is found in its neighbourhood, and is a populous, but a very dirty, black, smoky place, and we fancied the people looked as if they lived continually in the coal or lead mines. However, they are rich, and the place is very populous.[7]

Adding the last sentence captures the complexities of developmental prosperity. The impact of coal on the air was noted by Defoe more generally, as in descriptions of London and Newcastle. Roxana refuses to live in London, pretending "that it would choke me up; that I wanted breath when I was in London." Others such as John Evelyn similarly complained. In 1716, an ill Robert Walpole left London and gained "so great a benefit from the air that I gather strength daily."[8]

There were other issues with coal. In his *Tour*, Defoe noted fatalities in mining accidents, notably at Chester-le-Street.[9]

At the same time, there were efforts at improvement. Thus, established in 1723, the Chelsea Waterworks Company used a tidal watermill to pump up water from the Thames near Pimlico, with linked reservoirs in Hyde Park and St. James's Park. The system was later enhanced with pumping engines and an iron water main. The resulting supply helped in the expansion of the West End, but was challenged by the increasing demand caused by the rising population.

Adding to uncertainty came serious problems with particular harvests, not least in the late 1690s and late 1720s. A run of poor harvests was particularly difficult as there was then pressure on the seed corn for the next harvest. This was part of the commonplace tension between present need and future prospects. Alongside the seasonal variety in the provision and

7 *Tour*, 6.
8 Robert to Horace Walpole, 11 May 1716, BL. Add. 63749.
9 *Tour*, 9.

cost of food,[10] harvests were greatly affected by both climate and weather, and unpredictably so. Thus, the "little ice age" of the seventeenth century came to an end after a particularly malign bout of bad weather in the 1690s. Indeed, in the first quarter of the eighteenth century, average August temperatures were a full degree centigrade higher than in the previous quarter-century. This contributed to the agricultural fertility much commented on by Defoe, and did so as much as the work by the improvers that he noted. Agriculture was also affected by demand. Limited population growth caused farmers to face difficulties in paying their rents, although this could also be attributed to issues with liquidity, not least among issues with foreign trade.[11]

Agricultural vulnerability to the climate was part of a more general sense of precariousness. Defoe captured that most clearly with his accounts of storms, notably the notorious one of 1703, which is described at length and referred to frequently. So also with his novels. Thus, Moll Flanders loses wealth with storm damage. Crusoe, running away from Hull to London, fears for his life in a storm, only to be told that it was not particularly stormy. Sailing on to anchor off Great Yarmouth, a graver storm hits home and he faints under the pressure. The storm is described as a terrifying adventure of repeated danger, with the crew escaping onto a boat that puts out from shore, after which the boat sinks. Crusoe is compared to Jonah with references to Providence and Heaven. Storms hit both coastal waters and foreign trade; Walter Titley, envoy in Copenhagen, writing in 1730 of the important trade to the Baltic, notes: "the doubling of the Point of Jutland, and the passing of the Kattegat are so extremely dangerous."[12]

This was also an issue in the summer. Thus, Jonathan Wilson, a Cumbrian Quaker and malt dealer, recorded in July 1726:

> I set forward towards Cork … but I met with contrary wind and was driven into Wales and so after four days came home again and stayed about a week at home and so set sail again and

10 T. Gray (ed.), *Devon Household Accounts 1617–59, Part 1* (Exeter, 1995).

11 Broglie, French ambassador, to Chauvelin, Foreign Minister, 2 Jan. 1730, AE. CP. Ang. 369 f. 10.

12 Titley to George Tilson, 14 Jan. 1730, NA. SP. 75/54 f. 25.

> met with contrary winds again and was driven upon the coasts of Ireland near the mountains of Newry.... [B]ut after six days at sea got safe and well to Dublin.

Storms hit not only shipping, but also the land, notably coastal areas. There were serious floods on the Somerset coast in 1696 and again in 1703, with the sea water reaching as far inland as Glastonbury. The 1703 flood led to William Diaper's poem, "Brent," about the Somerset village of that name, which included the lines:

> And soon the waves assert their ancient claim.
> They scorn the shores, and 'ore the marshes sound,
> And mudwall cotts are levell'd with the ground.

The 1703 coastal floods were the consequence of a great storm that Defoe describes in *The Storm* (1704), a work that, like his *Essay on the Late Storm* (1704), includes an apocalyptic dimension, with the preface of *The Storm* seeing it as a way to offer a sermon. This was an era of very strong millenarianism.

At the governmental level, there were attempts at improvement, at least in the sense of coping. Thus, an Act of the Edinburgh Parliament of 1695 forbade pulling up plants by the roots, as that left areas exposed to the advance of sand. Leaving aside storms, strong winds could threaten or prevent the arrival of shipping and, with that, goods or mail.[13]

A sense of insecurity contributed to a widespread belief in an animistic world. It also threw to the fore issues of repentance and Providence, for there was no certainly in the path of individual lives nor in the fortune of communities. Life and death is a "given," but also greatly affected at the individual and collective level by the unpredictabilities that Defoe displays most clearly in his book on the Plague. The overall effect was to lessen life chances. This was especially so for infants and the young, those who were most exposed to infections. Colonel Jack married as his fourth wife a Mrs. Moggy "a plain country girl" of 33, who had been promised marriage and then deserted ten years earlier "by a gentleman of a great estate" by whom

13 Delafaye to James, Lord Waldegrave, 5 Nov. 1730, Chewton.

she had a child who had died. In turn, before she dies, Jack loses three children and a maid by smallpox, "so that I had only one by my former wives, and one by my Moggy, the first a son, the last a daughter." Life-expectancy figures improve for those who reached 20, but they were still much lower than those today, and still affected by unpredictability. That was the backdrop to the lives of novelists, readers, and their characters. It helps link their "external" life experiences to those of their own health and that of their families. There was an interaction in terms of the need to confront uncertainty, and the speeding up character of a life that would not necessarily wait for the prospect of a better future. Indeed, part of the remarkable nature of the lives of Robinson Crusoe and Moll Flanders was their longevity and the extent to which they avoided long periods of serious illness to match their tribulations. The facts of life and death helped encourage a response emphasizing providential factors.

With his concern with the built environment, Defoe focused on fire as an equivalent of the chance factors of life and death. Thus, for Alresford in 1689 "by a sudden and surprising fire, the whole town, with both the church and the market-house, was reduced to a heap of rubbish; and, except a few poor huts at the remotest ends of the town, not a house left standing." Five years later, it was the turn of Warwick to be "almost wholly reduced to a heap of rubbish," while Northampton had similarly been devastated in 1675. Defoe praised the rebuilding in each case.[14]

Had there been a major fire during his period of writing books, then it is possible that Defoe would have added a book on the Great Fire to that on the Great Plague. There was a similar novelistic character to both episodes, and, if anything, a stronger one to that of the Great Fire as it was more abrupt and visual. Raging for four days from September 1666, the Great Fire began in Thomas Faryner's bakehouse in Pudding Lane, near London Bridge, either as a result of the failure to extinguish an oven properly or because the temperature inside the bakehouse was so high that the flour dust in the air spontaneously combusted. Anti-Catholic propaganda blamed the fire on the Catholics, while the Protestant Dutch saw it as divine judgment on their English enemy. The context was a densely-populated city where regulations were widely ignored, and there was much low-quality

14 *Tour*, 3, 7.

building to cope with the rising population. Moreover, highly flammable goods in warehouses, such as tobacco, did not help the impact of building in wood.

The strength of the fire, fanned by strong easterly winds, was such that it was able to cross the Fleet River, and this spread destroyed early hopes that the fire would be only minor. Partly as a result of these hopes, the necessary measures to create effective fire-breaks by pulling down houses were not taken until late. Charles II and his brother, James the Duke of York (later James II), took an active role in fighting the flames, filling buckets and encouraging the fire-fighters, and there was success in preventing the spread of the fire, not least by the use of gunpowder to create fire breaks, saving the Tower; but the blaze swept on, defying the generally inadequate responses. It was only finally stopped on the night of 4–5 September when the wind dropped, which permitted the fire-fighters to rally and dowse the fires, although fires under the rubble remained for some time.

The fire left the City devastated, destroying St. Paul's, the Guildhall, the Royal Exchange, 87 churches, 44 livery company halls and about 13,200 houses, and burning 373 of the 448 acres within the City walls and another 63 acres to the west. Far more damage was inflicted in the area affected than in the Blitz of 1940–1, although the Blitz affected a far larger area. Moreover, in contrast to the thousands killed then, only five people definitely died in the Great Fire. Realistically, however, many poor people probably died as fire swept through places like Bridewell. Because Parish Clerks' Hall was burnt down, no bills of mortality were produced for some weeks, and it was difficult to work out who was dead and who had fled. As autumn nights drew in, the homeless camped in fields in Islington and Moorfields, while mercantile and other activities were relocated.

Rebuilding

In the aftermath of the fire, Charles issued a declaration promising that London would be rebuilt as better and would "rather appear to the world as purged with the Fire … to a wonderful beauty and comeliness, than consumed by it." More particularly, he declared that a handsome vista would be created on the river bank by banishing smoky trades. John Evelyn, Peter Mills, Christopher Wren, Robert Hooke, Richard Newcourt, and Valentine

Knight produced plans for rebuilding London to a more regular plan, the pattern followed in other leading European cities, and one that reflected the favor of the period for dramatic long streets and rectilinear town plans. Evelyn urged the value of zoning, especially the long-promoted idea of the removal of noxious trades from areas of polite habitation, while Wren proposed a City with two central points, the Royal Exchange and St. Paul's. Ten roads were to radiate from the former, while a piazza in front of St Paul's was to be the focus of three key routes in the western part of the City, which was laid out in a grid dependent on the major through-routes, with piazzas or rond-points playing a key organizational role. The river was to be faced by a "Grand Terras." Wren's plan influenced John Gwynn's 1776 proposal for a replanning of the entire city. Evelyn was also interested in piazzas, whereas Hooke (who later became City Surveyor) and Newcourt each proposed a regular grid.

Resources and will were lacking, while the existing property rights of individuals proved to be one of the chief stumbling blocks to an organized replanning. Yet, more positively, these rights stimulated the rebuilding. The need for a rapid rebuilding, not least to prevent merchants from remaining in the West End, rather than returning to the City, was paramount. With the government impoverished by war with the Dutch, this rebuilding involved tapping the resources that could be readily raised by property-owners, which, however, ensured that many faced serious debt. Despite the work of the Fire Courts which adjudicated competing claims to land, there was no equivalent to the commissioners empowered by Parliament to organize the replanning and rebuilding of Warwick after the devastating fire of 1694, an expedient that proved particularly successful in that case. Instead, the Rebuilding Acts for London of 1667 and 1670 were far more restricted in their scope. Nevertheless, they dispensed with the requirements of the trade guilds in order to aid rebuilding and also sought to limit the danger of a new fire by stipulating that buildings should have no projecting windows and should have at most four stories. Houses were to be built out of brick, and to be uniform in their frontages; and these regulations acted as the model for large-scale urban building elsewhere in England. The fire also greatly encouraged the taking out of insurance policies and the resulting insurance companies developed their own fire services, albeit without providing the necessary unitary provision.

In London, existing property rights ensured that boundaries did not change significantly in the rebuilding. Existing roads were also preserved. The opportunity was taken, however, to reduce the number of parishes, while numerous streets were widened. The sole new street, however, was King Street and, on from that, Queen Street, which created a new route from Guildhall to the river. Designed by Wren and Hooke, the 202 feet high Monument to the Fire followed in 1677, and remains an impressive legacy with its viewing platform. Inscriptions at the base originally blamed Catholics for the fire. The new Royal Exchange, an Italianate building with arcades, built in 1669 by Edward Jarman, was, in turn, to be destroyed by fire in 1838.

Wren, as King's Surveyor of Works, had to be content with designing the dramatic new St. Paul's—much of which was built in the 1700s—becoming the key work in the English Baroque. He was also responsible for designing fifty-one London churches, all in use by 1696, for long a high-point of London's architectural heritage; although, challenged by Victorian re-development and German bombing, only twenty-three now remain. The fifty-one were an affirmation of the Established Church in the face the Toleration Act of 1689 and Dissenter support in London. Finally completed in 1710, but in use from 1697, St. Paul's towered over the City and thus provided a key point in vistas from elsewhere in London and from the suburbs, but the absence of any coherent new-plan to the rebuilding ensured that St. Paul's could no more provide a clear center to the new London than any of the other buildings in the city.

Nevertheless, the rebuilding, which may have cost close to £6 million, left a city that was considerably more attractive visually than that after the air attacks in World War Two. The plan for the canalization of the River Fleet, so as to provide space for more wharves, failed, however, and the canal became a sewer that was to be covered over in 1733. The canal and the rebuilding of the churches and public buildings was financed by a coal tax. Beyond the reach of the Great Fire, much of medieval and Tudor London survived the seventeenth century, but this did not amount to much within the walls—as Hollar's 1669 print made clear—while the majority of London by 1700, let alone 1731, had been built outside the City onward from 1600. There were major developments in the East and West Ends, and the northern and southern suburbs.

It took time for London to be repopulated and rebuilt, a process in which the existing meanings of sites were both re-created but also altered.[15] Eighty-thousand people had fled and, by the end of 1672, a quarter had still not returned. The lower cost of living in the Middlesex suburbs, which stimulated the spread of the built-up area, was cited as a reason: taxes in the City were higher and indeed had become so even more as a consequence of the costs in London attendant on new churches, paving, and drains. As a result, in 1673, the City, mindful that over 3,000 of its new houses were unoccupied, took steps to ease the burdens on new freemen. Yet there was also a reluctance in the City to understand the extent to which Londoners now had alternatives as to where to live, and that citizenship, guild membership, and that of liveried companies, was not the only way to the privileges of London life. Meanwhile, as an important instance of the human ability to respond, there was the provision of anti-fire techniques in insurance and firefighting. The *British Mercury* of 4 February 1713 reported that a serious fire in Whitefriars in London was tackled by twenty-five "fire-men belonging to the Sun-Fire-Office … and some few of other fire officers." Moll Flanders finds "so many engines playing" when there was a fire.

The transformation of London, "this Phoenix" to use John Evelyn's words for St. Paul's, was a prelude to the account of national change presented by Defoe in the *Tour*. There was a similar interplay of structure and culture, and the prominence of London in the *Tour* was one that was obvious because of the range of changes that were of significance to Defoe. So also with his novels, which, with the exception of the very different *Robinson Crusoe*, were particularly metropolitan.

15 C. Wall, *The Literary and Cultural Spaces of Restoration London* (1998); E. McKellar, *The Birth of Modern London: The Development and Design of the City, 1660–1720* (Manchester, 1999).

3. A Changing Economy

> "The fate of things gives a new face to things."
> Defoe, *Tour*

There was much continuity in economic activity and social structure during Defoe's lifetime (1660–1731). Yet, as was only to be expected, the extent and prospect of change also, variously, interested, encouraged, and concerned contemporaries. At the same time, there was a degree of economic transformation, albeit in a longer-term pattern that contemporaries were apt to overlook, as well as less than was to happen over the following seventy years. Many changes had begun in the sixteenth century—namely, an increased use of coal for manufacturing and domestic fuel, a turn to the enclosure of farmland in order to raise agricultural production, and further innovation.

Change during Defoe's lifetime was both quantitative (more production and activity) and qualitative (new methods and routes), each of which interested him, as did an awareness of a more integrated national economy. Indeed, the last was a subject for Defoe and, at the same time, a means by which his works and arguments became national. The spread of a market economy, and the means to further this, were of great concern to Defoe, both as instrumental to national greatness and as the realization of individual potential. As such, there was a clear preference in Defoe's writing for signs of this activity and, commonly, an emphasis on London's market and capital as a pulsing basis for the resulting growth. In his pamphlets, Defoe sought to engage with the financial and economic changes of the period, and what appeared to be the monetarization of society. Similar points of course had been made by earlier writers, notably Ben Jonson in *Volpone* (1606), as well as by later ones. Financial instruments, notably bills of exchange, were important in *Roxana*, with value and credit— financial as well as moral, social as well as economic.[1]

Defoe could be critical of aspects of London, notably its financial ethos and role, but was less so than most writers. Defoe showed over this his classic ability to understand a question in the round, and to praise generalities while also attacking specific points. This was not a matter of inconsistency, but, rather, pertained to the complexity of issues. Thus, his pamphlet, *The Villainy of Stock-Jobbers Detected* (1701), was a revelational work, with the full-title continuing: *and the Causes of the late run Upon the Bank and Bankers discovered and Considered* (1701). Defoe offers a positive account of money:

> Trade in general is built upon, and supported by two essential and principal foundations, *viz* money and credit, as the Sun and Moon in their diurnal motion alternatively enlighten and invigorate the world, so these two essentials maintain and preserve our trade; they are the life and soul of trade, and they are the support of one another too. Money raises credit, and credit in its turn is an equivalent to money.

As a consequence, Defoe was critical of whatever hit paper-credit, indeed comparing stock-jobbing to a corporation of Hell and then as a form of social mobility by the dishonest.[2]

As with Defoe's work as a whole, there was an emphasis on political factors in economic matters, and notably so as far as the context was concerned. This emphasis looked back to Defoe's background and youth. The relevant context was that of the London Puritan-linked opposition to Court-based monopolies granted to individuals and other economic favoritism associated with the government of Elizabeth I (r. 1558–1603) and, even more, that of the Stuarts. The preference, instead, with Defoe, was not for a free-market individualistic liberal capitalism but, rather, for a structure of national protectionism, a structure that has been termed mercantilism. This

1 Mary Poovey, *Genres of the Credit Economy: Mediating Value in Eighteenth- and Nineteenth-Century Britain* (Chicago, 2008).

2 *Villainy*, pp. 1, 9, 26.

protectionism was notably associated with the London Puritanism of the Parliamentarians of the 1640s and early 1650s, a Puritanism that subsequently continued, notably among Dissenters. Nationalist economic legislation and a powerful navy were key aspects of policy under the Rump Parliament, and much of this was brought to fruition anew after the "Glorious Revolution" of 1688–9. This political dimension was not so much in the background of Defoe's writing on economic matters but rather its foreground. Defoe took forward the views of earlier Dissenter writers, such as Slingsby Bethel (1617–97), a merchant who became a London Whig and whose works included *The Present Interest in England* (1671), with its clear affirmation of the significance of overseas trade.

Alongside his mercantilism at an international level, Defoe, domestically, favored free market models against monopolies or cartels and guilds. Defoe's attitudes were also very much seen in his criticism of guilds and other specific privileges, as in:

> The greatest inconveniencies of British, are, its situation, and the tenacious folly of its inhabitants; who by the general infatuation, the pretence of freedoms and privileges, that corporation-tyranny, which prevents the flourishing and increase of many a good town in England, continue obstinately to forbid any, who are not subjects of their city sovereignty, (that is to say freemen,) to trade within the chain of their own liberties; were it not for this, the city of Bristol, would before now, have swelled and increased in buildings and inhabitants, perhaps to double the magnitude it was formerly of.[3]

In fact, by 1722, Bristol probably had doubled its size and population since 1650, but Defoe had really last seen it in 1705.

Trade worked at all sorts of literary levels. Thus, the most potent visualized image in Defoe's *Tour* was shipping, notably warships. The account in the *Tour* of the rapidity of preparing a warship for action was that of a purposeful and necessary activity.

As far as industry was concerned, Defoe was particularly interested in

3 *Tour*, 6.

coal-based activity, which was not surprising as he was a Londoner. He commented accordingly, not only in the *Tour* but also in the novels. In *Colonel Jack*, the young boys find warmth in the smoldering ashes resulting from coal-fired glass production in London. They live among rubbish. There are frequent references in the *Tour* to the coal trade. In the *Journal*, Defoe wrote of the coal trade from Newcastle to London: "without which the city [London] would have been greatly distressed; for not in the streets only, but in private houses and families, great quantities of coals were then burnt, even all the summer long and when the weather was hottest" in order to combat the plague.

For coal, as for other products, such as Cheshire cheese, sale to national markets circulated money and increased local demand, which therefore spurred activity elsewhere. Thus, the development of coal and lead mining in County Durham led to a rise in its population from about 35,000 in 1550 to about 70,000 in 1700, and to the enclosure of land so that it could be more easily farmed and, if necessary, adapted to new agricultural methods. By the end of the seventeenth century, most of the lowland east of the county was enclosed.

In most years, the demand for products was not driven down by the immediate need to cope with an increase in food prices. Indeed, on the longer-trend of Defoe's lifetime, consumption was not hit hard by the need to feed a growing population, as the latter only increased gradually. Nevertheless, that increase provided opportunities for agricultural improvers who sought to raise production. A key means was by enhancing fertilization and Defoe devoted considerable attention to this, seeing it as a major way by which wealth could be created. In particular, new crops contributed to improved productivity in individual fields which, in turn, fed through into increased aggregate production. Thus, the proportion of Norfolk and Suffolk farmers growing turnips or clover rose dramatically from the 1660s to the 1720s: probate inventories suggest a rise in the percentage of farmers growing turnips from 1.6 to 52.7. The resulting increase in fodder allowed heavier stocking, enhancing soil fertility. Defoe wrote of Suffolk: "the application of the people to all kinds of improvement is scarce credible,"[4] and of the journey from Winchester to Salisbury:

4 *Tour*, 1.

> ... 'tis more remarkable still; how a great part of these downs comes by a new method of husbandry, to be not only made arable, which they never were in former days, but to bear excellent wheat, and great crops too, though otherwise poor barren land, and never known to our ancestors to be capable of any such thing; nay, they would perhaps have laughed at any one that would have gone about to plough up the wild downs and hills, where the sheep were wont to go. But experience has made the present age wiser, and more skilful in husbandry; for by only folding the sheep upon the ploughed lands, those lands, which otherwise are barren, and where the plough goes within three or four inches of the solid rock of chalk, are made fruitful, and bear very good wheat, as well as rye and barley.[5]

At the same time, enclosure was limited in comparison to what was to follow later on in the century. Colonel Jack refers to the coach road from Bishop's Stortford to Cambridge: "the country was all open cornfields, no enclosures." Grain crops were significant for, as the fictional Colonel Jack noted, the poor were acutely concerned about the price of bread but "very seldom [had] any meat." New infrastructure reflected and contributed to the domestic market, such as the Cornmarket on Bristol's quay built in 1684.

There were also important developments in industrial capability, although little of what was to be understood as the Industrial Revolution. Socio-political factors that Defoe applauded were an important aspect of the equations of growth. These included a degree of political stability that helped guarantee the rights of property, as well as the removal of the fear that the Crown would expropriate investments and hand monopolies to political cronies. The role of the "Glorious Revolution" in ensuring the primacy of mercantile interests in trade and economic policy was significant. So also was it with the political union with Scotland in 1707 that Defoe saw as important in greatly expanding the domestic market, but over which he expressed concern about a failure up to his time of writing of many Scots to perceive and exploit possible opportunities. More generally, while relative

5 *Tour*, 3.

political stability from the 1690s and business-friendly policies promoted the growth of the domestic market, aggressive foreign policy and success in war greatly expanded their overseas counterparts, as well as protecting British trade from the attacks noted in several of his novels, including *Robinson Crusoe* and *Colonel Jack*. International tension could pose a significant challenge to the economy, which meant that its easing was important. The relationship between the economy and foreign policy was clearly summarized in a London report in *Farley's Bristol News-Paper* of 10 February 1728:

> Abundance of serges and other woollen manufactures are shipping off daily for the Streights;[6] and it is expected there will be a great demand for them this spring, on the prospect of an approaching peace.

Similarly, preparations for war affected the public funds. At the same time, the emphasis on state policy, which was necessarily the focus of pamphlet debate, should not lead to an underplaying of the efficiency of the private sector of the economy.

As yet, the developments in power sources related to domestic and not foreign strength. Steam power could replace water power, such as the "two vast engines" seen by John Evelyn in a Cornish tin mine in 1702:

> consisting of several wheels in the nature of pumps to draw the water out of the places they intend to search, they are continually going by the force of water which passing through several peoples grounds costs a great deal before it can reach the engines to which it is conveyed in a wooden trough very high.[7]

The coal-powered steam pump demonstrated by Thomas Savery in 1698 was of little practical importance, but Thomas Newcomen in 1712 introduced his Atmospheric Engine. This was particularly useful for pumping water out of mines, in the Cornish tin and copper mines, as well as in

6 Straits of Gibraltar en-route for Mediterranean markets.

7 BL. Evelyn papers, vol. 49, f. 23.

coal and lead mines elsewhere. The availability and cheapness of coal was an important factor in the use of these steam engines. By 1733, about 100 Newcomen engines had been built across the country, each an affirmation of the possibilities of the new. Newcomen (1663–1729) was an almost exact contemporary of Defoe and, like him, a Dissenter buried at Bunhill Fields.

Growing coal production was to help steam power, but this production, as Defoe noted, was largely for household heating, notably in London, where it ensured that the constraints produced by a reliance on wood could be overcome. The coal duty was the principal source of funds for the Commission for Building Fifty New Churches in London and Westminster established in 1711, and also financed the Dukes of Richmond. In 1700, British coal production was about three million tons, with the North-East of England the most important coalfield, accounting for half the national output. (East) Shropshire, (South) Yorkshire, and (South) Staffordshire, in that order, were the most important other coalfields.[8] Output was far greater than in any other European country.

Coal helped in the development of the iron industry. The smelting of iron and steel using coke, rather than charcoal, freed this important industry from dependence on wood supplies. However, this 1709 innovation by Abraham Darby at his blast furnace in Coalbrookdale was not widely applied at first, due to initial difficulties with the process as well as cost and quality considerations. Indeed, an aspect of the (understandable) degree to which Defoe did not spot economic trends came in his focus on the ironworks in Sussex, as well as his totally mistaken related confidence that timber supplies were inexhaustible,[9] a judgment he also offered on other occasions. Coal was also the major fuel in glass production, sugar refining, brewing, salt-boiling, and brick-making by 1700; with its availability explaining the significance of the production of glass in Newcastle, and that in London discussed in *Colonel Jack*. The Bear Garden in Southwark was replaced by a glassworks in the 1680s. As now, London was the high-wage center of the country, but, unsurprisingly in light of the technology of the times, the limited (by modern standards) output of the economy, and the nature of society, that did not translate to comfortable living standards for

8 J. Hatcher, *Before 1700: Towards the Age of Coal* (Oxford, 1993).
9 *Tour*, 2.

many Londoners. Edward, Lord Harley's party visited the coal-fired salt pans at South Shields.[10]

Despite the increased use of coal, water power remained more significant in much of the economy, notably the most important industry, textile manufacturing. Water power was important for new manufacturing, such as the silk-throwing machinery installed at Derby on the River Derwent in 1721 by Thomas Lombe, and also for more traditional textiles. For example, the export of serges, a popular type of cloth, from Exeter, the leading fulling and finishing center in the West Country and one that relied on water power, rose from 120,000 pieces annually in the 1680s to 365,000 in 1710, a quarter of England's entire cloth exports.[11] This cloth went largely to Mediterranean markets.

Water power, more generally, helped ensure the importance of rural industry. Water power was easier to utilize in areas of rapid water flow, which largely meant upland areas. In addition, wood supplies were more plentiful and less expensive in the countryside than in towns, as was coal in mining regions. In London, water power was of only limited use, which increased the significance there of coal. Raw materials could also be found in rural areas. This was not only the case with wood. Thus, the leather industry depended on cattle hides for tanning.

Moreover, labor was more flexible and cheaper than in the towns. Defoe wrote at some length about the cloth industry in the West Country, offering both description and explanation. The towns, notably rapidly-more-prosperous Frome, were presented as organizing the spinning by poor women and children of wool in their homes, a process he also found elsewhere, especially in Yorkshire and Lancashire. In *Moll Flanders*, the young Moll is taught to spin worsted, which was the chief industry in Colchester.

As Defoe noted, however, many rural areas (like many towns) did not become centers of industry. There were a number of reasons for this contrast, but human inputs were crucial. Entrepreneurial activity was a crucial factor in producing a symbiotic relationship between rural activity and urban investment, markets and, frequently, stages in manufacture. Family

10 HMC, *Portland Mss*, VI, 105.

11 W.G. Hoskins, *Industry, Trade and People in Exeter, 1688–1800* (Manchester, 1935).

connections as well as the fluid relations between merchants and gentry were important to this relationship.[12] Defoe proved an acute appreciator of this factor; although he tended to be more interested in urban activity than rural, and, both separately and overlapping this, in trade rather than industry. That was his focus despite a significant increase in industrial activity and employment in the early eighteenth century.

Defoe was committed to the exchange of goods, which he discussed in *The Complete English Tradesman* (1726), a work in which tradesmen are praised and their status affirmed. Aside from his concern about cultural preferences that limited the reputation of trade, notably the focus on the gentry, Defoe was also aware of practical economic constraints. In particular, there were those posed by poor transport links. The deficiencies of road traffic and the risks of its marine equivalent were frequent themes in his writings. This was most clearly the case in his formal discussion of transport in the *Tour*, but was also seen when his fictional characters travelled.

Road and water transport were brought together when crossing rivers in coastal regions. For these, Defoe's accounts can readily be supplemented by those of other travellers. Between Chester and Hawarden in 1698, Celia Fiennes "crossed over the marshes, which is hazardous to strangers." On her return from Wales, she:

> forded over the Dee when the tide was out … the sands are here so loose that the tides do move them … many persons that have known the fords well, that have come a year or half a year after, if they venture on their former knowledge have been overwhelmed in the ditches made by the sands, which are deep enough to swallow up a coach or wagon.[13]

So also for Defoe. Moreover, the Itchen ferry en-route to Southampton was "a very sorry boat,"[14] while, crossing the Tamar from Plymouth to

12 B. Purdue, *Merchants and Gentry in North-East England, 1650–1830* (Sunderland, 1999).

13 C. Morris (ed.), *The Illustrated Journeys of Celia Fiennes, c.1682–c.1712* (London, 1982), pp. 157–9.

14 *Tour*, 2.

Saltash in Cornwall, Defoe found a "very wide" estuary "and the ferry boats bad, so that I thought myself well escaped when I got safe on shore in Cornwall."[15] "The badness and danger of the ferries over the Severn,"[16] were noted, as was the route from Barton to Hull across the Humber:

> … an ill-favoured dangerous passage or ferry … in an open boat, in which we had about fifteen horses, and ten or twelve cows, mingled with about seventeen or eighteen passengers, called Christians; we were about four hours tossed about on the Humber…. I was so uneasy at it, that I chose to go round by York, rather than return to Barton.[17]

Ferries were not the only problem. Again anticipating Defoe, John Evelyn, travelling into Cornwall in August 1702 found "dirty or stony lanes."[18] Indeed, across Britain, we must be careful in using the term road in a modern sense since many were little more than bridle paths. There were no roads suitable for wheeled traffic, as opposed to horses, apart from the town and major routes, and this limited the efficiency of freight travel and the ease of passenger transport. Additional problems were caused by drainage and soil types. Thus, the greensand of the Weald ensured that Defoe "fatigued myself in passing this deep and heavy part of the country."[19] So also in Surrey and Northamptonshire. In December 1737, Edward, 2nd Earl of Oxford, travelled from Ipswich to Diss by a road "which would have been very difficult to have passed had not the frost borne."[20]

Defoe was particularly troubled about the heavy clay soils of the Midlands (which made much travel more difficult by road use) and the problems they caused for carriages and carts, not least the death of overworked horses. With his characteristic argument that London helped define national interests, Defoe accordingly argued the need for turnpikes. In doing

15 *Tour*, 3.
16 *Tour*, 6.
17 *Tour*, 7.
18 Evelyn Journal, BL. Evelyn papers, vol. 49, f. 21.
19 *Tour*, 2, 7.
20 HMC, *Portland Mss*, VI, 170.

so, he drew attention to the social equity of moving the burden from the local rates and economy. The passage was more generally symptomatic of his focus of concern and method of argument:

> The reason of my taking notice of this badness of the roads, through all the midland counties, is this; that as these are counties which drive a very great trade with the city of London, and one another, perhaps the greatest of any counties in England; and that, by consequence, the carriage is exceeding great, and also that all the land carriage of the northern counties necessarily goes through these counties, so the roads had been ploughed so deep, and materials have been in some places so difficult to be had for repair of the roads, that all the surveyors rates have been able to do nothing … it was a burthen too great for the poor farmers.[21]

Defoe also found travelling in Galloway "very rough, as well for the road, as for the entertainment."[22] The details of travel are used by Defoe in *Colonel Jack*, not least the swimming of the River Tweed by the villainous Captain Jack at Kelso, and his nearly drowning in Lauderdale. The situation varied by the season. Thus, on 5 January 1729, it was reported from Stamford that "the roads being so bad," it was not possible to travel from York,[23] and that on one of the country's leading roads.

Moreover, slopes caused major problems for vehicles, as Defoe noted in Lincoln: animals struggled with the steepness. He provided an account of the steep hill from Bath to the King's Down:

> the late Queen Anne was extremely frighted in going up, her coachman stopping to give the horses breath, and the coach wanting a dragstaff, run back in spite of all the coachman's skill; the horses not being brought to strain the harness again, or pull

21 *Tour*, appendix to volume 3.

22 *Tour*, 12.

23 John Young to Mr Brown, 5 Jan. 1729, J.W.F. Hill (ed.), *The Letters and Papers of the Banks Family of Revesby Abbey, 1704–60* (Lincoln, 1952), p. 101.

> together for a good while, and the coach putting the guards behind it into the utmost confusion, till some of the servants setting their heads and shoulders to the wheels, stopped them by plain force.

Other issues included the pears that gave one of the horses in Lord Harley's party a stomachache in Kent in 1723.[24]

As a very different problem, there was the highway robbery mentioned in *Moll Flanders*. The impact of robberies was magnified by the degree of uncertainty they caused for all travellers.

The limits of transportation encouraged the droving of livestock, and Defoe was particularly interested in the large-scale walking of turkeys from East Anglia to London.[25] Droving also featured in his novels. In Defoe's novel, Colonel Jack robs "an ancient country gentleman" in the London meat market at Smithfield "selling some very large bullocks" driven from Sussex.

His conviction of the problems created by poor transport led Defoe to show firm support for improving roads. In Britain, this was done by turnpike trusts, and Defoe favored these, using the *Tour* to argue strongly in their favor. Trusts were bodies, generally groups of local landowners and businessmen, who obtained Acts of Parliament to raise capital in order to repair and improve a road or network of local roads and to charge tolls to these ends. The capital was raised as loans, which, it was predicted (not always accurately) were to be repaid through income from the tolls. Each project reflected a confidence in the prospects for improvement and profit, as well as the need to spread costs. The first turnpike trust was created in 1663 and turnpiking increased in the 1690s. Thus, the first section of the London-Norwich road was turnpiked under an Act of 1696. Early eighteenth-century trusts dealt largely with repairs and widening, rather than the construction of new roads. To that end, many trusts, such as the Bath Trust that was established in 1707, had considerable success in improving the situation, which indeed was necessary. The Act of 1727 granting permission for the turnpiking of the Cirencester-Lechdale road,

24 HMC, *Portland Mss.* VI, 79.
25 *Tour*, 1.

a crucial route by which cloth from Stroud moved toward London, noted that the road:

> by reason of many heavy carriages frequently passing ... [has] become very ruinous and deep, and in the winter season many parts thereof are so bad, that passengers cannot pass and repass without great danger.

This turnpiking helped bring industry to south Gloucestershire as Defoe had hoped.

As so often with Defoe, what he called for was largely to come in later decades. By 1750, a sizeable network of new turnpikes, radiating from London, had been created, and, with even more growth in the 1750s and 1760s, there were 15,000 miles of turnpikes in England by 1770. The far more parlous situation in Defoe's lifetime was possibly a factor in the degree to which journeys within Britain by road played a lesser role in his stories than was the case for later novelists, although the more marginal nature of his characters and the extremes of their fate, including transportation to the New World, were also significant. The likely nature of transportation for the characters depicted in later novels, and thus the conventions for novelists, were not yet established.[26]

Within Britain, coastal transport was significant for Defoe's fictional characters, notably Colonel Jack, who takes the key East coast route. In the *Journal*, Defoe described London's grain supply in the 1660s:

> ... particularly carried on by small vessels from the port of Hull and other places on the Humber, by which great quantities of corn were brought in from Yorkshire and Lincolnshire. The other part of this corn-trade was from Lynn,[27] in Norfolk, from Wells and Burnham, and from Yarmouth, all in the same county; and the third branch was from the river Medway, and from Milton, Faversham, Margate, and Sandwich, and all the other little places and ports round the coast of Kent and Essex.

26 C. Ewers, *Mobility in the English Novel from Defoe to Austen* (Woodbridge, 2018).

27 King's Lynn.

> There was also a very good trade from the coast of Suffolk with corn, butter, and cheese.

Coastal transport suffered not only from a heavy dependence on the weather and a vulnerability to it, but also from the generally poorly-developed nature of docks and harbor facilities. These greatly interested Defoe and led him in particular to praise Liverpool which had the world's first commercial wet dock, built from 1710 and opened in 1715. The improvement of harbor facilities reflected opportunities and needs made dynamic by entrepreneurial activity and investment, and with significant governmental help. Thus, an Act of Parliament of 1717 established the River Wear Commissioners in order to develop harbour facilities on the lower Wear for the coal trade. The result was a much-improved harbor entrance and navigable channel that permitted a major growth in trade with the Wear, and thus aided the development of the port and economy of Sunderland and the expansion of the Durham coal-field. Both acted to greater national economic gain, not least by reducing the quasi-monopolistic control over the trade wielded by Newcastle.

Defoe uneasily counterpointed a sense of aggregate national improvement with the much more varied fortunes of particular communities. Thus, he wrote of the respective fortune of Somerset ports:

> since the increase of shipping and trade, bigger ships being brought into use, than were formerly built, and the harbour at Minehead being fairer, and much deeper, than those at Watchet and Porlock, and therefore able to secure those greater ships, which the others were not, the merchants removed to it.[28]

As well as across the estuaries already mentioned, ferries were crucial in crossing rivers prior to a major expansion in stone bridges from the mid-eighteenth century. Before that, there was the significance of very varied river conditions, a situation noted by Defoe, as in his discussion of Kelso:

> one of the greatest roads from Edinburgh to Newcastle lying through this town, and a nearer way by far than the road through

28 *Tour*, 4.

> Berwick. They only want a good bridge over the Tweed: at present they have a ferry just at the town, and a good ford through the river, a little below it; but, though I call it a good ford, and so it is when the water is low, yet that is too uncertain; and the Tweed is so dangerous a river, and rises sometimes so suddenly, that a man scarce knows, when he goes into the water, how it shall be ere he gets out at the other side; and it is not very strange to them at Kelso, to hear of frequent disasters, in the passage, both to men and to cattle.[29]

Defoe praised the bridges that were built, for example at Wadebridge over the River Camel in Cornwall.[30]

As another instance of change that was largely to come, there were coach services. These became more widespread and frequent from the mid-eighteenth century, as did the use of wagons, rather than the packhorses he had earlier noted as significant, for example in moving goods from Leeds, or salmon from Carlisle and Workington to distant London.

For Defoe, a key element in national improvement was that of inland waterways that were especially important for the movement of freight, and, unlike in the Netherlands, far less so for passengers. It was far cheaper to move freight by water than land, and thus crucial for bulky commodities that could not afford the price increase that land transport would have imposed. The inherited provision of waterways in the shape of rivers, such as the Severn, offered much for transport.[31] Thus, Defoe wrote of Nottingham:

> The Trent is navigable here for vessels or barges of great burden, by which all their heavy and bulky goods are brought from the Humber, and even Hull; such as iron, block-tin, salt, hops, grocery, dyers' wares, wine, oil, tar, hemp, flax, etc. and the same vessels carry down lead, coal, wood, corn; as also cheese in great quantities, from Warwickshire and Staffordshire.[32]

29 *Tour*, 12.

30 *Tour*, 4.

31 D. Hussey, *Coastal and River Trade in Pre-Industrial England. Bristol and Its Region, 1680–1730* (Exeter, 2000).

32 *Tour*, 8.

For Stourbridge fair, a major commercial event, near Cambridge, Defoe noted that the river Cam was navigable to Cambridge:

> and that by this means, all heavy goods are brought even to the fair-field, by water carriage from London, and other parts; first to the port of Lynn and then in barges up the Ouse, from the Ouse into the Cam, and so ... to the very edge of the fair.[33]

Yet, the rivers did not provide a national system and, separately, their flow was not predictable. Rivers were affected by freezing, spate or drought, and transport on them could have been limited by weirs. In response to their deficiencies, Defoe was an advocate for the canalization of rivers and, more expensively, for the construction of canals. The former approach suited the incremental nature of most achievement, a nature that contrasted with the bold prospects of wholesale rapid change outlined by most improvers and easiest to assert in pamphlets. There were peaks of activity in enhancing rivers in the late 1690s and in 1719–21. Thus, in Yorkshire, the improvement in the Aire and Calder navigation to Leeds and Halifax in 1699–1701 was a major step as noted by Defoe in the *Tour*:

> by which a communication by water was opened from Leeds and Wakefield to Hull, and by which means all the woollen manufactures ... is carried by water to Hull, and there shipped ... since the opening the navigation of these rivers ... they carry coal down from Wakefield (especially) and also from Leeds ... down into the Humber and then up the Ouse to York, and up the Trent.

Under an Act of 1699, the navigation of the Trent to Burton was improved, which enabled it to develop as a major brewing center. Taunton relied on transhipment five miles to the east until 1706, when an Act allowed the improvement of the navigation of the River Tone. There was another peak of activity in 1719–21. In his *Tour*, Defoe was impressed by the possibilities created by recent improvements in East Anglian rivers. Yet, as he

33 *Tour*, 1.

noted, alongside his sense of potential, there could be setbacks. There was the need to win political support, a need that led the corporation of Sheffield to press for parliamentary backing in 1731.[34]

Defoe was a great advocate for canals, and notably for a canal to link the Firths of Forth and Clyde and provide, as he argued, both advantages for Scotland and for Britain as a whole. Defoe's reflection on the scheme showed him able to relate ideas to the altering prospects brought by time:

> But [if] it is too much to undertake here, it must lie till posterity, by the rising greatness of their commerce, shall not only feel the want of it, but find themselves able for the performance.[35]

Similar bold schemes could be found elsewhere. Thus, the *Champion*, a London newspaper in its issue of 14 August 1740 noted that it had "heard some talk of a project to join the Avon in Somersetshire, to the Thames; and the Severn with the Trent."

However, for someone who prided himself on practicalities, Defoe was rather inclined to underrate them when it came to canals. Construction problems included the provision, support, and payment of a large number of workers, for canals had to be dug by hand as there were no steam shovels. There was also the need to plan for the provision and maintenance of an adequate water supply for the canals and for the prevention of leaks. The length of time involved in construction ensured that the financial burden involved could not be readily matched by revenues. Indeed, due to financial problems, the Forth and Clyde Canal, which was begun in 1768, was not finished until 1790, although it reached the outskirts of Glasgow in 1777.

Canals largely followed Defoe's lifetime, but he was in a position to note a major increase in international trade and in shipping tonnage. There is an overlap here with chapter eleven, that on Defoe's foreign worlds, as the imaginative engagement, most notably shown in *Robinson Crusoe,* drew heavily on the major change in British economic activity. At a time of generally low inflation, average annual exports rose from £4.1 million in the 1660s to £6.9 million in 1720, by which time imports were worth £6.1

34 HMC, *Portland Mss.* VI, 37.
35 *Tour*, 12.

million. London's commercial position reflected the dynamism of its traders. The value of London's imports from the East India Company and the English plantations (New World colonies) nearly doubled from the 1660s to the end of the century, while the percentage of London's total imports by value from these areas rose from twenty-four to thirty-four in the same period. But imports also posed economic and social problems. In *The Manufacturer* (1719–21), Defoe engaged in the issue of the import of textiles by the East India Company, which challenged British manufacturers.

The statistics given in the last paragraph reflected the rise in direct trade, rather than, as earlier, using intermediary traders, especially the Dutch, and intermediary ports, particularly Amsterdam. This rise in direct trade was a result of the legislation of mid-century, the Navigation Acts of 1650 and 1651, which were reprised in the Navigation Act of 1660 and the Staple Act of 1663, which in effect created a national monopoly as the form of commercial regulation, thus limiting the role of companies with royal monopolies, although they controlled trade with some important regions. London's role in the British economic system was enhanced by the prohibition of exports direct from the colonies to (European) Continental markets and, instead, the requirement that they be exported to Britain before re-export. Nevertheless, such measures were compromised by contraband, for smuggling occurred on a large scale, and by the extent to which the implementation of policies was distinctly *ad hoc*. Prohibiting the export of wool was seen as the only way to prevent competition from the French textile industry.[36]

Unlike in France, entrepreneurs also benefited from the absence of local tariffs, which helped create a substantial economic space. However, under a separate jurisdiction, Ireland was partly excluded from this national economic space, as Scotland was to be until 1707. Even then, although there was an aspiration to create a common framework in 1707 it was not fully operational until the nineteenth century, not least with significant difference in excise provisions.

Shipbuilding, another activity in which Thame-side concerns played the major role in this period, was helped by legislation in 1660 that all

36 Bevil Skelton, envoy in Paris, to Richard, 1st Viscount Preston, Lord President of the Council, 4 Feb. 1688, NA. SP. 78/151 f. 138.

foreign-built ships in English ownership be registered. Two years later, the purchase of ships from the Netherlands (the principal source of imported ships) was hindered when an Act decreed that ships of foreign build not registered by that date were to be deemed alien and to be subject to alien duties. In 1698, Peter the Great of Russia came to Deptford on the Thames (where the Howland Dock was begun in 1660), as well as to the Netherlands, in order to see shipbuilding in process, as he searched for foreign models for the industry he intended to establish. Shipbuilding reflected the powerful role of the Thames, not only in shaping London and in its transport links, within and outside the city, but also in its economy. In an echo of Venice, as Antonio Canaletto's painting of *The River Thames on Lord Mayor's Day* (1747–8) indicates, the river was also very important to the city's image and ceremonial, in this case showing an annual riverine procession of the City's leaders. There were other echoes of Venice in the arts, including in Handel's *Water Music* (1717).

Helped in part by Dutch investment after the Glorious Revolution of 1688–9, investment which both constituted an important aspect of a growing Anglo-Dutch co-operation and reflected the openness of the city's commercial culture, London's role in the multi-centered trading system was becoming more prominent. Direct trading with foreign countries, rather than via intermediaries, required more capital resources and expenditure, and a more sophisticated organizational structure. Yet, this trading enabled the British, essentially in the shape of London merchants, to bear the bulk of the transaction costs themselves and also to take much of the profit. This process can be seen with the India trade, which was largely financed with returns for bullion that could be obtained only from profits on other trades, for example the export of light draperies to the Mediterranean and of sugar to Hamburg, this sugar coming from the Caribbean colonies in return for goods and payment shipped to them. The profitability of these trades and the role of the Anglo-Dutch link helped provide a financial strength that underlined London's importance economically and politically. The *British Journal* on 28 March 1730 observed "Trade is the life of the nation's prosperity, so credit is the life of trade." On a pattern that was to remain the case down to the present day, London benefited from being an emporium, such that, far from being compartmentalized, the British trading system had important financial as well as economic interdependence. Indeed,

British re-exports rose from £2.13 million in 1700 to £3.23 million in 1750, as imported goods, such as tobacco from the Chesapeake or sugar from the West Indies, were re-exported to Continental Europe, notably to entrepots such as Hamburg and Livorno.

These figures, moreover, ignored the contraband commerce discussed by Defoe, both exports, notably wool, and imports. The latter contributed greatly to the deficit in trade with France, one that concerned commentators and notably so those of a mercantilist disposition, for example George Downing MP, the Teller of the Exchequer.[37] In Scotland, where it was large-scale,[38] there was a significant political dimension to smuggling, and in the Clyde prior to 1707 the tobacco business was heavily dependent on the capacity of the Scots' merchants and shippers to breach the rules.

Given the difficulties merchants encountered, difficulties discussed by Defoe, including natural disasters, war, dishonesty, and the problems in ensuring payment, the growth in trade was impressive. As Defoe and others noted, cloth exports were particularly important. Indeed, in *Moll Flanders*, stolen cloth and clothes operated as part of the domestic economy. When Peter Macskásy, a Transylvanian landowner but not an aristocrat, died in 1712, his effects included "fourteen measures of English cloth with collars of marten … a fine saddle blanket made of English cloth … a pair of London summer gloves, and a lined black English mantle."[39] In 1713, the proposed trade treaty with France proved the subject of successful attacks on the government, attacks that drew on the widespread argument—made by both Addison and Defoe—that trade, prosperity, and power were closely linked.[40] This helped account for the attention paid by foreign envoys to the state of public funds and for the significance of shocks such as the bursting

37 Parliamentary Diary, 30 Ap. 1675, M. Bond (ed.), *The Diaries and Papers of Sir Edward Dering* (London, 1976), p. 74.

38 R. Goring, "Eighteenth-Century Scottish Smugglers: The Evidence from Montrose and Dumfries," in *Review of Scottish Culture*, 3 (1987), pp. 53–9.

39 K. Verdery, *Transylvanian Villagers* (Berkely, 1983), p. 157.

40 J. Addison, *The Present State of War, and the Necessity of an Augmentation Considered* (London, 1708), p. 11; L. Dickey, "Power, Commerce, and Natural Law in Daniel Defoe's Political Writings, 1698–1707," in J. Robertson (ed.), *A Union for Empire: Political Thought and the British Union of 1707* (Cambridge, 1995), pp. 67–8.

of the South Sea Bubble. A pamphlet of 1722 referred accordingly to the Freemen of London: "as South Sea has stripped them of their superfluous riches, long wars, continued taxes, and high duties impaired their stock, and shocked their credit."[41]

Trade encouraged shipping, which was an interest of Defoe's. In January 1661, the diarist and naval bureaucrat Samuel Pepys took a barge to Blackwell and "viewed the dock and the new wet dock ... and a brave new merchantman which is to be launched shortly." The number of Glasgow's ships rose from thirty in the late 1680s to seventy by the 1730s. For both trade and shipping, there was protectionist legislation that reflected mercantilist ideas. Linked to this, there was a preference for imports of raw materials not manufactured goods, and for the reverse for exports. Thus, silk imports were banned in 1700 and imported printed fabrics in 1721. This operated to the benefit of the British cotton industry.

Defoe's public career as a writer reflected the role of trade in print, and the extent to which commerce involved ideological as well as prudential considerations.[42] He very much supported traditional mercantilist ideas, for example obtaining naval stores from British North America, and not the Baltic, and for developing transoceanic trade including in areas where it was hitherto non-existent or scanty, such as East Africa. Defoe also wanted a robust defence of trade, as in his proposal to destroy the Barbary pirates. He developed these ideas at length in his *A Plan of the English Commerce* (1728). In his Preface, Defoe complained about public ignorance on the topic, which was somewhat surprising as it had been much covered in the press. The theme of reaching out to new lands had an element of *Robinson Crusoe*:

> There are new countries, and new nations, who may be so planted, so improved, and the people so managed, as to create a new commerce; and millions of people shall call for our manufacture, who never called for it before.[43]

41 Anon., *Reasons against building a bridge from Lambeth to Westminster* (London, 1722), p. 6.

42 N. Glaisyer, *The Culture of Commerce in England, 1660–1720* (Woodbridge, 2006).

43 *A Plan*, Preface.

Meanwhile, merchant representation and mercantile business played a growing role in the House of Commons, while, after 1690, there was a massive increase in the number of petitions submitted covering overseas trade. The celebration of the patriot merchant helped make trade a potent political goal and platform, and this linked to the pursuit of maritime hegemony and imperial advantage. Defoe captured this, but his pamphlets revealed another reality, namely that the passage and implementation of foreign trade legislation was not easy, in part due to a continuing mistrust of the complete and lucrative world of international trade, and in part due to strong and persistent rivalries between commercial interests, rivalries that were crucial to their existence as much as their profitability.[44] The appropriate organization for trade remained particularly controversial. Privileged companies that possessed monopolistic rights in particular areas, such as the Royal Africa Company, the Hudson's Bay Company and the East India Company, had promoted investment. However, they aroused anger in those excluded from their benefit, principally the merchants of ports outside London, which were known as outports, but also from other interests in London. This was very much a world Defoe understood and, in his hostility to monopolies, he looked toward the arguments of Josiah tucker (1713–99), a clerical economist.

The distribution of activity and wealth varied, which was a topic of great interest for Defoe in his *Tour*. Academic research has underlined this perception. For example, in response to the rapid spread and increase in the consumption of tea, coffee, and hot chocolate, hot drink utensils, such as teapots and coffee pots, were appearing in Kentish inventories by 1685, although not in Staffordshire until 1725.[45] Alongside contrasts, there were more things available. The probate inventories of the Warwickshire village of Stoneleigh indicated that around 1700 goods appeared there that were produced for mass distribution, such as Ticknall ware for the dairy and tin dripping pans for the hearth.[46] These goods were sold through the retail

44 P. Gauci, *The Politics of Trade: The Overseas Merchant in State and Society, 1660–1720* (Oxford, 2001).

45 K. Wrightson, *Earthly Necessities: Economic Lives in Early Modern Britain* (New Haven, 2000), p. 298.

46 N.W. Alcock, *People at Home: Living in a Warwickshire Village, 1500–1800* (Chichester, 1993).

infrastructure on which Defoe commented so frequently, not least in novels, such as markets and fairs, for example that at Bury, which provided opportunities for criminals. The Coalbrookdale ironworks sold its pots, kettles, and firebacks through fairs in market towns such as Bishop's Castle, Congleton, Oswestry, and Wrexham, as well as to shops including, in 1718, in Birmingham, Bromsgrove, Evesham, Gainsborough, Ludlow, Macclesfield, Manchester, Newton, Shrewsbury, Stowe, and Welshpool.[47]

These were part of a situation that was at once change and continuity, but with the overall direction of travel being a continuation and strengthening of a national integration, one that, onward from 1707, also looked to Scotland as a part of a parliamentary-linked market. At the same time, the integration of Scotland was limited due to local political management, differential purchasing power, and the non-introduction of imperial measures until 1824.

With a characteristic understanding of the tensions within integration, an understanding that can too readily in some contexts be seen as inconsistency, Defoe had a mixed view of London's impact, as in his account of Ipswich, and with it many other towns:

> swallowed up by the immense indraft of trade to the city of London … if it be otherwise at this time, with some other towns, which are lately increased in trade and navigation, wealth, and people, while their neighbours decay, it is because they have some particular trade or accident to trade, which is a kind of nostrum to them, inseparable to the place, and which fixes there by the nature of the thing; as the herring-fishery to Yarmouth; the coal trade to Newcastle; the Leeds clothing-trade; the export of butter and lard, and the great corn trade for Holland, is to Hull; the Virginia and West India trade at Liverpool, the Irish trade to Bristol, and the like.[48]

In practice, as was commonplace with such commentary, this account of specialization was exaggerated, and, in practice, although this was not

47 B. Trinder, *The Industrial Revolution in Shropshire* (3rd ed., Chichester, 2000), p. 27.
48 *Tour*, 1.

generally his theme, there was much variety in the economies and commerce of the places he mentioned.

In considering the issue of change, Defoe wrote of Harwich, a town that had featured in his fiction:

> I cannot think, but that Providence, which made nothing in vain, cannot have reserved so useful, so convenient a port to lie vacant in the world, but that the time will some time or other come (especially considering the improving temper of the present age) when some peculiar beneficial business may be found out, to make the port of Ipswich as useful to the world, and the town as flourishing, as nature has made it proper and capable to be.[49]

Thus, the economy registered the joint responsibility seen more widely. At the same time, presenting this could challenge the author, for—as Defoe repeated in the preface to the second volume—the theme was that of change indeed, such that "as long as England is a trading, improving nation, no perfect description either of the place, the people, or the conditions and state of things can be given."

Visiting Helston in Cornwall on a very busy fair day in 1702, John Evelyn noted "where we dined was the Royal Oak Lottery which one could hardly have expected to have found in a country town so remote from London." He pressed on to Falmouth where he had "a small bowl of punch made with Brazil sugar."[50] Defoe was the prime chronicler of these developing networks. Capital energized, and was energized by, an entrepreneurialism that linked society, economy, government, politics, and religion. As Defoe emphasized both transport and knowledge were important to this entrepreneurialism. In the *Tour*, for example, he offered an account of the development of postal services that did not focus on London, notably those from Exeter to Bristol in 1696 and via Worcester to Chester in 1700. Defoe's account emphasized its value "to maintain the correspondence of merchants and men of business." Moreover, the ability to use the postal

49 *Tour*, 1.
50 BL. Evelyn papers, vol. 49 fols 36–7.

service which he depicted as running on via Manchester and Leeds to Hull meant that:

> the merchants at Hull have immediate advice of their ships which go out of the Channel, and come in.... The shopkeepers and manufacturers can correspond with their dealers at Manchester, Liverpool and Bristol, nay, even with Ireland directly; without the tedious interruption of sending their letters about by London.

Postal services helped increase visual knowledge of England as they led to the appearance of maps and other information. Thus, Captain Carr produced a map in 1668 from a draft by James Hicks, the Chief Clerk to the Post Office, covering all the postroads, their stages and distances, and advertised that it was possible to travel seven miles an hour in the summer and five in the winter.

Detailed mapping was very much on offer in John Ogilby's *Britannia.* A character out of fiction, Ogilby (1600–76), a Scot who ran a dancing school until lamed in a fall, became a tutor, founded Ireland's first theatre, and had his career derailed by the Irish rising of 1641, and turned to making money by translating, first Virgil, and then Aesop and Homer. The Stuart Restoration in 1660 in the person of Charles II brought Ogilby patronage, while he established a printing press in London publishing atlases, among other works. Appointed Cosmographer by Charles II in 1671, and His Majesty's Cosmographer and Geographic Printer in 1674, *Britannia* (1675) was the first volume of what was intended to be a multi-volume road atlas was based on surveys sponsored by the king. One hundred strip maps were shown, with a standard scale of one inch to a mile, and a standard mile of 1,760 standard yards, in place of the earlier frequent use of local measures. Such standardization was important to the understanding of distance and much else. More generally, Defoe's *Tour* was a work in and of such standardization, as it propounded national criteria and measures. The title page of *Britannia* depicted a surveyor instructing two subordinates pushing Ogilby's "Wheel Dimensurator," a measuring wheel that showed the distance travelled on a dial. About 7,500 miles of road were surveyed and the maps were supported by 200 pages of text, which included helpful information, notably a summary of the road, distances, facilities, and turnings to be avoided. In yet another instance of the overlap of art and cartography, the strips were presented as *trompe d'oeil* scrolls with the tops and bottoms furling over themselves. The maps offered considerable detail, including landmarks, the building material of bridges, the direction of slope, inns, fords, and whether roads were enclosed or open. As another warning to travellers, in the woods a haunt of highwaymen were shown.

Ogilby had hoped for the complete project to do more than 22,000 miles of road as well as twenty-five town plans, but died before the prospectus could be this developed. *Britannia* sold well, with four editions in the first two years, and pocket-sized versions appeared in 1719, 1720 and 1757. *Britannia Depicta* (1720), engraved by Emanuel Bowen, had the road maps on both sides of the page, which reduced the bulk, and also included small maps of each of the English and Welsh counties. Other route maps that could have been used to help understand Defoe's *Tour* included William Berry's *The Grand Roads of England* (1679), John Seller's *A New Map of the Roads of England* (c.1690), and George Wildey's *The Roads of England according to Mr Ogilby's Survey* (1712).

Established in 1680, the Penny Post scarcely covered the entire country, but it benefited from the existing road system and from improvements to it. Stage-coaches stopped at inns at each stage of the journey, obtaining fresh horses, and thereby travelling faster. So also did the press, which expanded greatly from the lapsing of the Licensing Act in 1695, and saw London newspapers being sent round the country. The Ogilby maps demonstrated the salience of London, which was far from central geographically, in the national transportation system.

As a parallel with Ogilby, and another aspect of political economy, *Great Britain's Coasting Pilot* (1693), also called *The English Pilot*, was the work of Captain Greenville Collins (*c.* 1634–1694). The sense of mapping as a vital aid to national defence was seen in 1681 when the government appointed Collins, a naval officer and commander of the eight-gun yacht HMS *Merlin*, "to make a survey of the sea coasts of the kingdom by measuring all the sea coasts with a chain and taking all the bearings of all the headlands with their exact latitudes." In some respects, a Crusoe-like figure in his engagement with the wider world, Collins had extensive experience of navigation, including on a failed attempt to reach Japan by a North-East passage north of Asia, an attempt that was wrecked off the island of Novaya Zemlya. He had also served in the Mediterranean against Algerine privateers, who were a major and conspicuous threat to trade, and Collins drew maps on his mission.

Collins lobbied for an improved survey of Britain's coast, not least to rectify mistakes, to provide a centralized system for collecting and disseminating improved maps, and to give himself something to do in the years of peace that began in 1674 and lasted until 1688. The survey, which lasted seven years, faced many problems due to the speed with which it was accomplished, the limited manpower available, and the lack of an available comprehensive land survey of the coastline as the basis for a marine survey. Collins published his results in *Great Britain's Coasting Pilot,* which contained sailing directions, tide tables, coastal views and charts, thus offering a codification of information that often hitherto had been a matter of the local "secret" knowledge of pilots. The complete work was first published in 1693. Collins was allowed to style himself Hydrographer in Ordinary to the King from 1683, while the survey was reprinted frequently in the eighteenth century.

The interest in such mapping was utilitarian in an economic sense, as well as military and political. In 1670, Charles II ordered the Council of Plantations, "to procure maps or charts of all … our plantations abroad, together with the maps … of their respective ports, forts, bays and rivers," in short to prepare a cartographic record of empire.

Capitalism, in the sense of the creation, mobilization and direction of capital, was crucial to the development of Britain internally as well as of its global links and, more specifically, to the ability to make overseas activity and colonies work and, in particular, work in accordance with the global economy.

4. The Society of Outsiders

> "The people who work in the coal mines in this country [Scotland], what with the dejected countenances of the men, occasioned by their poverty and hard labour, and what with the colour or discolouring, which comes from the coal, both to their clothes and complexions, are indeed, frightful fellows at first sight."[1]

As this passage shows, one that could almost have come from George Orwell's *The Road to Wigan Pier* (1936), or, with less of a separation, William Cobbett's *Rural Rides* (1830), Defoe was far more conscious of social differences than most other prominent writers of his age. Indeed, his attitude in the *Review* frequently reflected the stance of a Dissenter criticizing gentlemanly betters.[2] In turn, he was to be attacked by Alexander Pope in the *Dunciad*, as part of an attack on popular literature and what Pope held to be the associated mediocrity of all. It was understandable that Defoe should concentrate on outsiders, and, in this, there is part of his comparison with Dickens. This was also the case in their commitment to reform, their journalism, and various aspects of their novels. In particular, *Colonel Jack* anticipates *Oliver Twist*, although Jack shows more resolve. The major difference is that Dickens could not get inside his female characters as Defoe did.

An outsider himself, Defoe was also well-attuned to the degree to which life, fortune, and therefore problems, opportunities, and status were all precarious. This awareness was notably so because he did not start writing until he reached middle-age and already by then had experienced a range of for-

1 *Tour*, 13.

2 J.E. Evans, "Mr Review on the 'Glorious' *Tatler* and the 'Inimitable' *Spectator*," in *Journal of Newspaper and Periodical History*, 3,1 (1986): pp. 2–9.

tune, including highly precarious circumstances. That awareness was taken forward in his depiction of the often astonishing transformations in the lives of his novelistic protagonists, each of whom was anyway supposed to be a real person, and all of whom were involved in a struggle for survival that could be harrowing and bleak.[3] The preface of *Colonel Jack* promises "the various turns of his fortunes in the world, make a delightful field for the reader to wander in," and, in this, Defoe prefigured Tobias Smollett's novels, just as he anticipated that writer's industry and outsider status, in his case as a cantankerous Scotsman.

Added to this was the degree to which Defoe's most stable novelistic subject, Robinson Crusoe, was, in practice, an outsider whose time in his new world was far longer than any who mention the novel appreciate. Social stability, in this case, required being a real outsider, indeed solitary for most of his time on the island and a director of just one other for most of the remainder.

Any account of society in Defoe's Britain can begin with a sense of this society as having stable structures and norms, but in practice that sense served as well—or even in part instead—as a context for a far more unstable and certainly uncertain reality. Indeed, categories that might appear stable, notably that of gentleman in *Colonel Jack* or respectability in *Roxana*, were brilliantly shown by Defoe to be anything but. In each case, indeed, they are heavily dependent on contingencies, on the standard contrasts between reality and illusion, and on the extent to which the categories themselves were subject to different readings. The last was further brought to the fore by the contingencies already mentioned. Fiction used property issues to ask questions about identity.[4]

These different readings of social and moral categories were a significant theme in Defoe's fiction, and notably so as options were discussed by and for protagonists, including in the *Journal* how best to respond to the Great Plague. These different readings were also part of the process by which characters experienced and responded to possibilities, flux, and change. Far from being a matter of inconsistency on the part of Defoe or his characters, these

3 I. Watt, *The Rise of the Novel* (London, 1957), p. 134.
4 W. Schmidgen, *Eighteenth-Century Fiction and the Law of Property* (Cambridge, 2002).

different readings were important to their stories. They were also significant in his evaluation, or rather re-evaluation, of society in the *Tour*. In that study, social position—and notably aristocratic rank—attracts praise in terms of the use of status and wealth for the cause of improvement. Defoe offered this scrutiny, which is very much that of his values: urban, Dissenting, and entrepreneurial.

There was also in Defoe's work the discussion of gender, not only as a source of contested attitudes to sex, marriage, and motherhood, particularly in *Roxana* where they are articulated at length,[5] but also a powerful cross-current to male issues and priorities of status. Thus, in *Roxana*, there is the use of Amy to give the protagonist influence over the lascivious and exploitative landlord. In contrast, not least in tone, the assumptions of the reader of the *Tour* might have been challenged by the lengthy account of the Derbyshire lead miners, which was somewhat different from the outside perception of the Scottish coal miners cited at the start of this chapter. The cave-dwelling Derbyshire miners are approached in terms of the wife of one, who is praised as worker, mother, and housekeeper and who provides a source of observation different from that of Defoe as narrator. Defoe continued:

> We asked her, if she had a good husband; she smiled, and said, Yes, thanked God for it, and that she was very happy in that, for he worked very hard, and they wanted for nothing that he could do for them; and two or three times made mention of how contented they were. In a word, it was a lecture to us, and that such, I assure you, as made the whole company very grave all the rest of the day. And if it has no effect of that kind upon the reader, the defect must be in telling the story in a less moving manner than the poor woman told it herself.[6]

This was not only an exemplary account of acceptance, an equivalent to the explicit moral politics of much of Defoe's work, but also tellingly the

5 L. Linker, *Dangerous Women, Libertine Epicures, and the Rise of Sensibility, 1670–1730* (Farnham, 2011), pp. 115–39.

6 *Tour*, 8.

exemplary insight of a poor woman and told in terms sympathetic to her. It stands implicitly as a comment on the world of stuff, fashionable but socially useless elegance, seen in Court, but possibly also of the widely-diffused consumerism that is one of Defoe's themes. This consumerism both allows him to repurpose in more beneficial and economic terms the insistent moral discourse against luxury, but also could lead Defoe to consider the perspectives of those who were too poor to participate.

Especially in his London-set novels, Defoe also very much advanced a harsh view of consumerism and notably one that presented it in moral terms. Economic priorities were presented as the dominant reality for women by presenting the choice for many between loss of life and prostitution. Marriage could be a form of intermediate status, one that could be lost by widowhood or separation, and that provided anyway a type of limited control and rights that, while different from those of spinsterhood,[7] were not necessarily easier. Thus, the process by which Roxana considers her options, as commodity, moral agent, and possessor of only so much free will, is presented at great—possibly excessive—length. These options bring to the fore the classic moral issue of temptation, an issue that makes the work conservative only for some of the responses from Roxana to be anything but.[8] So also with the choices that Moll Flanders repeatedly has to make. In her case, crime is part of the matrix: a choice for criminal acts was as part of a world in which sexual acts to advantage were part of the process for self-advancement and could also involve criminal acts and relationships with criminals. This overlap provides a dynamic of that novel.

The role of deception in the presentation of status was frequently present, not only in Defoe's fiction—and more especially but not only with his female characters—but also in the crime reports of the period. Thus, the *Weekly News and Register* of 19 June 1730 provides an account that could have come out of a novel:

> On Tuesday last was held a Board of General Officers at the Horse Guards, Whitehall; at which were present the Right Honourable

7 B. Hill, *Women Alone: Spinsters in England, 1660–1850* (New Haven, 2001).
8 E. Peraldo (ed.), *Daniel Defoe – Roxana: The Fortunate Mistress* (Paris, 2017).

> the Earl of Orkney,[9] President … when one Mary Armitage, wife of Mr Joseph Armitage, cornet in the Lord Stanhope's Dragoons, now in Ireland, moved the said Board, as she had several times before, for a maintenance: But upon examining several witnesses relating to her character, she was proved to have been before married to one Walker a foot soldier; and when married to the said Armitage, she pretended to be a £3000 fortune; instead of which she appeared to have been a person of ill fame; for she was twice in Newgate, and tried at the Old Bailey, about four or five years ago, once for robbing a Jew of a considerable quantity of plate and other things, for which she was burnt in the hand; and a second time for defrauding several persons under false pretences, for which she was fined 20 marks, and ordered to stand in the pillory for the space of one hour. Upon a full hearing, the Board did not think fit to allow her anything; and so dismissed her.

Authorship also involved deception, in part necessarily so due to potential legal penalties. Defoe did nothing to match George Psalmanazar who passed himself off from 1703 as Formosan (Taiwanese) and published a description and an invented language accordingly in 1704, only being discredited in 1708.

Defoe's account of women was far more gritty than that of the later novels of sentiment. He tried to get "inside" the minds of his female characters, albeit with the significant exception of *Robinson Crusoe.* This, instead, becomes a buddies' novel with the arrival of Friday, a process that would have been very different had the latter instead been a woman. There was no inherent reason why that should not have been the case: a woman, as well as a man, could have been brought to the island for slaughter and have escaped as Friday did. Indeed, we are not told the gender of those who are slaughtered. It is interesting to consider how the relationship between the two would have developed had Friday been a woman, but that suggestion may well be regarded as very much of the present moment. As a related

9 George, 1st Earl (1666–1737), a veteran of the conquest of Ireland and of the battle of Blenheim. He was the non-resident Governor of Virginia.

point, there were women in the world of Atlantic piracy, although many were badly exploited in this highly masculine sphere.[10]

Traditionally, when the focus in scholarship was on a class-based approach to social status,[11] women were subsumed within the position of fathers and husbands. That, indeed, captured one reality of their property rights and of the degree of an inequality in society that was ignored by most contemporary commentators. For example, at a time of a French scheme to invade on behalf of the Jacobites, the *York Gazetteer* of 3 April 1744 begins with an essay on how British women backed the present political establishment, arguing that arbitrary power and Catholicism were both antipathetical to women, and continuing:

> It has been observed that the laws relating to them are so favourable, that one would think that they themselves had given votes in enacting them. All the honours and indulgences of society are due to them by our customs, and by our constitution they have all the privileges of English born subjects, without the burdens.

This antipathy was more generally seen as encapsulated in the regulations for Catholic clerical celibacy, which was held to encourage fornication.

More realistically than the *York Gazetteer*, "nothing but money now recommends a woman," as one noted in *Moll Flanders*; another dismissing Moll as a spouse for her son for "she is a beggar." Defoe presents Moll as learning that the situation was even bleaker in London: "that marriages were here the consequences of politic schemes for forming interests and carrying on business ... as the market ran very unhappily on the men's side, I found the women had lost the privilege of saying No."

Yet, this approach also failed to represent the range of possibilities and independences that in practice existed: from moving social status, permanently

10 J. Appleby, *Women and English Piracy, 1540–1720: Partners and Victims of Crime* (Woodbridge, 2013).

11 P. Earle, *The Making of the English Middle Class: Business, Society and Family Life in London, 1660–1730* (London, 1988).

or temporally, through presentation, subterfuge, sex, or matrimony, to the experiences of acting without an automatic dependence on men. Indeed, the use of language was frequently an aspect of a sense of fluidity in status. Engine, a maid in Edward Ravenscroft's play, *The London Cuckolds* (1681), explains:

> this employment was formerly named bawding and pimping, but our age is more civilised and our language much refined. It is now called doing a friend a favour. Whore is now prettily called mistress. Pimp; friend. Cuckold-maker; gallant. Thus the terms being civilised the thing itself becomes more acceptable. What clowns they were in former ages.

However, as Defoe repeatedly makes clear, there was a pronounced element of male control in wielding the financial benefits of marriage and prostitution, and the women could be left out of the story other than as anonymous figures given scant apparent agency. Thus, on 2 February 1702, George Hilton (1674–1725), a Westmorland Catholic gentleman, recorded in his journal: "went to George Dix at the Sandside with Geo Wilson. Broke three of my resolutions, vizt eat flesh, laid with a woman, up till 2 o'clock in the morning."[12] In contrast, Defoe provided women with perspective, reflection and agency.

So also it was with the links between masters and servants. They might be close, but, for most commentators, the latter were largely anonymous or, at most, of only secondary importance. *Roxana* is highly unusual as a novel because Amy, the servant, is a key player, indeed often the key player, in the story. Moreover, Roxana's habit of sharing her bed with Amy, a habit which is not glanced over, and her key role in the latter's sexual initiation, gives not only an intensity in their relationship, but also a directness as well as psychological complexity that was different from that of most writers. Amy scarcely prefigures Pamela, another servant, either in Samuel Richardson's novel or, once enhanced socially by marriage, in Henry Fielding's *Tom Jones.*

Defoe was habitually direct and dynamic in his writing, but in this case there is a sense of pressing on limits. Yet, he was far from alone in this. Eliza

12 A. Hillman (ed.), *The Rake's Diary: The Journal of George Hilton* (Barrow, 1994).

Haywood offered frank discussions of female desire in *The City Jilt* (1726) and *The Mercenary Lover* (1726). *The City Jilt*, with its account of the seduction and abandonment of Glicera, provides a "secret history" to match that of Moll Flanders. In contrast, the standard literature of social norms did not describe what in practice were more variable values and, even more, a diverse set of practices, both of which were revealed by readers to the periodical *Athenian Mercury* in 1690–6, a periodical in which Defoe was involved by his schoolfellow Samuel Wesley.[13] Female writers such as Haywood became more significant than hitherto. They did not constitute a bloc but overlapped in their interests and commitments with male writers. The poet Mary Astell is possibly definable in modern terms, however anachronistically, as a feminist, but also had strong Christian faith.[14]

As another aspect of female prominence, actresses took over female roles from the late seventeenth century, and this led to a more realistic presentation of women and of gender relationships.[15] Both presumably became more relevant to women play-goers, a process encouraged when oratorios gained popularity at the expense of operas onward from the 1730s. Ann Oldfield, who played the title role in Nicholas Rowe's *The Tragedy of Jane Shore* (1714), was an important figure. The practice of presenting women in tragedies as passive heroines, still more the marginal figures that the dramatizations of Classical stories usually allowed, was qualified. George I attended Oldfield's benefit performance in 1724, just as he attended benefits for two actresses in 1720.

At the same time, the emotional position of many women was difficult and that could be captured in the arts. There were romanticized "love matches" in such works as Henry Purcell's opera *Dido and Aeneas* (1689), while Shakespeare's plays were "improved." Thus, *King Lear* appeared in Nahum Tate's version of 1681, with a happy ending in which Cordelia survives and is betrothed to Edgar. In comedies, tensions might be defused and social role-playing presented with humorous consequences and no long-term difficulties thanks to benign fortune. In George Farquhar's *The*

13 H. Berry, *Gender, Society and Print Culture in Late-Stuart England: The Cultural World of the "Athenian Mercury"* (Aldershot, 2003).

14 R. Perry, *The Celebrated Mary Astell, an Early English Feminist* (Chicago, 1986).

15 Elizabeth Howe, *The First English Actresses: Women and Drama 1660–1700* (Cambridge, 1992).

Beaux' Stratagem (1707), the death of Aimwell's brother ensures that he can be an affluent peer and marry Dorinda without her losing status.

The assertiveness of women could be presented sympathetically on the stage—Millamant in William Congreve's play *The Way of the World* (1700) appearing impressive when she makes it clear that marriage to Mirabell (a man) would only be acceptable under certain conditions. With Congreve's comedy *Love for Love* (1695), this has been taken as an example of John Locke's contract theory in drama. At the same time, in *The Way of the World*, Lady Wishfort's desire for a lover is made to appear ridiculous, while the anger of Mrs. Marwood at Mirabell's failure to reciprocate her desire helps provide the malice that drives the malign counter-plot thwarting the benign plot provided by Mirabell's quest for Millamant.

Many men presumably would have preferred their wives to focus on needlework and other traditional activities such as managing the household. Indeed many did, although relatively little needlework survives. In Wallington, however, there are ten panels of needlework done by Julia, Lady Calverley, in the 1710s for the drawing room at Esholt Hall, the family seat. Wallington also has a substantial needlework screen worked in 1727 by Lady Calverley. These reflect the influences of the period: the scenes on the screen are from engravings from editions of Virgil's *Georgics* and *Eclogues*, while the designs of the panels were influenced by imported Oriental textiles.

In many cases, the portrayal of marriage to a callous husband as imprisonment, offered in Thomas Southerne's play, *The Wives Excuse* (1691), was not fanciful: Mrs. Friendall, the perceptive and wronged protagonist, declares, "But I am married. Only pity me," and speaks of the "hard condition of a woman's fate." This was a classic instance of what in 1714 the playwright Nicholas Rowe was to term "She-Tragedy,"[16] a genre to which Defoe contributed in prose. Colonel Jack could have a harsh view of marriage:

> I talked to myself thus; if I marry an honest woman, my children will be taken care of; if she be a slut and abuses me, as I

16 Jean Marsden, *Fatal Desire: Women, Sexuality, and the English State, 1660–1720* (Ithaca, 2006).

> see everybody does; I'll kidnap her and send her to Virginia to my plantations there, and there she shall work hard enough, and fare hard enough to keep her chaste, "I'll warrant her."

This captured not only the sense of marriage as slavery, but also of the American colonies as on the troubling edge of civilization. Roxana, indeed, refers to the marriage contract as making a woman "a slave," a comparison that is repeated.

This depiction was not an exaggeration, and the situation could be even bleaker. A Dutch visitor in 1662 witnessed the treatment of a woman convicted of murdering her husband, a crime treated with particular severity and scant consideration of provocation:

> We saw a young woman, who had stabbed her husband to death … being burned alive.… She was put with her feet into a sawn-through tar barrel.… A clergyman spoke to her for a long time and reproved her and said the prayer. Then faggots [sticks] were piled up against her body … and finally set alight with a torch … and it was ablaze all round.

In 1702, Mary Pierrepont was intended by her father, Evelyn the Marquess of Dorchester, for Clotworthy Skeffington, heir to Viscount Massereene. She felt she "had rather give my hand to the flames than to him," whom she described as Hell, but Dorchester, "the disposer of men," refused to accept her decision for a single life. To escape, Mary eloped.[17]

The content and context of legal relationships over both divorce and women's separate property were complex and unstable, not least affected by the tension between common law and church courts.[18] As with Defoe's accounts, there were also the conventions of stated behavior expected by the courts, with all the problems these posed of establishing the agency and

17 I. Grundy, *Lady Mary Wortley Montagu: Comet of the Enlightenment* (Oxford, 1999), pp. 46–8.

18 S. Staves, *Married Women's Separate Property in England, 1660–1833* (Cambridge, Mass., 1990); L. Stone, *Road to Divorce. England 1530–1987* (Oxford, 1990) and *Uncertain Unions: Marriage in England, 1660–1753* (Oxford, 1992).

purposes of individual men and women. The majority of actions for divorce brought in the London Consistory Court were brought by women against their husbands for cruelty. This was an aspect of women's role as outsiders, for power disproportionately rested with men, and notably so in the Established Church that policed moral codes, seeking to determine Dissenters' behavior as well as Anglicans. There were many women in Dissenter congregations, including the one that Bunyan joined in Bedford, but they also were dominated by men. Defoe criticized the disposal and treatment of women in matrimony, notably in *Conjugal Lewdness or Matrimonial Whoredom* (1727), which includes a criticism of contraception, and also in *Roxana* (1724), in which the protagonist is married off at 15. Defoe also used images from hunting, as in *Moll Flanders* where a son of the house knows "how to catch a woman in his net as a partridge," and Moll suffers accordingly. There was a clear social dimension to this reference, as the Game Act of 1671 made hunting the exclusive preserve of the landed gentry in England and Wales, and was matched by legislation in Scotland and Ireland. There was supplementary legislation in 1707, and the Acts were enforced by the use of gamekeepers.

In another instance of discrimination as well as female vulnerability, women were commonly held responsible for the birth of illegitimate children, a situation in which servants and other female employees proved particularly exposed. Established in 1649, the County House of Correction at Stafford had held ten prisoners between the Easter Sessions of 1678 and the previous session: three men for being pilferers and two for being idle and leading a bad course of life; one woman for pilfering, two for being idle and disorderly, one for being very disorderly and one for having bastards. The last was a frequent problem for the parish authorities, not least as it led to an extra cost for the Poor Rate, and this problem led at Stafford and more generally to the incarceration of some of the women in question.[19] This situation proved of great interest to writers, including Defoe.[20] Sexuality often focused on the use of servants. In *Roxana*, Amy remarks on how the terror of a storm at sea leads to the confession of sins, as with a maid who revealed "that she had lain with her master, and all the apprentices."

19 A.J. Standley, "The Staffordshire House of Correction," in *Staffordshire History*, 15 (1992): pp. 5–8.

20 I. Bell, *Literature and Crime in Augustan England* (London, 1991).

Aside from the difficulties specifically facing unmarried pregnant women, fear of pregnancy itself frequently figures for Defoe's female characters. That makes his Dissenter support for the nuclear family, as in the account of the Derbyshire miner earlier, more impressive because he was fully aware of the difficulties confronting this ideal.

Furthermore, married men had a greater propensity than their spouses to abandon their families. The breakdown of marriage, and desertion by the spouse, commonly featured in accounts of women vagrants. Prostitution, full or part-time, was the fate of many, and in *Moll Flanders* Defoe describes this as of considerable scale in London, as well as presenting it as without any pleasure, the men generally drunk and the women necessarily concerned with money; and the risk of venereal disease being part of the disastrous bargain: "… sowing the contagion in the life-blood of his posterity … when he is, as it were, drunk in the ecstasies of his wicked pleasure, her hands are in his pockets," supplementing her income. Furthermore, although its incidence is very hard to quantify, abortion was an aspect of the world of prostitution, which was blamed largely on women and not on their clients.

There were women who gained wealth by prostitution, and also women involved in responsible economic positions, such as, in the 1690s and 1700s, Elizabeth Hervey, the London agent of her family's cloth manufacturing business in Taunton. Whether as independent agents or as key elements in family businesses, women could play key economic roles. They, however, were atypical, as were heroines. In Delarivier Manley's play, *Lucius: The First Christian King of Britain* (1717), a tale of love and war, Queen Rosalinda, the female lead, is instrumental in the conversion of Lucius to Christianity. Women could rise to be sovereign through inheritance as with Mary and, more clearly, Anne, while others manoeuvred successfully as wives. Yet, the habitually caustic Sarah Marlborough could be brutal about the men of her social standing:

> What a sad thing it is for men that had an opportunity of knowing everything that is valuable be able to talk of nothing but hunting; and … to know so little of accounts or business as to be afraid of their stewards.[21]

21 Sarah Marlborough to Humphry Fish, 13 Mar. 1727, BL. Add. 61444 f. 110.

More common was the exclusion of women from many activities, whether economic or social, for example access to coffee houses as customers. Mary Astell depicted wives as having to flatter their husbands. Those who lived with men but did not become their wives faced uncertainty during marriage and many difficulties afterwards as in the case of the partner of the never-married John, Lord Somers (1651–1716), a key Whig politician who rose to be Lord Chancellor and later Lord President of the Council, and was also, as an instance of the frequent overlaps of the period, President of the Royal Society. He left sisters, but also the situation described by Sir Richard Steele in a letter of 1716 to Charles, 2nd Viscount Townshend, a Secretary of State, sent six months after Somers' death:

> The case I would lay before is that of Mrs Blount,[22] whose name has been for many years mentioned with that of Lord Somers by common fame, to her advantage or disadvantage according as men have been acquainted with her circumstances. She is a woman of the first understanding, daughter of Sir Richard Fanshawe, who died English and Ambassador in Spain. Her commerce with the noble Lord I mention would appear in a very different light from that wherein the world views it, were his letters to her to appear in public. She has volumes of paper which represent the most ardent affection and the highest respect imaginable towards her, a manner in which so wise and good a man could not treat a woman, without having in his own mind satisfaction that from the particularities of their condition, he lived with her without guilt, though not without reproach.
>
> The lady has a spirit and understanding as great as his, and to this is owing her present calamity for she was incapable of reminding him to provide for her, when she knew he loved better than life itself.
>
> The other day I made her a visit and found her sitting amidst her household furniture, dispersed on the floor in order to sell it

22 Conventionally, women above a certain age were referred to as Mrs. whether married or not.

> by parcels to buy bread. She has a son whom our lord proposed to make an equal match to a woman of fifteen thousand pounds a little before his death. But dying intestate that part of his estate which he designed for his family is fallen among his heirs at law ... what I take the presumption to lay before your lordship is that the greatest character of the age wherein we live is likely to be subjected to busy tongues in the most cruel manner by reason of this lady's indigence, and you may rescue the fame of a man who loved and honoured you, from disgrace and infamy by bestowing some employment on the son to support the mother. The gentleman will dishonour no favour done him and an action of so great humanity will lay up for you a right in Providence to be protected in your self and family from the like calamities. The reproaches, misinterpretations and perplexities which always surround men in such stations as your lordship is in, are not worth suffering for anything grandeur can bring with it, except you sweeten your lives, with the consciousness of doing acts like these.[23]

Such accounts made novels plausible.

Inequalities of opportunity separately arising from social status were not the same as those stemming from wealth. Status and wealth were not identical, a difference that caused tension, but was also welcomed by Defoe and other improvers who saw the makers of wealth as enjoying a real status irrespective of their inherited and ostensible one. This was not only an aspect of Defoe's Dissenting background, but also of his concern with individual responsibility. To that end, he also subscribed to a concern with the meritorious rich as well as their poor counterparts. Thus, for Defoe there was a focus on trade and industry, both seen as meritorious, and not, despite the later reading of his work as pro-capitalist,[24] on finance. Defoe, however, was not as hostile to finance as Jonathan Swift who, in his pamphlet, *The Conduct of the Allies* (1711), referred to:

> undertakers and projectors of loans and funds. These, finding that the gentlemen of estates were not willing to come into their

23 Steele to Townshend, 1 Nov. 1716, BL. Althorp papers E6.
24 B. Dijkstra, *Defoe and Economics* (Basingstoke, 1987).

> measures, fell upon those new schemes of raising money, in order to create a moneyed interest, that might in time vie with the land, and of which they hoped to be at the head.[25]

To a degree, Swift was capturing the sense that there was a rivalry over the composition and purpose of the élite, one that subverted any apparent stability and, more profoundly, social stability. In practice, despite Tory claims to the contrary, the Whigs were a party of great landowners, as well as of bankers, Dissenters, and the urban interest; just as the Whigs also included many supporters of the Church of England. Thus, the Whigs were able to find members of the social élite to act as Lords Lieutenant, the key figure of authority and prestige in their counties. The Lords Lieutenant played an important role in rallying and leading local forces in any crisis. Thus, in September 1715, in the face of Jacobite moves, all Lords Lieutenant were ordered to their counties,[26] although not all did so.

At the same time, however defined, the social élite was scarcely fixed. Creations kept up the overall size of the peerage as well as reflecting political favor and success: there were 43 by William III, 42 by Anne, and 66 by George I. The peerage were important across the settings and means of power. Thus in 1699, Edward, 1st Earl of Jersey, suggesting new Lords Lieutenant for the three Ridings of Yorkshire, sent William III "a list of some people of quality of that county, and in what riding their estates lie."[27]

There was only limited challenge to their position.[28] In 1719, the Peerage Bill sought to fix the size of the English nobility, only to be defeated, in part because of the heavy representation in the Commons of gentry who aspired to ennoblement and, in their own terms, were already members of the élite. Display by and of the élite was captured in John Wootton's painting of *The First Duke of Dorset Returning to Dover Castle after Taking the Oath as Lord Warden of the Cinque Ports*. Painted immediately after the

25 H. Davis et al (eds.), *The Prose Works of Jonathan Swift*, 16 vols (Oxford, 1939–68), VI, 10.

26 James, 1st Duke of Montrose to 3rd Earl of Loudoun, 20 Sept. 1715, HL. LO. 11669.

27 Jersey to William, 9 June 1699, BL. Add. 63630 f. 136.

28 J. Cannon, *Aristocratic Century. The peerage of eighteenth-century England* (Cambridge, 1984).

event in 1728 and sumptuously framed with family devices atop the frame, it was displayed in the family seat at Knole.

Members of the élite could crash financially. Defoe noted that some families lost "fine parts and new-built palaces" due to ruin in the "South Sea deluge."[29] Nevertheless, the élite generally were protected by their wealth and borrowing capability. They were able to afford new stately homes. Newly-established families asserted their position with ostentation expressed in stone. The banker Henry Hoare marked the transition stemming from his purchase of the Stourton estate in 1717, and the foundation of a new landed dynasty, by pulling down the old Stourton House and calling in the fashionable Scottish-born architect Colen Campbell to build a Palladian house at Stourhead in 1720–4. Blenheim asserted the new status of the Churchills as Dukes of Marlborough. The initial plan for the salon included niches containing ten-foot-high Italian statues representing the Virtues. So too with Vanbrugh's work for Admiral Delaval at Seaton Delaval, while Castle Howard—which he gained the commission to build for the Earl of Carlisle in 1699—was the first private house in England to be built with a dome, and its hall is seventy feet high.

More generally, although the homes of the élite, both rural and urban, proclaimed hierarchy, permanence and status, they also reflected a concern to be up-to-date, which indeed was part of this status.[30]

Conversely, many of the élite ignored their castles, which were uncomfortable to live in. In 1672, two hundred and seventy-two wagon loads of lead and timber were taken from Warkworth Castle when Elizabeth Percy, the widow of Jocelyn, 11th Earl of Northumberland, gave the materials to one of the estate auditors. On the death of the last Earl of Lincoln in 1693, Tattershall Castle passed into the ownership of the Fortescue family who did not live there, and the abandoned castle became derelict, with part used as a cattle shed.

The less affluent landed gentry shared in aspects of élite culture, although in a less ostentatious and conspicuous manner. In Berkshire, much of the building was undertaken by gentry families favoring solid, four-square

29 *Tour*, 1.

30 C. Christie, *The British Country House in the Eighteenth Century* (Manchester, 2000).

houses, such as Ardington House built in 1719–20, all probably designed by local builders, such as Thomas Strong and William Townsend, although they could be influenced by Wren and Vanbrugh.[31]

The middling orders found themselves in a more vulnerable position,[32] and, linked to that, were challenged by the porosity of social boundaries. This included the impact on younger sons of primogeniture (inheritance by the eldest), of the relative openness of marital conventions, and of the active nature of the land market. The notices in the *London Journal* of 27 November 1725 include one for Thomas Rogers, "Agent for Persons that Buy or Sell Merchandises, Estates etc," who was willing to meet customers at the Rainbow Coffeehouse in London. The notice very much represented a society where land and money were easily exchanged, the very element captured by Defoe:

> Any person that has twenty thousand pounds to lay out, may be informed where a good estate in land very improvable, may be purchased.... A person wants to buy a large estate with a seat, fit for a gentleman in any pleasant healthy county. Another an estate from about £6,000 to £8,000 value not far from Bath. Another a good house with some farms near Reading of from £200 to £500 a year. Another an estate of £2,000 value, or upwards, in Middlesex, Essex or Hertfordshire.

At the beginning of *Robinson Crusoe*, the young protagonist is rebuked by his father for planning to seek his fortune away by going to sea. The father, instead, wants him to be a lawyer and praises:

31 T. Williamson, "Estate Management and Landscape Design," in C. Ridgway and R. Williams (eds.), *Sir John Vanbrugh and Landscape Architecture in Baroque England, 1690–1730* (Stroud, 2000), p. 28; G. Tyack, "Country Houses, *c.*1500–*c.*1750," in J. Dils (eds.), *An Historical Atlas of Berkshire* (Reading, 1998), p. 60.

32 M. Hunt, *The Middling Sort: Commerce, Gender and the Family in England, 1680–1780* (1996); A Sippel, "*Aurea mediocritas?* The Middling Sort of People in the English-Speaking World in the Seventeenth and Eighteenth Centuries," in *XVII–XVIII*, 72 (2015): pp. 29–39.

> … application and industry…. He told me it was for men of desperate fortunes on one hand, or of aspiring, superior fortune on the other, who went abroad upon adventures, to rise by enterprise, and make themselves famous in undertakings of a nature out of the common road; that these things were all either too far above me, or too far below me; that mine was the middle state, or what might be called the upper station of low life, which he had found by long experience was the best state in the world, the most suited to human happiness, not exposed to the miseries and hardships, the labour and sufferings of the mechanick part of mankind, and not embarrassed with the pride, luxury, ambition, and envy of the upper part of mankind … not subjected to so many distempers and uneasiness, either of body or mind, as those were who, by vicious living, luxury and extravagancies on one hand, or by hard labour, want of necessaries and mean or insufficient diet on the other hand, bring distempers upon themselves by the natural consequences of their way of living.

The virtuous nature of "the middle station of life" is one of Defoe's themes not only here but also more widely, and it captures his social politics and, indeed, aspiration for the whole of society. Compared to most novelists, Defoe was more critical of the gentlemanly status, in part because he was concerned about how it set a model for others while many who had the rank were reprobates.[33]

There is in the depiction of the "middling" orders an aspect of Defoe's Dissenting politics, as this group is that which would be most accessible to religious guidance. In *Roxana*, Sir Robert Clayton—a real person, a Whig Lord Mayor of London, and thus part of Defoe's overlap of history and fiction—is used to offer Defoe's perspective on the relationship between merchants and the nobility:

> a true-bred merchant is the best gentleman in the nation; that in knowledge, in manners, in judgment of things, the merchant

33 H.J. Shroff, *The Eighteenth-Century Novel: The Idea of the Gentleman* (London, 1983).

> out-did many of the nobility; that having once mastered the world, and being above the demand of business, though no real estate, they were then superior to most gentlemen … that an estate is a pond; but that a trade was a spring.

In *Moll Flanders*, the young Moll has a very different sense of true value to that of the élite:

> I understood by being a gentlewoman was to be able to work for myself, and get enough to keep me without that terrible bugbear going to service, whereas they meant to live great, rich and high, and I know not what…. I understood by it no more than to be able to get my bread by my own work.

Moll, in contrast, later finds her ex-highwayman husband unwilling, as a would-be gentleman, his most distinctive virtue, to cope first with the prospect of transportation to America— "that servitude and hard labour were things gentlemen could never stoop to." Thereafter, he proves unable to cope with the nature of life there because he is not business-like:

> he was bred a gentleman, and by consequence was not only unacquainted, but indolent, and when we did settle, would much rather go out into the woods with his gun, which they call there hunting, and which is the ordinary work of the Indians, and which they do as servants … he would much rather do that than attend the natural business of his plantation.

Defoe could be very harsh about the poor, as in the Journal:

> it was impossible to beat anything into the heads of the poor. They went on with the usual impetuosity of their tempers, full of outcries and lamentations when taken [by the plague], but madly careless of themselves, foolhardy and obstinate, while they were well. Where they could get employment they pushed into any kind of business, the most dangerous and the most liable to infection.

Defoe was also harsh in his account of Charlton Horn Fair, a scene of popular festivities, which was held at Cuckold's Point on the Thames east of London until, in 1872, it was closed for its disorder. Defoe provided a harsher account than that by Ned Ward in his *A Frolick to Horn-Fair* (1700). Defoe was blunt:

> … the yearly collected rabble of mad-people, at Horn-Fair; the rudeness of which I cannot but think, is such as ought to be suppressed, and indeed in a civilised well-governed nation, it may well be said to be unsufferable. The mob indeed at that time take all kinds of liberties, and the women are especially imprudent for that day; as if it was a day that justified the giving themselves a loose to all manner of indecency and immodesty, without any reproach, or without suffering the censure which such behaviour would deserve at another time…. I recommend it to the public justice to be suppressed, as a nuisance and offence to all sober people.[34]

The sense of a precarious order was repeatedly, but variously, captured by Defoe. In the *Tour*, Cornwall was very much seen by Defoe as remote and as less active than Devon, albeit offering prospects from trade, notably at Falmouth, its major port. He wrote:

> The game called the Hurlers, is a thing the Cornish men value themselves much upon; I confess, I see nothing in it, but that it is a rude violent play among the boors, or country people; brutish and furious, and a sort of an evidence, that they were once, a kind of barbarians.

Characteristically, Defoe does not see a Classical route as a cause of praise:

> It seems, to me, something to resemble the old way of play, as it was then called, with whirle-bats, with which Hercules

34 *Tour*, 1.

> slew the giant, when he undertook to clean the Augean stable.[35]

Defoe added the colonial dimension to his praise of the middling orders, with characters pursuing wealth in the Americas, wealth that was a matter of trade, land, and the control over labor that was present in indentured workers and, even more, slavery. In *Moll Flanders*, where wealth comes and goes, it is difficult to find emotional and financial constancy, and crime, marriage, and inheritance are ways to acquire capital. An exacerbation of a sense of precariousness was unsurprising given the financial crash of 1720, the South Sea Bubble. Moll's third husband:

> finding his income not suited to the manner of living which he had intended, if I had brought him what he expected, and being under a disappointment in his return of his plantations in Virginia, he discovered many times his inclination of going over to Virginia to live upon his own.

Very often, the action in the novels, that which set the background both for success or failure, and for reflection and repentance, exemplified the argument Defoe had earlier advanced in *Jure Divino* (1706): "Self-Love's the Ground of all things we do." This point was underlined in a footnote: "self-interest is such a prevailing bond, especially when reason concurs, that it never fails to open men's eyes to their own advantage."[36]

Yet, that individualism, with everything it could offer for good and bad, had to be constrained by the natural order implanted in men by God. That order, once breached, opened the path to havoc. Defoe could see a direct parallel between poor practice and civil war, the latter a threatening frame of reference in light of recent history. Attacking stockjobbers, he asked:

> What safety can we have at home, while our peace is at the mercy of such men, and it is in their power to job the nation into feuds among ourselves, and to declare a new sort of civil

35 *Tour*, 4.

36 Defoe, *Jure Divino* (London, 1706), IV, 8.

> war among us when they please? Nay, the war they manage is carried on with worse weapons than swords and muskets; [mortar] bombs may fire our towns and troops overrun and plunder us. But these people can ruin men silently, undermine and impoverish by a sort of impenetrable artifice, like poison that works at a distance.... They can draw up their armies and levy troops ... and the poor passive tradesmen, like the peasant in Flanders, are plundered by both sides, and hardly knows who hurts them.[37]

The references to the economic damage being akin to being a casualty of war was a pointed one. The overlap between the "middling orders," and, on the other hand, the varied groupings of the "people" and the "labouring poor" was captured by Defoe. This overlap reflected, but brought to the fore, other aspects of precariousness. A pamphleteer of 1730 observes:

> I believe there is no sober man doubts but there is a difference, a very material one, between liberty and licentiousness, and that the latter ought to be restrained ... the ruin of free governments has been owing to nothing more than to the degenerating of liberty into licentiousness.[38]

Defoe very much presented prosperity as linked to employment, as in his account of rural industry near Halifax where, alongside the fulling mills owned by the clothiers, there are, as part of an industrial structure directed by them:

> an infinite number of cottages or small dwellings, in which dwell the workmen which are employed, the women and children of whom, are always busy carding, spinning, etc. so that no hands being unemployed, all can gain their bread, even from the

37 *Villainy of Stockjobbers Detected*, p. 21.

38 Anon., *The Treaty of Seville and the measures that have been taken for the four last years, impartially considered* (London, 1730), p. 30.

> youngest to the ancient; hardly anything above four years old, but its hands are sufficient to itself.[39]

Yet, the nature of employment could also be dire, as with the Fifeshire coal-field, regarding which see the quote at the start of this chapter. Similarly, in *Colonel Jack*, the owner of the London glassworks refers to "my black wretches that work there at the furnace." Alongside similarities in the sense of work and limited returns, there were also very different milieux for the poor, notably those of town and country.[40] The various modes and sites of employment of these milieux had a major impact on experience, living standards, and life chances.

Defoe could take a stance on issues involving the unfortunate that had consequences for other sections of the poor. This situation was, and is, scarcely unusual, but it also reveals the personal preferences of the "improvers." Thus, Defoe's scheme, drafted in 1709 for a new town of German Protestant refugees in the New Forest reflected his concern with Protestant refugees and was rooted in utopian ideas of improvement. Yet, the scheme was doomed to failure because of his disregard for local common rights, even though he was aware that they were of value to local people.[41] The New Forest was to him a "vast wilderness,"[42] a sort of internal frontier of improving settlement, which provided a parallel with his views of the New World. In practice, Defoe's views of the New Forest were inconsistent and, more profoundly, unrealistic as the soil was poor and badly-drained.[43] Defoe did not tend to be good on the issue of soil quality, which given the limited range, by later standards, of fertilizers, was of particular significance.

Although the fictional discussion of crime and criminality[44] generally

39 *Tour*, 8.

40 C. Estabrook, *Urbane and Rustic England: Cultural Ties and Social Spheres in the Provinces, 1660–1780* (Stanford, 1999).

41 R. Hoyle, "Daniel Defoe, the Palatine refugees and a projected new town in the New Forest, 1790," in *Southern History*, 38 (2016): 130–49; T. Speller, "Violence, Reason, and Enclosure in Defoe's *Tour*," in *Studies in English Literature*, 51 (2011): pp. 585–604.

42 *Review*, 5 July 1709.

43 Hoyle, "Defoe," p. 149.

44 I. Bell, *Literature and Crime in Augustan England* (London, 1991).

did not focus on this social level, those who could not support themselves were regarded as a problem that, alongside charity for the "deserving," required deterrence as part of the solution. Thus, John Locke proposed to the Board of Trade that the poor should be made to work, and that those who refused be whipped. The Poor Law put responsibility on individual parishes, a system that provided little ease for itinerants travelling to seek work or for other reasons. The Poor Relief Act of 1662 made the right to relief dependent upon the pauper being settled in the parish, a practice that led to the exclusion of paupers deemed non-resident. Individuals could only remain in a new parish if they had a settlement certificate stating that their former parish would support them if they became a burden on the Poor Rate. The rest of the poor were liable to be driven away unless they could find work, which contributed to a more general pattern of widespread migration, albeit in general over relatively short distances of under twenty kilometres. Young women moving for marriage was an important cause.[45]

The care offered by parishes was very varied, and having preferred the French care of orphans in *Moll Flanders*, Defoe has Roxana worry about the likely fate of her children: "a hundred terrible things came into my thoughts; *viz* of parish-children being starved at nurse; of their being ruined, let grow crooked, lamed, and the like, for want of being taken care of." The position of children captured Defoe's concern and presented an awareness of social differences, as more generally was the case in *Roxana*. In this novel, perceptions of morality are shown as overly affected by harsh social practices and norms:

> Great Men are delivered from the burthen of their natural children, or bastards, as to their maintenance: This is the main affliction in other cases, when there is not substance sufficient, without breaking into the fortunes of the family; in those cases, either a man's legitimate children suffer, which is very unnatural; or the unfortunate mother of that illegitimate birth, has a dreadful affliction, either of being turned off with her child, and be left to starve etc. or of seeing the poor infant packed off with a piece of

45 B. Stapleton, "Migration in Pre-Industrial Southern England: The Example of Odiham," in *Southern History*, 10 (1988): p. 89.

> money, to some of those she-butchers, who take children off of their hands, as, it is called; that is to say, starve them, and, in a word, murder them.

The position of children, and their capacity to be moral agents, came center-stage in *Colonel Jack*, with the differing courses and responses from him and his companions. Defoe drives the point home in the preface, with the second and third paragraphs announcing:

> Here's room for just and copious observations, on the blessing, and advantages of a sober and well-governed education, and the ruin of so many thousands of youths of all kinds, in this nation, for want of it: also how much public schools, and charities might be improved to prevent the destruction of so many unhappy children, as, in this town [London], are every year bred up for the gallows.
>
> The miserable condition of unhappy children, many of whose natural tempers are docile, and would lead them to learn the best things rather than the worst, is truly deplorable, and is abundantly seen in the history of this man's childhood.... If he had come into the world with the advantage of education, and been well instructed how to improve the generous principles he had in him, what a man might he not have been.

A growing institutionalization of poor relief from the 1690s involved the designation of specific facilities, in part to ensure work and in part in order to distribute poor relief. These "corporations for the poor" began with one in Bristol in 1696, a public workhouse and hospital earlier used as a mansion, then a sugar processor, and then a mint for the recoinage of 1696. Similarly, an increase in the number of the poor led Worcester in 1703 to establish a workhouse in which "beggars and idle people" could be compelled to work. The Workhouse Test Act of 1723 encouraged parishes to found workhouses to provide the poor with work and accommodation. All Nottingham's parishes built workhouses under the Act in the 1720s, and Lancaster one in 1730. Nevertheless, "out relief," the practice of providing help to the poor in their own homes rather than in institutions, was cheaper and remained more common. In his *A Journal of the Plague Year* (1721), Defoe pressed the case for a charitable treatment of the poor.[46]

The precariousness of prosperity and status looked toward other aspects that concerned contemporaries, including religious observance and political order. In 1693, James Vernon, the confidential figure in the offices of the Secretaries of State, drew unsympathetic attention to the extent to which the poor, in the face of weather-related dearth, were engaged in food riots:

> the insolence of the common people has risen to a great height about the carrying out of corn especially at Worcester where they not only force the prisons to let out some of their companions that were committed for these riots but they went in a body where they heard there was a great magazine of corn which they took away and sold it by proclamation for two shillings per bushel.[47]

A month later, Vernon added his worry that Jacobites would exploit the anger of London silk weavers at parliamentary measures to obstruct the import of raw silk from the Netherlands.[48]

During the 1722 elections, John, Lord Perceval, a Whig, reported, "The mob which is generally High Church have where they are strongest been insufferably rude, as at Westminster, Reading, Stafford etc."[49] He thus brought together social, religious and political criteria in order to depict a general crisis, the depiction, in turn, contributing to a sense of alarm. That year, Defoe referred "to the rage of the street" in *Moll Flanders* in describing the London response to a pickpocket. Yet, he presented this popular justice as less harsh than the judicial hanging, which that novel frequently mentioned as the return for crime.

Conversely, the firmness of the law was a product of a general sense of lawlessness and of the more specific difficulties encountered by royal

46 V.L. Wainwright, "Lending to the Lord: Defoe's Rhetorical Design in *A Journal of the Plague Year*," in *British Journal for Eighteenth-Century Studies*, 13 (1990): pp. 59–72.

47 Vernon to William Blathwayt, 4 May 1693, Beinecke, Osborn Shelves, Blathwayt Box, 19.

48 *Ibid.*, 2 June 1693.

49 Egmont to Daniel Dering, 27 Mar. 1722, BL. Add. 47029 f. 110.

officials, for example the armed resistance by smugglers seeking to export wool near Hastings in 1697.[50]

A sense of precariousness was captured in the response to the large-scale Glasgow Malt Tax riots of 1725 of Charles Cathcart, a member of the Scottish nobility and of the circle of George, Prince of Wales, later George II:

> If the disturbers of the public peace there are not soon brought to condign punishment I am much afraid a thorough disregard and contempt to all laws will obtain over the whole country.

Cathcart also feared that the social sway of the gentry was at risk: "If any wrong step is taken at Edinburgh, it will hardly be in the power of our gentry to keep our folk from following any bad example that may be set to them."[51] Alongside general disquiet, there was a feeling that particular areas were lawless, especially rural areas where settlement was sparse. Thus, visiting Brent Tor on Dartmoor, James Yonge claimed in 1674 that the locals were "rude and brutish."[52]

Yet, far from being restricted to remote areas, the cities, most notably the largest, London, also posed many issues of conduct and control, as well as creating a strong sense of the presence, even threat, of outsiders, and of the extent to which they set their own rules.[53] Defoe proved particularly adept at capturing this dimension.

In addition, aside from the many private editions of works in copyright, piracy was an aspect of the world of outsiders that affected Britain; in this case not only trade but also norms of behavior. Piracy became particularly prominent and serious in the late 1710s, and it is unsurprising that Defoe, who was fascinated by marginal environments, employed it as a plot device capable of producing radical plot shifts, notably in *Robinson Crusoe* and

50 H. Rawlings (ed.), "Extracts from Sussex Quarter Session Records, 1626–1800," in *Sussex History*, 32 (autumn 1991): pp. 38–41.
51 Cathcart to Earl of Loudoun, 4, 29 July 1725, HL. LO. 7897, 7943.
52 F. Poynter (ed.), *The Journal of James Yonge* (London, 1963), p. 145.
53 T. Hitchcock and H. Shore (eds.), *The Streets of London: From the Great Fire to the Great Stink* (London, 2003).

Colonel Jack. Defoe's attitude could be very relaxed, which was a major contrast to that of the government. Thus, in *Colonel Jack*, which was published in 1722 against a background of much, largely successful, government action aimed at piracy, the protagonist is on a ship en-route from Liverpool to Virginia that is "met with" by pirates:

> who plundered us of everything they could come at that was for their turn, that is to say, provisions, ammunition, small arms and money; but to give the rogues their due, thought they were the most abandoned wretches that were ever seen, they did not use us ill; and as to my loss, it was not considerable, the cargo which I had on board, was in goods, and was of no use to them; nor could they come at those things without rummaging the whole ship, which they did not think worth their while.

At greater length, Jack subsequently discusses being chased by pirates off Antigua, but escaping due to the intervention of a British warship. Piracy brought together the adventures of fiction, both plot and style of writing, with Defoe's commitment to a mature discussion of interests affecting trade.[54] The character of Defoe's novels as at once spiritual autobiographies and adventure stories was such that although the pirates led to abrupt plot shifts, their actions were a context for the developing spiritual autobiography rather than replacing it. Indeed, the struggle with the exigencies of repentance became the key adventure in the novels. These adventures were made more humane by a lack on Defoe's part of the misanthropy seen with Swift.

54 J.H. Baer, "'The Complicated Plot of Piracy': Aspects of English Criminal Law and the Image of the Pirate in Defoe," in *The Eighteenth Century*, 23 (1982): pp. 3–26.

5. Christians and Values

"Time, the great devourer of the works of men."[1]

Defoe was born against the backdrop of 130 years of acute religious division, tension, and disorder. Far from the Protestant Reformation creating an agreed new order, it had established a rift with those who remained Catholics. This rift was not only a matter of national attitudes and laws, and questions about loyalty. As recorded by Defoe, the rift also involved a sense of local memory. The Marian persecutions of Protestants in 1553–8 were remembered where they had occurred, and Defoe linked this to the contemporary challenge from Jacobitism which he presented as characterized by Catholicism, although most Jacobites were not Catholic. This was seen in his account of Hadley [Hadleigh] and his linkage of it to the Atterbury Plot of 1721–2:

> From Ipswich I took a turn into the country to Hadley, principally to satisfy my curiosity, and see the place where that famous martyr, and pattern of charity and religious zeal in Queen Mary's time, Dr Rowland Taylor, was put to death [1555]; the inhabitants, who have a wonderful veneration for his memory, show the very place where the stake which he was bound to, was set up, and they have put a stone upon it, which nobody will remove; but it is a more lasting monument to him that he lives in the hearts of the people. I say more lasting than a tomb of marble would be, for the memory of that good man will certainly never be out of the poor people's minds, as long as this island shall retain the Protestant religion among them; how long that may be, as things are going, and if the detestable conspiracy

1 *Tour*, 6.

> of the Papists now on foot should succeed, I will not pretend to say.[2]

This was scarcely Defoe as a proto-Enlightenment modernizer, however that dubious category is to be defined. Antipathy to Catholics is triggered soon after by a visit to Framlingham Castle where Mary Tudor rallied support in 1553 against a Protestant coup:

> when the Northumberland faction, in behalf of the Lady Jane [Grey], endeavoured to supplant her; and it was this part of Suffolk where the Gospellers, as they were then called, preferred their loyalty to their religion, and complimented the popish line at [the] expense of their share of the Reformation; but they paid dear for it, and their successors have learned better politics since.[3]

A visit to Ripon leaves Defoe more balanced, praising the charity of the monastery but attacking the right of sanctuary there.[4] Furthermore, in decrying what he saw as the total lack of religious observance in northern Scotland, Defoe praised, as the sole exception, "the diligence of the Popish clergy" in this matter.[5] His general theme, however, was very clearly anti-Catholic, and certainly so in comparison with the later fascination for monastic ruins, as in his visit to the impressive remains of Melrose Abbey in Scotland.

Defoe was far from alone in his comprehensive criticism. *The Weekly Journal: or British Gazetteer* of 2 May 1724 carries a long letter from "Mithridates," a pseudonymous correspondent living in Croydon, who argues that praying to saints and angels dethroned Jesus as the sole mediator, that the "written word of God" should be the only rule, and, with several examples, that some saints were "such scandalous persons, that a good Christian would not very willingly keep company with them when living, much less desire their prayers or intercession when dead."

2 *Tour*, 1.
3 *Tour*, 1.
4 *Tour*, 8.
5 *Tour*, 13.

At the same time as anti-Catholicism, Protestant divisions had become more acute from the late sixteenth century. Indeed, some Catholics were banned (in theory) and divisions between Protestants were much more visible. Religious differences between Protestants is a crucial factor in the civil wars that began in 1639 in Scotland and from 1642 in England. That in Ireland from 1641, in contrast, began as a Catholic rebellion. Religious differences encouraged people to turn to violence against kin and neighbors, and also helped define areas of control. Thus, the Puritanism of much of Northamptonshire was crucial in its support for the Parliamentary cause. The civil wars were accompanied by iconic violence as in 1646 when Chester surrendered and the victorious Parliamentarians vandalized the cathedral, breaking the stained glass, and damaging the organ and much else. In his *Tour*, Defoe refers to some of the battle sites of the wars, for example Marston Moor (1644), as well as to other events such as the Royalist siege of the Parliamentary stronghold of Taunton, a center of Dissent.

Parliamentary victory was followed in 1653 by a military coup carried out by Oliver Cromwell and this sought to enforce an oppressive Puritanism that, for the sake of continued reformation and godliness, repressed popular rituals deemed superstitious or profane, such as Christmas and dancing round the maypole. The Puritan "Cultural Revolution," however, was an unpopular failure, several preachers comparing England to Israel after Moses, ungrateful for the gifts of God. This was a troubling legacy for Puritanism.

This unpopularity contributed greatly to the return of monarchy in 1660, in the person of Charles II, which was not a propitious background for Puritans or indeed the Dissenting world that expanded, as Puritans such as, notably with the Act of Uniformity of 1662, Defoe's family, left the Church of England or were driven from it. The new regime incorporated some former Cromwellians, but others were purged. The Act for the Well Governing and Regulating of Corporations of 1661 provided for the purging from borough offices of those regarded as disaffected, which was established primarily by their unwillingness to take the oaths of supremacy and allegiance. Moreover, if it was "expedient for the public safety," they could be purged even though, as with Gloucester Corporation, willing to take the oaths. Thirteen of the twenty-four burgesses of Tewkesbury were purged in 1662.

The revived Crown-Church order lasted until the 1670s when Charles II changed tack, returning to his promise of toleration made in the Declaration of Breda in 1660, in part now due to his Catholic inclinations rather than the need to win Puritan support for his Restoration. In 1672, Charles issued a Declaration of Indulgence in which he claimed the prerogative right to vary the parliamentary settlement of religious affairs. He suspended the enforcement of the laws against worship by Dissenters and permitted Catholics to practice in their own homes. Hundreds of Defoe's fellow Dissenters registered their place of worship as legal meeting houses. Easing the plight of Dissenters was regarded as a way to rally support against the Church of England, but most Dissenters were more concerned about Catholicism.

In turn, the warp and weft of politics, regarding which see chapter eight, led Charles to surmount the political crisis of 1678–81, that of the Popish Plot followed by the Exclusion Crisis. To do so he moved to the Tories who were very much the party of the Church of England. In return for their support, Charles was willing to allow Tory churchmen to initiate prosecutions of Dissenters in the early 1680s on a more extensive scale than at any point in the reign.

His brother and successor, James II (and VII), however, broke with the Tories from 1685 as he sought to Catholicize government, both central and local, and to establish full religious and civil equality for Catholics. The Declaration of Indulgence (1687) granted all Christians full equality of religious practice, which was a challenge to the position of the Established Church and one again to the benefit of Dissenters as well as Catholics. Catholics were made Lords Lieutenant, while Catholics and Dissenters were installed as members of corporations. This policy divided the Dissenters, for many—especially in London—distrusted James and did not want to be part of a situation in which Catholicism was resurgent.

The fictional Robinson Crusoe returned to England in 1687, and published in 1719 when Britain was at war with Spain, the novel provided Defoe with opportunities to make anti-Catholic remarks. Thus, Crusoe, who is presented as saved by his conversion to faith, would "rather be delivered up to the savages, and be devoured alive, than fall into the merciless claws of the priests, and be carried into the Inquisition," the claws very much an animalistic image. At the same time, as with Mary Tudor's reign, it is difficult to know what would have happened had James's reign been longer, while the private opinions of individuals during the reign are also unclear. As Defoe bookended his response to James's reign by participation in two rebellions, his view is readily apparent.

The "Glorious Revolution" ensured a Presbyterian ascendancy in Scotland where episcopacy was abolished, in England and Wales a loosened hegemony for the Church of England, and in Ireland a further weakening of the Catholic position. Under the Act for Exempting their Majesties Protestant Subjects, Dissenting from the Church of England, from the Penalties of Certain Laws, the concessionary but restrictive formulation of what is better known as the Toleration Act (1689), Dissenters (Protestant Nonconformists who believed in the Trinity) could obtain licences as ministers or schoolmasters. The Act was followed by the registration of numerous Dissenting meeting-houses—at least 113 in Devon alone by 1701. Yet, even under the Toleration Act, there were still significant restrictions for Dissenters. To obtain the licences as ministers or schoolmasters, applicants had to take the oaths of Supremacy and Allegiance, accept thirty-six of the thirty-nine Articles, make the Declaration against Transubstantiation, and be registered with a bishop or at the Quarter Sessions, both of which posed problems. More generally, the Test Act remained in force and Dissenters were in many ways outsiders because they had to conform in order to obtain marriage and burial, although not baptism. The implications for Defoe would have been considerable.

The Presbyterians, Independents (Congregationalists), Quakers and Baptists were the leading Dissenting churches. Dissenting thought was scarcely free from differences and paradoxes, notably over the doctrine of the Trinity against those who looked toward what was to become Unitarianism. In theological terms that were of direct relevance for the history and salvation of individuals, there was in particular the rivalry between determinism and free will that was central to the discussion of predestination. What that meant for redemption was unclear, but it was certainly constrained.[6] In terms of fiction, these issues were inherently imaginative in their potential, and this provided a very different stance and approach from

6 S. Sim, *Negotiations with Paradox: Narrative Practice and Narrative Form in Bunyan and Defoe* (London, 1990).

that of the theological disquisitions with which from his upbringing Defoe was clearly familiar.

In *Robinson Crusoe*, Crusoe reflects in favor of the changes stemming from the Glorious Revolution and in contrast to clerical intolerance: "My man Friday was a Protestant, his father was a pagan and a cannibal, and the Spaniard was a Papist; however, I allowed liberty of conscience throughout my dominions." The novel also provided Defoe with an opportunity to attack the nature of established churches:

> As to all the disputes, wranglings, strife, and contention, which has happened in the world about religion, whether niceties in doctrines, or schemes of church government, they were all perfectly useless to us; as for ought I can yet see, they have been to all the rest of the world. We had the sure guide to heaven, viz the word of God; and we had, blessed be God, comfortable views of the spirit of God teaching and instructing us by his word, leading us into all truth, and making us both willing and obedient to the instruction of his word.

The range of religious practice was extensive, although there were very few professed atheists. Thus, John Toland, the author of *Christianity Not Mysterious* (1696) and a radical, nevertheless still suggested a God as a force that had created a world and a humanity capable of goodness and not intervening through revelation or miracles. To Toland, the universe had purpose, but no need for priests.[7]

Many members of the Church of England regarded the changes from 1689 as a threat not only to their position, but also to the religious orthodoxy, moral order and socio-political cohesion that the Church was seen as representing and sustaining. This perception that the Toleration Act was but part of a longer-lasting crisis contributed to a feeling of malaise and uncertainty. The individual quest for salvation depicted by Bunyan sidetracked—and thus evaded—the intercessory role of the Sacraments, administering clergy, and the ceremonial context in formal sacral spaces. Thus,

7 J.A.I. Champion, *Republican Learning: John Toland and the Crisis of Christian Culture, 1696–1722* (Manchester, 2003).

clerical ideology was challenged, although some clerics (and laity) refused to accept the new system and became Non-Jurors. The writings of radical Whigs, such as Toland, sharpened a sense of anxiety, as did Dissenter practices and alleged ambition. Occasional Conformity, the loophole that allowed Dissenters to avoid restrictions on non-Anglicans, particularly troubled many commentators favorable to the Church of England.[8] Sir John Pakington, a Tory MP, in 1703 told the House of Commons that Occasional Conformity was "scandalous and knavish, that the Dissenters would soon control the Commons," and "then I'll venture to pronounce the days of the Church of England few." The practice was called "playing bo-peep with God Almighty." Defoe saw an element of institutional as well as personal hypocrisy in Occasional Conformity. Moreover, it could lead to permanent conformity, as well as encourage the marriage of Dissenters into the Church of England families.

Defoe's political thought has been seen as primarily focused on his Dissenter concern with the issues of religious toleration.[9] This also provided a way for Defoe to consider earlier Stuart rulers, notably Charles I, and also to argue in favor of resistance theory, which was his response not to kingship, but to bad kings.[10]

Defoe's ecclesiology was scarcely the view of the Church of England which, after 1689, could not enforce church attendance, and saw irreligion as both cause and consequence of the erosion of its position. This led to the foundation in 1698–9 of the Society for Promoting Christian Knowledge (SPCK), an Anglican missionary society. The preamble to its charter in 1699 claimed that "gross ignorance of the Christian religion" was responsible for a threatening "growth of vice and immorality," a situation the Church sought to combat by making active use of the Church courts. There was a strong wish among many in the Church of England for Dissenters to return in order to strengthen it against Catholicism, but alongside talk about church reunion that did not mean any strong interest in compromise.

8 Defoe, *An Enquiry into the Occasional Conformity of Dissenters, in Cases of Preferment* (London, 1697).

9 R.P. Clark, "Defoe, Dissent, and Early Whig Ideology," in *Historical Ideology*, 52 (2009): 595–614, esp. 614.

10 Defoe, *Jure Divino*.

In contrast, and to the alarm of the Dissenters, there were significant defections to the Church of England—including Samuel Wesley, the son of a minister deprived in 1662 and the father of John and Charles, who had conformed and entered Oxford accordingly and with whom Defoe had a furious debate over Dissenting Academies. Two future Archbishops of Canterbury, John Potter (r. 1737–47) and Thomas Secker (r. 1758–68), also defected. Potter, who conformed in 1688, became Regius Professor of Divinity at Oxford in 1708, and though a Whig willing to accept toleration, became a High Churchman.[11] John Tillotson, Archbishop from 1691 to 1694, had Dissenter parents.

Tory concerns looked toward the 1709 sermon by Dr Henry Sacheverell, a Tory High Anglican cleric, who argued that the Church was in danger under the (Glorious) Revolution settlement, as interpreted by the Whigs. Indeed, Thomas, 1st Earl of Wharton and Whig Lord Lieutenant of Ireland, was sufficiently pro-Dissenter in this period that the Irish House of Lords, where the bishops were influential, complained to Queen Anne. He was recalled in 1710, although this would have happened anyway with the new Tory government. Defoe was concerned about divisions between Protestants, arguing that the Church's hostile treatment of Dissenters in Ireland would help Catholics,[12] an argument rejected by Jonathan Swift. Defoe also repeatedly attacked Sacheverell, notably in the *Review*. The Sacheverell Riots in 1710 saw High Church mobs attack Dissenter meeting houses in London. Many of its thronging streets were in the shadow of an architectural masterpiece that was both new and built for the glory of God, Wren's rebuilt St. Paul's Cathedral, which with one of the first domes erected in England, was a triumph of architectural accomplishment. It borrowed the style of church architecture seen in Baroque Rome, but did so to the glory of the Church of England. Built in 1711–24, Thomas Archer's St. Philip's in Birmingham was another major Baroque work.

The politics of religion were very much at the fore, and increasingly so in the 1710s. The Tory ministry of 1710–14 sought to restrict religious

11 S. Taylor, "Archbishop Potter and the Dissenters," in *Yale University Library Gazette*, 67 (1993): pp. 118–26.

12 Defoe, *The Parallel: or, Persecution of Protestants. The Shortest Way to Prevent the Growth of Popery in Ireland*, p. 20.

toleration in the Occasional Conformity (1711) and Schism (1714) Acts, which were measures unwelcome to Dissenters. Given Defoe's links with Robert Harley, 1st Earl of Oxford and a key member of the ministry, these put him in a very difficult position. Yet, Defoe was correct to feel that Tory parliamentarians and ministerial rivals of Harley were the drivers, and not Harley with his different pre-Tory background. Moreover, aside from the press and political ambiguities he might adopt, there was in the 1710s scant consistency among either Tories or Whigs.

In turn, the Whigs, in power from 1714, took a different, more favorable, position toward Dissent, leading to bitter Tory criticism as well as widespread anti-Dissenting riots in 1715. In his pamphlet, *Elements of Policy Civil and Ecclesiastical, In Mathematical Method* (1716), Matthias Earbery, a Nonjuring cleric whose title was an ironical tribute to the fashion for Political Arithmetic, attacked Whig notions that power came from the people, as it had, he argued, serious consequences in Church government.[13] A Tory pamphleteer of 1724 had a Whig declare, "The Church of England and her clergy were ever objects of my most implacable aversion."[14] In 1719, during the Whig Stanhope-Sunderland ministry of 1717–20, a particular period of reaching out to Dissenters, the Corporation Act was diluted, so that many Dissenters were able to play a role in local government, although Whig ministerial interest in repealing the Act, as well as the Test Act, did not come to fruition. From 1722, as a reward for loyalty, a small *regium donum* (king's gift) was given annually in England to trustees from the Baptist, Independent, and Presbyterian churches, the funds being used to supplement the incomes of their indigent clerics. From 1726, there were annual Indemnity Acts protecting the Dissenters from malicious prosecution, especially office holders who had failed to take communion, and effectively extending toleration further.

At the same time, despite many Whigs being Dissenters, as Defoe noted was unusually not the case in Northallerton,[15] the Whig position did not mean hostility to the Church of England. Some prominent Whig politicians,

13 [M. Earbery], *Elements*, p. 87.

14 Anon., *The True Character of a Triumphant Whig both in his Religion and Politics* (London, 1724), pp. 7–8.

15 *Tour*, 9.

such as Thomas, 1st Duke of Newcastle, were devout, and there were many who were "Church Whigs."[16] There could be "inconsistencies" between political and religious beliefs, at least in terms of standard definitions of being a Whig and Tory—for example, in the case of William Nicolson, Bishop of Carlisle, who as a reminder of the overlapping nature of interest and activity was also a Fellow of the Royal Society.

Meanwhile, thanks to toleration, the Church of England had to operate more effectively if it was to resist the challenge of other churches. Some bishops, such as Henry Compton and Gilbert Burnet, consciously responded to the idea of competition from Dissent—Burnet's *Discourse of the Pastoral Care* (1692) for clerics being written in this vein. The duty of the Church to teach the faith was much emphasized: religious activism for clergy and laity alike was stressed in Anglican propaganda. Indeed, the Church continued the themes established at the Reformation of strengthening piety and education, the two contributing to the central role of the Church in issues of identity and politics, but also leaving room for significant tension between clergy and laity.[17] The role of the Church involved continued effort, not least in providing a clergy and churches able to serve all. At the start of the eighteenth-century, in the Northamptonshire parish of Upper Boddington the roof was repaired at the rate of a bay per four years. The plastering was mended, the Creed was put up, and the windows repaired—the vicar, Edward Maynard, recording it "not being half-glazed," gave them new glazing: "I made it at last a lightsome, decent church which was before a most squalid rueful place."[18]

Defoe offered the different perspective of a Dissenter, but with a particular emphasis on lay piety that suggested a contrasting context for spiritual guidance. Indeed, *Robinson Crusoe* shows a Christian society without a priesthood, indeed presenting a very potent image of a God-fearing utopia. Defoe provided very few clergy as characters in his novels. There

16 Edward Carteret to Charles, 2nd Viscount Townshend, Secretary of State for the Northern Department, 2 July 1725, NA. SP. 35/57 f. 9.

17 D. Spaeth, *The Church in an Age of Danger: Parsons and Parishioners, 1660–1740* (Cambridge, 2000); Spaeth is less optimistic than W. Gibson, *The Church of England 1688–1832: Unity and Accord* (London, 2001).

18 B. Hornby, "A Place in History through Memoirs," in *Northamptonshire Past and Present*, 51 (1998): pp. 31–2.

was no equivalent at length to the benign Parson Adams in *Joseph Andrews*, although, far more briefly, Moll Flanders owed much in her repentance to the clergyman who in Newgate brought forward her capacity for repentance.

In the *Tour*, Defoe commented about the unusual piety shown in a Cameronian [Covenanter] preaching to near 7,000 in the open in Scotland: "… if there was an equal zeal … our churches would be more thronged, and our ale-houses and fields less thronged on the Sabbath-Day than they are now."[19] This was a counterpart to his earlier remark on "this idle generation."

Yet, there was widespread piety in the British Isles, as well as observance of the formal requirements of the churches. Despite criticism, this was the case in England with the Church of England. So also with the Dissenters who remained focused on the areas and groups earlier characterized as Puritans, while also joining new activist institutions such as Societies for the Reformation of Manners. Dissenters differed among themselves on theological and organizational points—notably over Trinitarian and predestinarian beliefs—but there was a common focus on personal piety and a direct relationship with divine grace.[20] Defoe offered both, as well as criticism of the wealth of the Established Church, as in the very fine housing of the clergy in Lichfield.[21] Conversely, he praised Quakers in *Roxana*; while, in America, Moll Flanders finds a "honest Quaker, who proved a faithful, generous, and steady friend to us," and is very important to the *denouement*.

Towns were often centers of Dissent, challenging the Church's religious-cultural hegemony in the locality and region, just as they could seek to resist the attempts of the local gentry to control their parliamentary representation, and were also centers of a changing economy. Defoe captured all those elements. In Taunton, 11 May, the anniversary of the raising of the siege of the Parliamentary-held stronghold in 1645 during the English Civil War—a result that was seen as a great providential salvation against

19 *Tour*, 12, 6.

20 M. Watts, *The Dissenters: From the Reformation to the French Revolution* (Oxford, 1978).

21 *Tour*, 7.

the Royalists—was celebrated with sermons preached into the 1720s and an annual celebration into the 1770s. Politically, these events were a Dissenter radical expression of opposition to the Tory Corporation (town government). These local politics relived, and were enlivened by, historical divisions.[22]

Nevertheless, aside from Whig bishops who preached moderation in dealing with Dissenters, so did Tories such as Compton. Protestant unity, indeed, remained a prominent theme in public polemic, not least against Jacobitism. Defoe was part of this broad, Protestant patriotism, one in which Dissenters found many ways to integrate.

However, slowing down the account to be more chronologically specific, at the very time in which Defoe moved toward novels, the Dissenters were under pressure from public reports due to the ministerial wish to assist them. Largely advanced by alarmists—such as Sir Jonathan Trelawny, Bishop of Winchester—troubling rumors began to circulate that the Dissenters would demand the abolition of bishops or equality between the Church of England and the Dissenters. There were increasing problems for the ministry in the House of Lords where many bishops, including Archbishop Dawes of York, began to display considerable independence in the winter of 1717–18, not least by signing protests, which offered a way to publicize their views.

Identity and Integration were not only issues for Dissenters. So also, despite many initial difficulties, did foreign Protestant refugees find various ways to integrate. In 1685, Louis XIV's abrogation of Huguenot (French Protestant) rights had led to a flood of refugees, so that, by 1690, Huguenots were about 8–10 percent of London's population. There were tensions in the short term, notably pressure on housing and competition for jobs. However, in the long term, the Huguenots were to integrate well into London society, a process helped along by their being Protestants, although not of the Church of England. Alongside new ideas, unfamiliar foods were introduced, including caraway seeds, garlic, oxtail soup, and pickles. After the Huguenot influx followed that of German Protestants fleeing Catholic persecution, especially in the Palatinate, and by 1709 over

22 W. Gibson, *Religion and the Enlightenment 1600–1800: Conflict and the Rise of Civic Humanism in Taunton* (Berne, 2007).

13,000 Palatine refugees had reached London—about 6,500 of them housed in army tents on Blackheath, and about 5,100 in the navy's ropeyards at nearby Deptford. Defoe supported the idea of a new town for them in the New Forest, a theme to which he returned in the *Tour.* Many of the Palatines went on to settle in Britain's colonies. Immigration contributed for Whigs a sense that mixture brought progress, one that Defoe underlines in his satirical *The True-Born Englishman* (1701), which in part was a defence of William III against xenophobic attacks.[23]

The Tories, in contrast, were hostile to Protestant immigrants. In part, this hostility was religious in character, with the Church of England depicted by Tories as under threat from Whig attitudes and policies. A dilution of the Englishness of the Church of England was an important aspect of this apparent threat, with the Huguenots and the Palatines presented as allies of the Whigs, who ensured by the General Naturalisation Act of 1709 that they could be granted naturalization if they conformed to the Church, although few were and the unpopular act was repealed in 1712.[24] In practice, the Latitudinarians within the Church of England were sympathetic to Continental Protestants, but polemicists did not do subtlety. There was also concern about a threat of competition to English workers, a theme raised in the Commons in 1697 when two Whigs introduced a General Naturalisation bill.

Religion was important to identity at many levels. The Scots in part defined themselves by successfully pursuing and defending a distinctive religious settlement. In turn, this settlement encouraged a sense of separation in—and from—England. As a result, much that focused on the Church was in effect a pursuit of nationalism. This was differently true of anti-Catholicism, with *The Preservative Against Popery* tracts of the 1680s enormously popular and influential in the eighteenth century. Other religious works sold extremely wel—including *The Church Catechism Explained by Way of Question and Answer, and Confirmed by Scripture Proofs* (1700) by

23 W. Schmidgen, *Exquisite Mixture: The Virtues of Impurity in Early Modern England* (Philadelphia, 2012).

24 D. Statt, "The birthright of an Englishman: the practice of naturalization and denization of immigrants under the later Stuarts and early Hanoverians," in *Proceedings of the Huguenot Society*, 25 (1989): pp. 68–70.

the Kent cleric John Lewis, a keen defender of the Church of England. Ten thousand copies of Robert Nelson's *A Companion for Festivals and Fasts of the Church of England* (1704) were printed in four and a half years.

Newspapers provided frequent accounts of the mistreatment of Protestants in Catholic-ruled countries, and if notably so in France, not only there.[25] In January 1725, the envoy of the Elector of Saxony, who was also King of Poland, reported that the recent judicial execution of Protestants in Thorn, Poland, had made "a devil of a clamour. All the nation complains loudly and accuse us of persecution and cruelty." Anglican congregations were urged to raise funds for them in "Church briefs."[26]

The *London Journal* was typical in trying to link Catholicism abroad with a threat at home and in arguing that all Protestants were involved: "Every advance of the power of bigotry abroad threatens us with a Popish pretender at home.... [T]he blows of the Jesuits are meant against Protestants of all denominations."[27]

Moreover, British diplomats were instructed to support foreign Protestants. Jacobite activity encouraged bouts of anti-Catholic comment. Thus, the Atterbury Plot was accompanied by much criticism of Catholicism, including calls for reprisals against the Pope.[28]

Earlier, in his *Memoirs of a Cavalier; or A Military Journal of the Wars in Germany, and the Wars in England. From the Years 1632 to 1648* (1720), Defoe again returns to the seventeenth century, but brings it up to date as he is writing against the background of religious tension in Europe. The story, which Defoe presents as the truth, has its English protagonist witness the murderous and vividly described sack of Magdeburg by Catholic forces in 1631 and then enter the army of King Gustav Adolph of Sweden, later a Protestant hero. Offering an account of martial culture,[29] Singleton continues a military career. He proves far less committed in the British civil conflicts from the late 1630s, but serves in the Royalist forces, albeit having

25 *Craftsman*, 26 Dec. 1730.

26 Jacques Le Coq, Saxon envoy, to Count Lagnasc, Saxon Foreign Minister, 9 Jan. 1725, Dresden, Staatsarchiv, Geheimes Kabinett, Ges. 2673.

27 *London Journal*, 9, 23 Jan. 1725, see also 2 Jan.

28 *Applebee's Original Weekly Journal*, 15 Dec. 1722.

29 R. Manning, *The Martial Ethos in the Three Kingdoms* (Oxford, 2003).

a critical view of Charles I and Prince Rupert of the Rhine. Unusually for Defoe, the hero is a second son from the landed upper orders, discusses conflict, and is opposed to the Parliamentary side—but more typically the hero perspective is that of a loner.

Religious identities and differences were a context for political rivalries, and, as Defoe's work shows, for the fate of fictional characters. Nevertheless, in local communities, such as Great Yarmouth, a workable accommodation with Dissenters was gradually teased out after the Toleration Act,[30] and the decline in ecclesiastical authority provided more opportunities for Dissenter activity. Indeed, Defoe found it:

> … a very well governed town; and I have nowhere in England observed the Sabbath-Day so exactly kept, or the breach so continually punished as in this place, which I name to their honour. Among all these regularities, it is no wonder if we do not find abundance of revelling, or that there is little encouragement to assemblies, plays, and gaming-meetings.[31]

By the 1720s, the national situation was very different from that of the 1660s, and there was scant interest in any enforced uniformity. Defoe benefited from this transition and contributed to it. There was also a degree of compromise in the treatment of Catholics—although in the 1740s, Jaques Sterne, the Whig Archdeacon of Cleveland, broke up a Catholic convent in York. Defoe notes that Durham was:

> full of Roman Catholics, who live peaceably and disturb nobody, and nobody them; for we being there on a holiday, saw them going as publicly to mass as the Dissenters did on other days to their meeting-house.[32]

Characteristically, very different emphases can be found from the same period, but consistency was not the nature of the world on which Defoe

30 P. Gauci, *Politics and Society in Great Yarmouth, 1660–1722* (Oxford, 1990).
31 *Tour*, 1.
32 *Tour*, 9.

reported, nor, indeed, always central to his content and even tone. Thus, considering bigamy in the long absence of her husband, Roxana presents the Devil as linked to the Catholic option:

> the same Devil that put this into my head, bade me go to any of the Romish clergy, and under the pretence of confession, state the case exactly, and I should see they would either resolve it to be no sin at all, or absolve me upon the easiest penance. This I had a strong inclination to try, but I know not what scruple put me off of it, for I could never bring myself to like having to do with those priests; and though it was strange that I, who had thus prostituted my chastity, and given up all sense of virtue … should scruple any thing.… I argued with myself that I could not be a cheat in anything that was esteemed sacred … in short though I was a whore, yet I was a Protestant whore, and could not act as if I was Popish, upon any account whatsoever.

The remark about being a Protestant whore echoed one by Nell Gwyn, an actress who became a mistress to Charles II, when contrasting herself with the Catholic Louise de Keroualle, whom Charles II made Duchess of Portsmouth.

Moll Flanders does not have the same concern as Roxana with repentance, but the novel is again about the divine economy of good and bad, more specifically of the inability "to preserve the most solemn resolutions of virtue without divine assistance." Alongside the curiosities of literary criticism, for example *Moll Flanders* as a "heroic myth … of capitalist society" analogous to Soviet art in the 1920s,[33] comes the exemplary purpose outlined by Defoe in the Preface:

> Throughout the infinite variety of this book, this fundamental is most strictly adhered to; there is not a wicked action in any part of it, but is first and last rendered unhappy and unfortunate; there is not a superlative villain brought upon the stage, but either he is brought to an unhappy end, or brought to be a

33 Juliet Mitchell, "Introduction" to the 1978 Penguin edition of *Moll Flanders*, p. 25.

> penitent; there is not an ill thing mentioned but it is condemned, even in the relation, nor a virtuous, just thing but it carries its praise along with it.

Defoe understands that this point might not be welcome to the readers:

> … the mercy of God in sparing my life, and a greater detestation of my past sins…. This may be thought inconsistent in itself, and wide from the business of this book; particularly, I reflect that many of those who may be pleased and diverted with the relation of the wild and wicked part of my story may not relish this, which is really the best part of my life, the most advantageous to myself, and the most instructive to others. Such, however, will, I hope, allow me the liberty to make my story complete. It would be a severe satire on such to say that they do not relish the repentance as much as they do the crime; and that they had rather the history were a complete tragedy, as it was very likely to have been.

Roxana presents such a tragedy, but in *Moll Flanders* "more than secret assistance from the grace of God" is provided to help her repent truly, in the shape of hard efforts, by a good clergyman. He is very different to the drunken ordinary of Newgate, and is therefore able to break into her very soul.

Alongside his concern in particular for Dissenters, Defoe had a more general conviction that Providence plays a key role in the details as well as generalities of life, a conviction that was widespread in the period. This provided a context for his consideration of religion but also of other factors. Thus, in the discussion of Nottingham in the *Tour*, he writes:

> There was once a handsome town-house here for the sessions or assizes, and other public business; but … being over-crowded upon occasion of the assizes last year, it cracked … it must be said (I think) that Providence had more care of the judges, and their needful attendants, than the townsmen had.[34]

34 *Tour*, 8.

Providence as a concept was potentially morally ambiguous, but it was understood as not dispensing with the need for good and appropriate conduct. This is captured with the *Journal* in the discussion of the response to plague, as Defoe advises the reader:

> he should keep his eye upon the particular providences which occur at that time, and look upon them complexly, as they regard one another, and as all together regard the question before him: and then, I think, he may safely take them for intimations from Heaven of what is his unquestioned duty to do in such a case; I mean as to going away from or staying in the place where we dwell, when visited with an infectious distemper.

Uncertain, the narrator turned over the pages of the Bible and appealed for divine guidance, the 91st Psalm leading him to believe that the protection of God should lead him to stay put.

The question of "Which Church?" dominated much discussion, but such discussion rested for many, probably most, and certainly for Defoe, on a commitment to fundamentals of faith in a universe determined by divine rules that were implanted in human society. This led to dramas of sin, repentance and redemption, ones that were driven home most strongly by Defoe in *Roxana*, his last novel. Defoe very much set the personal behavior of his protagonist in terms of a consumerism that could extend to a failure to grasp the realities of faith:

> I had no sense of repentance, from the true motive of repentance; I saw nothing of the corruption of nature, the sin of my life, as an offence against God; as a thing odious to the holiness of his being.

The novel offers a history of Roxana, one in which time is very specific and yet also general, recording events and their links:

> What a glorious testimony it is to the Justice of Providence, and to the concern Providence has in guiding all the affairs of men, (even the least, as well as the greatest) that the most secret crimes

> are, by the most unforeseen accidents, brought to light, and discovered.
>
> Another reflection was, how just it is, that sin and shame follow one-another so constantly at the heels, that they are not like attendants only, but like cause and consequence, necessarily connected one with another; that the crime going before, the scandal is certain to follow; and that it is not in the power of human nature to conceal the first, or avoid the last.

There was an instructive degree of Calvinist concerns, even orthodoxy, in the novel.[35] Defoe's theme, here and elsewhere, was not that of a religious resignation, but instead a more active engagement.

Repentance was the theme earlier when Colonel Jack meets his divorced wife who had been sent as a criminal to Virginia:

> she said, as her breach with me began first in folly, and ended in sin, so her whole life afterward, was a continued series of calamity, sin and sorrow, sin and shame, and at least misery; that she was deluded into gay company, and to an expensive way of living which betrayed her to several wicked courses to support the expenses of it; that after a thousand distresses and difficulties, being not able to maintain herself, she was reduced to extreme poverty.

She adds a clear Biblical reference and lesson: "now she was with the Prodigal brought to desire husks with swine."

Defoe used *Colonel Jack* to offer a clear link of fiction with religion, the two providing an exemplary sermon. He reflects at the close:

> Perhaps, when I wrote these things down, I did not foresee that the writings of our own stories would be so much the fashion in England, or so agreeable to others to read, as I find custom and the humour of the times has caused it to be; if anyone that

35 S. Sim, "Opposing the unopposable: Roxana and the paradox of reprobation," in *British Journal for Eighteenth-Century Studies*, 8 (1985): pp. 179–86.

> reads my story pleases to make the same just reflections, which I acknowledge, I ought to have made; he will reap the benefit of my misfortunes, perhaps, more than I have done myself; it is evident by the long series of changes, and turns, which have appeared in the narrow compass of one private mean person's life, that the history of men's lives may be many ways made useful, and instructing to those who read them, if moral and religious improvement, and reflections are made by those that write them … in collecting the various changes, and turns of my affairs, I saw clearer than ever I had done before, how an invisible overruling power, a hand influenced from above, governs all our actions of every kind, limits all our designs, and orders the events of everything relating to us…. [M]y story, I would have all that design to read it, prepare to do so with the temper of penitents.

Criminality offered much of the fascination and contingency of event in *Moll Flanders* and *Colonel Jack*. At the same time, the novelistic ability to add the psychology of the protagonists, provided their subjectivity and, separately, a means for readers to identify with them.[36] Yet, the reiterated drive of themes of sin and repentance meant that this identification was probably in part voyeuristic.

Defoe's concern with the Devil was seen at length in his *Political History of the Devil* (1726),[37] a lengthy work in which the nature of the protagonist is probed from the perspective that he exists, and that Milton's account is inadequate. This was not the England that was to feature prominently in the stays made soon after by Montesquieu and Voltaire. Far from Defoe's emphasis on religion appearing redundant in a "polite" world, such language was frequently present across society, not least in politics. Britain might ally with Catholic powers, but a strong element of confessional consciousness was provided by history as well as a sense of a present threatened by Jacobitism. The latter was repeatedly criticized as Catholic, and Protestants who

36 H. Gladfelder, *Criminality and Narrative in Eighteenth-Century England: Beyond the Law* (Baltimore, 2001).

37 Defoe, *The Political History of the Devil,* Irving Rothman and Michael Bowerman (eds.) (New York, 2003).

supported the Jacobite cause were castigated accordingly as in *The Flying Post* of 12 January 1720 in an essay that attacked Tories for suggesting "to the brainless mob that the Church is in danger" and drew on Stuart failures to support Continental Protestants in the late 1610s and 1620s. Similarly, "Anti-Jack" in the *London Journal* of 16 January 1720 refers to the Popish Plot and to the Irish rising of 1641.

The sense of Catholic threat was made far more serious by Catholics being within British society as well as challenging it from without. As such, Catholicism matched the assault from diabolical agencies, which also benefited from being able to adopt disguise. Defoe, in contrast, saw himself as valiant for truth, stripping society down in his analysis and his characters through their being made to confront this morality. While Providence served, as with Crusoe, to help structure the past of his characters, the future provided opportunities for a free-will bound up in moral (and other) choice,[38] and without being able to have recourse to the later indulgence of a sensibility without piety as a lived experience. Moreover, there was not to be a reliance on hedonism. In 1716, Benjamin Hoadly, Bishop of Bangor and chaplain to George I, a firm Whig of a latitudinarian character, observes: "Self-interest ought to govern us all, and will govern us, either real, or mistaken. My happiness is my self-interest."[39]

This was a self-interest of morality, one that Defoe's fiction and characters came to understand and follow. Reason and faith were his conjoined, mutually-reinforcing weapons in life and necessarily so because, as he affirms in an assault on masquerades: "We live in a general disguise."[40] Faith and the willingness to repent were key guides in this human maze.

38 S. Sim, "Interrogating an Ideology: Defoe's *Robinson Crusoe*," in *British Journal for Eighteenth-Century Studies*, 10 (1987): p. 172.

39 Hoadly to Charlotte Clayton, 1 Sept. 1716, Beinecke, Osborn Shelves, fc 110 2.

40 Defoe, *A System of Magic; or A History of the Black Arts* (London, 1727).

6. Enlightenment and Science

A sense of moral purpose and responsibility is made clear by Defoe in the *Review* of 2 October 1711, in which the true ends for which learning and wit "are given"—in other words, bestowed by God, as "the establishing virtue in and the shaming vice out of the world." This was the rationality that Defoe affirmed, and while it might in "modern" terms be seen as religious in character—and therefore for some reason irrelevant—in practice it was one that related to important currents of thought in seventeenth-century English intellectual society. These included the overlapping arguments of Francis Bacon, the so-called Scientific Revolution, the focus on reform associated with Political Arithmetic, and seen differently, with the foundation in 1660 of the Royal Society for the Promotion of Natural Knowledge. Generally known as the Royal Society, the latter was designed to provide progress from the discovery of God's creation, notably in the form of the objective account of experiments,[1] and thus to help overcome the religious and political divisions of recent years, and in doing so offer a latitudinarian improvement.

Each of these currents was of significance to Defoe's writing, more particularly in his reform literature. They were also of consequence for his methods of explication. Defoe's deep understanding of Baconian ideas in part reflected his attendance, from 1674 to 1679, at the Dissenter academy in Stoke Newington near London. Charles Morton, who founded this academy, had been part of the Baconian circle that was significant in mid-century Oxford, and Morton went on to produce *Compendium Physicae* (1687), which in part reflected Baconian scientific concepts. *Robinson Crusoe* is in many respects a Baconian text.[2] Morton insisted his students had a scientific education that would be the first resort over the supernatural.

1 W. Lynch, *Solomon's Child. Method in the Early Royal Society of London* (Stanford, 2001).

2 I. Vickers, *Defoe and the New Sciences* (Cambridge, 1996).

At the same time, Morton was a Dissenting minister who suffered from the Act of Uniformity, under which he lost his living, and that played an important role in his legacy toward Defoe. Indeed, the harshness of the ecclesiastical order as well as concern about James II led Morton to emigrate in 1686 to New England where he taught at Harvard and became a minister, being prosecuted for sedition in 1687 when James's allies were in control. Morton supported the conversion of Native Americans, a policy that Defoe was to support both for explicit religious reasons and for the implicit reason of fulfilling human potential—not just in the shape of those converted but also in helping British colonialization. Defoe took a similar view in his attitude to the Highlands and Islands of Scotland, which were presented in the *Tour* as barbaric.

There was no attempt on the part of Defoe or others to exclude a divine role for Providence, and the divine intention expressed in the workings of the natural order was all-important to his argument. Far from seeing reason and religion as incompatible, most intellectuals and churchmen shared John Locke's view that a rational appreciation of man's situation would lead people to be Christians. By treating reason as a divine gift, and the universe as a divine creation, they established a framework in which—far from observation being hostile to faith—the two were each part of God's creation. Understandably given the prominence of Locke, Defoe was influenced by his ideas on how facts, ideas, and experience were perceived and incorporated, and thus how education occurred. This involved an element of naturalism but more particularly fostered the transformation of sensation into thought.[3] Enlightenment was part of the religious worldview and vocabulary; the closely intertwined literatures of religion and science sought to engage not only with existing issues, but also with the questions created by encounters with new environments.[4] This process is dramatized by Defoe, not only in *Robinson Crusoe*, but also in *Farther Adventures of Robinson Crusoe*, *Captain Singleton*, and *A New Voyage*. In doing so, Defoe's account overlapped with the methods and insights offered by captive narratives.[5]

3 E. Tavor, *Scepticism, Society and the Eighteenth-Century Novel* (London, 1987).
4 D. Van Renen, *Nature and the New Science in England, 1665–1726* (Oxford, 2018).
5 L. Colley, *Captives: Britain, Empire and the World 1600–1850* (London, 2002);

Locke was widely read in Dissenting Academies, while many Church of England clerics—notably Tillotson and his imitators—offered strongly rational sermons rather than any form of mystical spiritualism. In *Roxana*, Defoe refers to "a Supreme Power managing, directing, and governing in both causes and events in this world." This approach was able to save humanity from despair, which was one of Defoe's themes. Indeed, both in generalities and specifics, that approach was very much the case with his novels. Thus, in *Robinson Crusoe*, he reflects via Crusoe:

> So little do we see before us in the world, and so much reason have we to depend cheerfully upon the great Maker of the world, that He does not leave his creatures so absolutely destitute, but that in the worst circumstances they have always something to be thankful for, and sometimes are nearer their deliverance than they imagine; nay, are even brought to their deliverance by the means by which they seem to be brought to their destruction.

This approach extended to all aspects of creation. Thus, *Robinson Crusoe* provided Defoe with an opportunity to consider the nature of the subconscious, when Crusoe felt dubious about whether an approaching English boat was hostile, having been possibly taken over by others, an image that was of more general resonance:

> Let no man despise the secret hints and notices of danger, which sometimes are given him, when he may think there is no possibility of its being real. That such hints and notices are given us, I believe few that have made any observations of things can deny; that they are certain discoveries of an invisible world, and a converse of spirits, we cannot doubt; and if the tendency of them seems to be to warn us of danger, why should we not suppose they are from some friendly agent, whether supreme, or

L. Voigt, *Writing Captivity in the Early Modern Atlantic: Circulations of Knowledge and Authority in the Iberian and English Imperial Worlds* (Chapel Hill, 2009).

> inferior, and subordinate, is not the question; and that they are given for our good?

Such warnings by spirits are discussed by Defoe in his *History of Apparitions* and other writings. In *Robinson Crusoe*, he then adds a novelistic flourish in order to insert his reflection in the narrative and move the reader forward:

> The present question abundantly confirms me in the justice of this reasoning; for had I not been made cautious by this secret admonition, come it from whence it will, I had been undone inevitably, and in a far worse condition than before, as you will see presently.

This literal, plot-based, approach to Defoe's account of Crusoe is far more plausible than any attempt to suggest that a subconscious fear is revealed—namely, that of being rescued and thus losing both island dominion and the solitude that aided redemption.

God appears alongside astronomy in Defoe's *A New Voyage Round the World*, a late novel in which the protagonist does not successfully provide immediacy or even much focus for the reader:

> I know some are of opinion that before the full period of the Earth's existence all the remotest and most barren parts of it shall be peopled; but I see no ground for such a notion, but many reasons which would make it appear to be impracticable, and indeed impossible, unless it should please God to alter the situation of the globe, as it respects the sun, and place it in a direct, as it now moves in an oblique, position; or that a new species of mankind should be produced who might be as well qualified to live in the frozen zone as we are in the temperate, and upon whom the extremity of cold could have no power. I saw, as there are several parts of the globe where this would be impracticable. I shall say no more than this, that I think it is a groundless suggestion.

The power of God comes to the fore in Defoe's explanation of the end of the Great Plague:

> Nor was this by any new medicine found out, or new method of cure discovered, or by any experience in the operation which the physicians or surgeons attained to; but it was evidently from the secret invisible hand of Him that had at first sent this disease as a judgment upon us; and let the atheistic part of mankind call me saying what they please, it is no enthusiasm; it was acknowledged at that by all mankind. The disease was enervated and its malignity spent; and let it proceed from whencesoever it will, let the philosophers search for reasons in nature to account for it, and labour as much as they will to lessen the debt they owe to their Maker, those physicians who had the least share of religion in them were obliged to acknowledge that it was all supernatural that it was extraordinary, and that no account could be given of it.

The *Journal* gave Defoe the opportunity and need to consider the nature of reality and the causes of events and explain his views clearly:

> But when I am speaking of the plague as a distemper arising from natural causes, we must consider it as it was really propagated by natural means; nor is it at all the less a judgment for its being under the conduct of human causes and effects; for, as the Divine power has formed the whole scheme of nature and maintains nature in its course, so the same power thinks fit to let his own actings with men, whether of mercy or judgment, to go on in the ordinary course of natural causes; and he is pleased to act by those natural causes as the ordinary means, excepting and reserving to himself nevertheless a power to act in a supernatural way when he sees occasion.

Reason and religion were aligned by clerics. In his sermon, "The Use of Reason in Religion," George Smalridge, Tory Bishop of Bristol 1714–19, used reason to support the doctrine of the Trinity. Similarly, sermons were often analytical examinations of the meaning of Biblical texts, sometimes quite explicitly championing the cause of reason. John Wynne, Bishop of St. Asaph 1715–27 and of Bath and Wells 1727–43, published an *Abridgement of John Locke's Essay on the Human Understanding* (1696), which was praised by Locke but banned in Oxford. In his *Sermon before the Society for the Reformation of Manners, January 1726*, Wynne claims that men and women need to call on their reason and intelligence to overcome any sense of shame or embarrassment for their faith: reason must conquer irrational feelings for the benefit of religion. This was also an aspect of a more widespread public education. Thus, the hymnist Isaac Watts writes *The Knowledge of the Heavens and the Earth Made Easy* (1726), believing that to introduce beginners to astronomy would reinforce religious knowledge. A sense of contrast with solely secular accounts was presented with the emphasis on God, and the Great Chain of Being, at the conclusion of *Colonel Jack*:

> as he guided, and had even made the chain of causes and consequences, which nature in general strictly obeyed, so to him should be given the honour of all events, the consequences of those causes, as the first mover, and maker of all things.

Defoe's lesson was clear, as earlier with his presentation of "the laws of honour, printed by the laws of nature in the breast of a soldier, or a man of honour."

Defoe's emphasis on the role of God was central to the tensions in his work, and presumably his life. He had a lasting struggle with Hobbes's *Leviathan*, both in its engagement with a nasty, brutish, and short philosophy of life that, in practice, Defoe so often found to be quite true, and in addressing a spectre of atheism of which Defoe was fearful for Britain and which, despite his strongly Protestant background and profession, he might himself have worried about. Defoe was attracted and repulsed by Restoration libertines acting out Hobbesian qualities, by which he was compelled even into the 1720s. Defoe had read the libertine John, 2nd Earl of Rochester, even at times quoting him in his works,[6] and he had probably

6 J. McVeagh, "Rochester and Defoe: A Study in Influence," in *Studies in English Literature, 1500–1900*, 14, 3 (1974): pp. 327–41.

been exposed to some of Lucretius's Epicurean writings as a youth. The fear of a godless world creeps into all his major novels, and alongside the religious doubts he may have harbored, Defoe sometimes philosophically turns to the materialists and the atheists.

This tension was linked with that between the material and spiritual world. The novels show the cost of everything—it obsesses his narrators and plagued his doubts. Alongside expressions of certainty, Defoe can be seen as quite sensitive, almost neurotic, in his writings, a very conflicted person, and a writer torn by varying allegiances, legal troubles, and spiritual crises. In *Roxana*, his last and darkest novel, all of this is brought together in a deeply conflicted character, perhaps not unlike Defoe himself.

The very fabric of the world itself also appeared rent with struggle. The geological history of the Earth involved Biblical creation teaching. Thomas Burnet, who was Chaplain in Ordinary and Clerk of the Closet to William III, explains in his *Sacred Theory of the Earth* (1681–90), the Earth's development in large part with reference to Noah's Flood, following in 1692 with *The Ancient Doctrine Concerning the Origin of Things*, an attempt to reconcile his theory with Genesis. That year, the London and, far more damaging Port Royal, Jamaica, earthquakes were widely presented as warnings of God's anger, responses of retribution that can be located in the politicized culture of the period. The breach in the succession and the strains of war with France provided occasion and cause for bitter debate about the role of Providence.

There were indications in Defoe's writings, both fictional and, even more, factual, of what would later be termed the Enlightenment, and, in his preface to the *Tour*, Defoe refers to "the improvement, as well in culture, as in commerce," although improvement and enlightenment were not to be co-terminous. Defoe was critical of popular accounts he deemed unenlightened, as with caverns, a longstanding cause and site of superstition:

> As to the stories of a witch dwelling here [Wookey Hole, Somerset], as of a giant dwelling in the other [Pool's Hole, Derbyshire], I take them to be equally fabulous, and worth no notice.[7]

7 *Tour*, 4.

Yet, a mysterious past is alluded to in *Robinson Crusoe* without such criticism: "I fancied myself now like one of the ancient giants which are said to live in caves and holes in the rocks, where none could come at them." This was a reference to an unknown that could be highly troubling.

The overlapping of scientific ideas and information with other forms of explication seen in the *Tour* was an overlapping likewise offered in the local histories of the period.[8] To a degree, indeed, the *Tour* transforms these histories by focusing on the contemporary and on the national scale. Defoe shows in that book a knowledge of scientific discussion, as in Merionethshire in Wales:

> We enquired here after that strange phenomenon which was not only seen, but fatally experienced by the country round this place, namely, of a livid fire, coming off from the sea; and setting on fire, houses, barns, stacks of hay and corn, and poisoning the herbage in the fields; of which there is a full account given in the Philosophical Transactions,

the last a reference to those of the Royal Society for 1694. Defoe offered such accounts without comment as they were endorsed by this authoritative source. In *Moll Flanders*, there is in the description of the prison at Newgate a very powerful geological image:

> like the waters in the cavities and hollows of mountains, which petrify and turn into stone whatever they are suffered to drop upon, so the continual conversing with such a crew of hell-hounds as I was [with], had the same common operation upon me as upon other people. I degenerated into stone.

Defoe was far more sceptical about popular beliefs, and did not hesitate to criticize them as, in the *Tour*, with the monastery at Crowland:

> a great many stories are told of the devils of Crowland also, and what conversation they had with the monks, which tales are

8 S. Mendyk, *"Speculum Britanniae": Regional Study, Antiquarianism, and Science in Britain to 1700* (Toronto, 1989).

> more out of date now, than they were formerly; for they tell us, that in ancient times those things were as certainly believed for truths, as if they had been done before their faces.

The monks were rumored to have poisoned King John in 1216. A nearby river confluence led to the comment "that there is a whirlpool, or bottomless pit.... I see no reason to give credit to."[9]

Such remarks were amplified by other references to the Devil or to superstition. The presence of standing stones, an interest of Defoe's and one that puzzled him and others due to their weight and the difficulty of moving them, could be attributed to the Devil, and such reports were also noted by other travellers.[10] Nevertheless, Defoe's approach saw skepticism about Catholic accounts, for example of the miraculous and much-visited Well of St. Winifrid in North Wales.[11] In other cases, Defoe could engage more actively, as in Poole's Hole, a Peak District cavern:

> occasioned by the fortuitous position of the rocks at the creation of all things, or perhaps at the great absorption or influx of the surface into the abyss at the great rupture of the Earth's crust or shell, according to Mr Burnet's theory; and to me it seems a confirmation of that hypothesis of the breaking in of the surface.[12]

The reference to Thomas Burnet's *Sacred Theory of the Earth* shows Defoe as knowledgeable, and also the extent to which eighteenth-century works sought to integrate theology with other perspectives. Conversely, Defoe was not really engaged with apocalyptic thought and millenarian writing, unlike many others writing in this period, notably William Lloyd, Bishop of St. Asaph (1680–92), Lichfield (1692–9), and Worcester (1699–1717). As a reminder of how categories could overlap and therefore of the need for caution before decrying apparent inconsistency, Lloyd, who came from a

9 *Tour*, 7.
10 *Tour*, 6; HMC *Portland Mss*, VI, 92.
11 *Tour*, 6.
12 *Tour*, 8.

Royalist family—his father imprisoned in the 1640s for his support for Charles I—was one of the seven bishops acquitted in 1688 and a keen supporter of the Glorious Revolution,[13] but also actively prophesied—including to Queen Anne, Robert Harley, and John Evelyn—and was indeed known as "Revelation Lloyd" and "Old Mysterio." Lloyd predicted the fall of the Antichrist in 1717, earning newspaper criticism and mockery as a result. Earlier, interest in millenarianism and also in the occult were very much part of the intellectual repertoire of the virtuosi of the Royal Society.

Popular interest in the world of spirits and witches, and in elements of white and black magic, was also not completely removed from respectable culture. It has been assumed that, due to the Scientific Revolution (which is classic as a modern description of a much more complex past), belief in the supernatural was now weak. If so, many at all social levels had not noticed this injunction. In the early decades of the eighteenth century, there was still much writing about the world of spirits. Far from this being seen as necessarily antipathetic to science and the progressive cause it supposedly presented, spirits and witchcraft were presented as scientifically proven by empirical means and therefore requiring explanation. Different ways to understand the world were believed to run in parallel—testimony through history providing one, theology through revelation and the Bible another, and psychology through the senses a third. The latter could be instructed, thus enabling those trained to experience what others could not, including the occult. John Beaumont, a Fellow of the Royal Society, published in 1705 his *An Historical, Physiological and Theological Treatise of Spirits, Apparitions, Witchcrafts, and Other Magical Practices: containing an account of the genii or familiar spirits, both good and bad, that are said to attend men in this life, and what sensible perceptions some persons have had of them (particularly the author's own experience for many years). Also of appearances of spirits after death, divine dreams, divinations, second sighted person, &c; likewise the power of witches and the reality of other magical operations, clearly asserted.*[14] Similarly, Newton's mystical and religious views were less incompatible with his physics than might appear to modern commentators.

13 I have benefited from reading "Prelate Plotter in 1688: William Lloyd of St Asaph," an unpublished paper by Bill Gibson.

14 I have benefited from listening to a paper on Beaumont by Jonathan Barry.

Indeed, while in some respects it may appear a conservative aspect of a superstitious popular culture, an emphasis on occult skills as a means to learn the secrets of the universe and nature could also be found in Freemasonry. This was a new cult (the Grand Lodge was established in 1717) and channel of sociability. Freemasonry, moreover, was very popular among the male social élite and the Hanoverians quickly joined the cult.

In England, the last successful prosecution for witchcraft, that of Jane Wenham in Hertfordshire, occurred in 1712; whereas in Scotland prosecutions and executions declined after 1662, the last major witch-hunt was in 1697–1700 and the last recorded prosecution was in 1727, and that in Dornoch, which was far distant from the centers of Scottish power and society. Yet, there was much still published arguing the case for witchcraft, as in two works by the Lockean doctor Richard Boulton, his *A Complete History of Magic, Sorcery, and Witchcraft* (1715) and *The Possibility of Magic, Sorcery and Witchcraft Demonstrated* (1722). There was a political aspect to the debate, as in 1712 over the Wenham case, with Tories arguing that Whig positions demonstrated religious weakness, while the Whigs presented the Tories as superstitious. In practice, views were not constrained by politics, as a belief in the Devil might be part of the new science as well as shared across the political spectrum; and this belief also frequently encompassed a conviction that witchcraft existed.[15]

Defoe, in his writings, provided frequent reference to the Devil and as a real presence, an approach that was to be echoed in some later novelists—notably some of the Gothic novelists, for example Matthew Lewis's *The Monk* (1796). References to the Devil occur in *Colonel Jack*, as in:

> The subtle Devil never absent from his business, but ready at all occasions to encourage his servants, removed all these difficulties, and brought me into an intimacy with one of the most exquisite divers, or pickpockets in the town,

or "this was the high road to the Devil," or "as the Devil is certainly an

15 I. Bostridge, *Witchcraft and Its Transformations, c.1650–c.1750* (London, 1997); J. Sharpe (ed.), *English Witchcraft 1560–1736* (London, 2003), volumes 4–6.

apparent prompter to wickedness, if he is not the first mover of it in our minds." These were conventional arguments.

Yet, there was far less mention of the Devil in *Colonel Jack* than in Defoe's other novels. Moreover, there was a sense of moral progress; Jack prayed to God to give him repentance for having robbed a poor old woman, and he comes to have "a solid principle of justice and honesty, and a secret horror at things passed, when I looked back upon my former life ... reflections upon Hell and the damned spirits." This remorse for the robbery and subsequent apology are important episodes.

Reflections by the protagonist upon sin were less measured, restricted, and efficacious in *Roxana*, where Amy—Roxana's servant and confidant—is repeatedly presented as a diabolical figure who provokes the moral weakness within the protagonist, notably toward bigamy:

> Had I now had my senses about me, and had my reason not been overcome ... I should have repelled this Amy, however faithful and honest to me in other things, as a viper and engine of the Devil; I ought to have remembered that neither he [a potential husband] or I, either by the Laws of God or Man, could come together, upon any other terms than that of notorious adultery. The ignorant jade's argument, that he had brought me out of the hands of the Devil, by which she meant the Devil of poverty and distress, should have been a powerful motive to me, not to plunge myself into the jaws of Hell, and into the power of the real Devil.... But poverty was my snare.

Again for *Roxana*: "the Devil, who had found the way to break-in upon me by one temptation, easily mastered me now."

To Defoe, the Devil was opposed both to Providence and to the reason implanted in Humanity by God. By being "enslaved" to the "rage" of "vicious appetite," a person, however, welcomes in the Devil: "defaces the image of God in his soul; dethrones his reason; causes conscience to abdicate the possession, and exalts sense [meaning sensation] into the vacant throne; how he deposes the man, and exalts the brute." Reason is seen as under threat from the emotions, the latter providing the Devil with his opportunities. Repeatedly, Roxana both demonstrated and commented on this point:

> Thus blinded by my own vanity, I threw away the only opportunity I then had, to have effectually settled my fortunes, and secured them for this world; and I am a memorial to all that shall read my story; a standing monument of the madness and distraction which pride and infatuations from Hell runs us into; how ill our passions guide us; and how dangerously we act, when we follow the dictates of an ambitious mind.

Subsequently she referred to a "violent fermentation" in her blood, a traditional approach and in a linkage of personality and health to those who were "lunatic with their pride." The idea of dying with grief or running-mad with joy—which was to be seen repeatedly with Romanticism—was presented by Defoe in *Roxana* as a failure arising from the hold that pride and ambition could gain. Less dramatically, "the hand of God" led to repentance in *Moll Flanders*, whereas more generally the "diligent Devil" repeatedly provided temptation. In Defoe's novels, the use of frequent reversals as plot devices captured both a sense of the moral struggle and yet also an underlying set of moral rules.

The frequent references to the Devil helped make *Roxana* an early Gothic novel, a style that comes to the fore in the 1790s, and although very much a character from this genre of a novel, it is not Amy alone who is at fault. Roxana reflects: "I had been the Devil's Instrument, to make her wicked; … I had stripped her and prostituted her." She subsequently referred to the passage from the *Book of Daniel* in which Belshazzar sees the warning handwritten on the wall, to the "Justice of Heaven" to "a Dart struck into the Liver," a reference to the *Book of Proverbs*, to "a secret Hell within," and to an immediacy of perdition:

> … it never lightn'd or thundered, but I expected the next flash would penetrate my vitals … it never blew a storm of wind, but I expected the fall of some stack of chimneys, or some part of the house would bury me in its ruins … the arms of Hell … my fears of vengeance.

To a modern mind, this account might read like a description of mental illness, but the consciousness of sin that Defoe deploys is one in which there is purpose:

> dreamed continually of the most frightful and terrible things imaginable. Nothing but apparitions of devils and monsters; falling into gulfs, and off from steep and high precipices, and the like; so that in the morning, when I should rise, and be refreshed with the blessing of rest, I was hagridden with frights, and terrible things, formed merely in the imagination.

References to Fall and Blessing, each capitalized in the original, were clearly religious, and were followed by the lengthy passages leading to the killing of Roxana's daughter, and with appropriate imagery and language: "the clouds began to thicken about me … a She-Devil … a blast from Heaven."

There was no sense in *Roxana* that women were not capable as men of the full range of immoral behavior, nor without the ability to reflect on their situations but also be trapped by them. Indeed, women were offered complexity.

The cast and tone in *Roxana* are very different from those in *Robinson Crusoe*, in which the barbarism is found in the actions of native peoples, notably their slaughter of prisoners, regarding which see chapter eleven. For many contemporaries, barbarism, instead, existed in the "prejudice and superstition" associated with Catholicism,[16] and this approach linked national history to current affairs, and attitudes to knowledge to religious differences.

More generally, much that was printed would not strike modern readers as enlightened. Thus, the "Observations on March" 1706 in *Rider's British Merlin*, a popular work of astrology—which was then a very active field—followed advice on the harvest with: "It is good to purge and let blood, for in this month the humours and block increase, and gross feelings breeds gross block and humours." Two months later, "Green whey excellent against cholar [sic]," and in August, "red wine and claret are excellent remedies for children against the worms."

At the same time, such works were evidence of the entrepreneurship

16 Charles Whitworth, envoy to the Imperial Diet at Regensburg, to Luke Shaub, envoy to Vienna, 27 Dec. 1715, New York, Public Library, Hardwicke papers vol. 42.

that print facilitated. Thus, the September item includes an advertisement for "Buckworth's [sic] for loxinges, famous for the cure of coughs, colds, catarrhs and hoarseness etc."[17] Thanks to *Rider's British Merlin*, this London-made and authenticated product could be advertised around the country. It had been first made in the 1650s and was the first such proprietary medicine extensively advertised in the press during the 1650s.

This example provides a different instance of the overlap of categories and topics generally treated as separate, in this case "tradition" and capitalism. Looked at from another angle, the extent to which there was a disjuncture between current ideas and categories of the modern and those at the time emerges clearly. This disjuncture (by modern standards) was highlighted in the range of its practice between quackery and established medical procedures, a range that very much involved writers as it provided opportunities for satire as well as for earning through puffery.[18]

Newton scarcely enjoyed a universal following. Thus in 1728, the mathematician Joseph Morgan published *The Immobility of the Earth Demonstrated, Proving the Earth to be the Centre of the Universe.* More generally, for Newton, scientific research was not regarded as necessarily incompatible with traditional forms of Christian and occult knowledge—for example miracles and astrology. Indeed, in Defoe's lifetime, there was a strong interest in the miraculous, an interest bringing together claims by Protestant sects, such as the Baptists, the role of healers, and the active engagement of intellectuals such as Robert Boyle (1627–91), who very much reflected Baconian views. An active practitioner of scientific experimentation, Boyle was also—like Morton and Defoe—a committed supporter of the proselytization of Native Americans in North America, backing the translation of the Bible for that end. Conversion of the Native Americans was seen as a religious good in itself, and therefore a rationale for imperialism and as strengthening England's colonies. Such interests on the part of Boyle and others serve as a reminder of the vitality of traditional beliefs and the extent to which there was no linear progression from superstitious belief to the cult and practice of enlightened reason, in so far as the two categories

17 BL. Add. 74642 fols 18, 26, 39, 43.

18 F. Doherty, *A Study in Eighteenth-Century Advertising Methods* (Lewiston, 1992).

can be readily defined, reified, and treated as chronological blocs, let alone as opposed such.

The absence of a linear progression was not a situation invalidated by Locke's perception that man was actively shaped by outside forces, a view that increased interest in phenomena and the environment. Locke's *Essay Concerning Human Understanding* (1690) argues that all knowledge consist of ideas that originate in sensation. From this comes the suggestion, one with which Defoe wrestles in his novels, that man, both as an individual and as a social being, could be improved by education and a better environment, at once bringing and reflecting progress. And all this in a way that would have made much sense to Dissenters. Activity was stressed, rather than the passive acceptance of divine will and an unchanging universe. Locke's theory of personal identity, however, faced the question of whether dependence of the senses on perception—a somewhat determinist approach—challenged the independence of the mind's reason. Emphasis on the senses or reason varied.

A parallel with the attempt to establish an explanation of the individual through perception was provided by the emphasis on a mechanized cosmos associated with Newton. This emphasis also reflected a focus on regular, precise, measurable, and predictable processes and forces. Nature's "secrets" could now be scrutinized and readily explained, a process that extends to identifying the role of Providence. In a rejection of what were held to be Classical norms, all knowledge was now utilitarian—including the understanding of divine purpose. By integrating physical processes on Earth and in the solar system, Newton lessened differences between the two spheres.

Political arithmetic was an aspect and product of this utilitarianism, an attempt that draws on Bacon's ideas to use knowledge for the public good. Information was to help provide the means for a rational statecraft, with rationality understood as grounded in mathematics, and therefore precise and clear. There was a wish to re-form the present and thus repurpose the impact of the past by means of projects that ranged from the practical to the implausible; and many writers of the period, including Defoe, engaged with this aspect of projecting.[19] William Petty (1623–87), who

19 D. Alff, *The Wreckage of Intentions: Projects in British Culture, 1660–1730* (Philadelphia, 2017).

coined the term "political arithmetic" in 1672, had close connections with Hobbes and Boyle, and the idea of power as an essentially rational pursuit based on functional values was adopted by Defoe in his work.

Petty was not alone. His friend John Graunt (1620–74), a cloth merchant, analyzed London's mortality figures, a source also used by Defoe, in terms of what would now be called a time-series. This involved assessing change through time in order to try to understand disease, and thus help ensure stability. In doing so, Graunt captured the potential of political arithmetic for understanding social developments. This was part of a more general trend, part of which reflected the possibilities and needs of public finance and of new financial instruments. In *Colonel Jack*, there is reference to "insurance offices, as they call them" the phrase, however, suggesting unfamiliarity. Graunt's work may have encouraged others to analyze population—for example John Imber, a Hampshire cleric who analyzed some of the local parishes for the episcopal visitation return of 1725.[20]

Far more politically significant and closer to Defoe's world of political polemic, Charles Davenant (1656–1714), appointed Inspector-General of Imports and Exports in 1703, was responsible for producing fiscal data intended to inform government, and in that respect parliamentary policy. As with the work of Defoe, arguments and indeed information was often partisan. Statistical information played an overt role in public debate, as with that of the cost of war, which was addressed in Robert Walpole's Whig pamphlet, *A State of the Five and Thirty Millions mentioned in the Report of a Committee of the House of Commons* (1711). Yet in contrast, and as with so many not the easiest of men to pigeonhole, Davenant's *Reports to the ... Commissioners for ... Public Accounts* (1712) served the agenda of the Tory government in demonstrating that trade with France, which the Tories were pursuing in an ultimately unsuccessful attempt to ensure a trade treaty, might be beneficial; whereas that established with the Dutch, an ally of the Whigs, had harmed Britain.

The varied strategies of analysis and explication were not separate but interacted. Thus, political arithmetic interacted with Newtonian physics in the use of the concept of the balance of power. This reflected a commitment

20 B. Stapleton, "Age Structure in the Early Eighteenth Century," in *Local Population Studies*, 34 (spring 1985): pp. 28–32.

to understanding and explication through measurement. The extent to which controversies related to issues of trade ensured this process of using statistics. These controversies become particularly common onward from 1713, with that of the Anglo-French Commercial Treaty of the same year beginning the process. That particular controversy highlighted the need for accurate statistics as well as conceptual methodological guidance for commercial issues and the extent to which they may be weaponized. As one official noted of the parliamentary defeat:

> Many boroughs [which elected MPs] are strangely possessed with an opinion of great prejudice threatened by this treaty to our woollen manufactures abroad, which others think they can prove will be advanced by it.[21]

Referring to the struggle over textile imports that was then peaking, the *London Journal* of 2 January 1720 notes: "there are a great number of writings and papers published every day … dispersed gratis about both town and country." There were moral dimensions to this question, not just in terms of the employment of fellow-Britons, but also with reference to concerns about the corrupting nature of luxuries and luxury.

Defoe's "political arithmetic," although in his view based on the "just reasoning"[22]—as seen in lengthy discussion in the *Tour* of the value of the Union as well as of other points—possesses a degree of partisanship. However, that did not prevent him from making some highly pertinent points, as of Castle-Rising: "an old decayed borough town with perhaps not ten families in it, which yet (to the scandal of our prescription right) sends two members to the British Parliament, being as many as the city of Norwich itself."[23] Similar points about a lack of equity were made elsewhere in the *Tour*, including about Queenborough, Winchelsea, Gatton, Bletchingly, Old Sarum, Boroughbridge, Aldborough, and the South West as a whole. There were even more extreme examples in Scotland.

These points harken back to the attempt under Cromwell to transform

21 R. Warre to Mr Birch, 19 June 1713, BL. Add. 46546 f. 74.
22 *Tour*, 13.
23 *Tour*, 1.

parliamentary representation, a move that clashed with property rights as well as traditional practice. As a result of the Cromwell link, a reform of representation became an impossible theme politically, and all that despite the significant constitutional changes involved in the "Glorious Revolution." Defoe's repeated interest in the *Tour* would probably have struck readers as unusual, which it was, although there had been prior instances of the same theme—as in a 1702 pamphlet that drew on political arithmetic, *The Representative of London and Westminster in Parliament, Examined and Considered. Wherein appears the antiquity of most of the boroughs in England, with the proportions, whereby every county is over or under represented according to a scale from the Royal Aid Assessments; by which it appears that Middlesex is found to be represented but one tenth part of its due.*

Defoe's interest in improvement was also present in his discussion of economic matters, as in sheep-grain agriculture:

> If this way of folding sheep upon the fallows, and ploughed lands were practised, in some parts of England, and especially in Scotland, they would find it turn to such account, and so effectually improve the waste lands, which now are useless and uncultivated, that the sheep would be more valuable, and lands turn to a better account than was ever yet known among them.[24]

At the same time, Defoe's presentation of change was one of an inherent instability —"The fate of things gives a new face to things," the "new turns" given "even to nature itself," reflected a sense that Humanity could change the environment and therefore had a key role in God's plans.[25] Yet, as a comment on a frequent lack of human grace, Defoe was unimpressed by the failure to respect God: "in England, nothing is more frequent, or less regarded now, than the most horrid oaths and blasphemies in the open streets, and that by the little children that hardly know what an oath means."[26] Such comments about the rise of irreligion are common across the ages.

24 *Tour*, 4.
25 *Tour*, Preface.
26 *Tour*, 12.

A failure to respect God was not the sole reason for disquiet. The apian utilitarianism of Bernard Mandeville's *The Fable of the Bees* (1705) provides a disconcerting social parable. Similar to the debates over Church affairs, and most prominently the Bangorian Controversy of the late 1710s, discussion of more explicitly social and political issues and solutions captured a sense of flux that worried many and provided ample challenges for writers.

7. Culture and the Arts

> "Streets of booths were set up on the Thames … all sorts of trades and shops furnished and full of commodities. Coaches plied [on the Thames] full from Westminster to the Temple, and from several other stairs [to the river] to and fro, as in the streets; sledges, sliding with skates, a bull baiting, horse-and-coach races, puppet plays and interludes, cooks, tippling and other lewd places, so that it seemed to be a bacchanalian triumph, or carnival on the water."

John Evelyn's description of the frost fair held on the River Thames resulting from the great freeze of 1683–4 serves as a reminder of the quite varied milieux and contents of culture. These have to be borne in mind when resorting to aggregation by abstractions.

Defoe's cultural impact is very much located in terms of the rise of the novel, which was for a long time discussed in terms of his work, and later that of Samuel Richardson and Henry Fielding. However, doing so neglects a far greater range of early novels—many written by women—and this limitation misleadingly simplifies the origins of the genres. Although English writers played the key role in its eighteenth-century development, there were important seventeenth-century precursors, including Cervantes' *Don Quixote* and indeed a range of literary types to which the novel looked. Notably, these were picaresque-tales, travel books, and romances. Yet as part of the novel's hybrid and varied character it is also important when exploring its origins to consider letters[1] and the Bible, as well as other long-established story-telling patterns, including the epic.[2]

1 R. King, *Writing to the World: Letters and the Origins of Modern Print Genres* (Baltimore, 2018).

2 K. Seidel, *Rethinking the Secular Origins of the Novel: The Bible in English Fic-*

The common feature of the early English novels was their claim to realism. In that context, Defoe's subjects were very different, and they looked back to varied influences. He drew on the strong canon of Dissenter writing—one looking back to the Reformation—and more notably its determination to communicate and to do so clearly.[3] There was, however, a range of thematic influences. More specifically, *Robinson Crusoe* is affected by travel literature and the spiritual autobiography, and *Colonel Jack*, *Moll Flanders,* and *Roxana* by picaresque tales. However, the common theme in these alleged autobiographies was authenticity, and so they revealed affinities with criminal biographies, a very popular genre: *The Lives of the Highwaymen* was first published in 1714. And Defoe was not alone. The romantic tales of the period, such as those by Eliza Haywood, also claimed to be accounts of real life and manners. Moreover, the most distinctive, if not idiosyncratic, novelistic work, Swift's *Gulliver's Travels* (1726), proclaims itself to be a true account.

The production of novels was encouraged by a range of developments in the period. The sale of novels benefited from the distribution networks provided by and for newspapers, and the press was also valuable for advertising books. Thus, a Leeds item in the *Leeds Mercury* of 3 October 1727 declares:

> On Monday next, will be exposed to sale by way of auction at Mr Richard Nottingham's at the King's Arms in Leeds, a parcel of books consisting of 997, with maps and pictures, together with bibles and common prayer books. NB. A great many of the books are bound extraordinary well, and gilt on the back and lettered.

The latter captured the varied consumerism bound up in the book, but the distribution and sale of books and newspapers readily spread ideas among the literate.

tion (Cambridge, 2021); N. Horejsi, *Novel Cleopatras: Romance Historiography and the Dido Tradition in English Fiction, 1688–1785* (Toronto, 2019).

3 N.H. Keeble, *The Literacy Culture of Nonconformity in Later Seventeenth-Century England* (Leicester, 1987).

The variety of cultural milieux and means is striking. For example, the Cotswold Games, which included cudgel-playing, horse-racing, hunting and walking on the hands—and had been founded as a protest against Puritanism—were revived after the Restoration, but they were not the product of any single political or cultural impulse. So, too, is was with the English Baroque, against the background of which Defoe grew up and lived—and which, variously, included the works of Dryden and Wren, Purcell and Vanbrugh, the last of whom was not alone in building Baroque stately homes. Work by other architects included Boughton House in the late seventeenth century, and in the new century appears Beningbrough, and the 1720s work on Wentworth Woodhouse. At the same time—as Vanbrugh, and even more so Dryden, showed—there could be very different works and resonances in the career of any one individual. Baroque style as well as deception in life, behavior, art, and fiction overlapped from the mid-1710s in the fashion for masquerades, a cultural reality of which Defoe disapproved.[4] The priorities of established culture were shown by the activities of successive Poet Laureates. Nicholas Rowe (1715–18) completed a verse translation of Lucan's *Pharsalia*, a project that testified to the prestige of work on classical texts. His successor, Laurence Eusden (1718–30), gained the post through political patronage unencumbered by merit. He had signalled his loyalty with *The Royal Family* (1714) and won the support of a key patron, the Lord Chamberlain, Thomas, Duke of Newcastle, with a poem about his marriage. Another Whig, John Hughes, wrote *An Ode for the Birthday of Her Royal Highness the Princess of Wales* (1716), and was appointed Secretary to the Commission of the Peace by Lord Chancellor Cowper.

As an aspect of a classicism that concerned some commentators who worried about the departure of the élite from established patterns, a rejection of the distinctive national past was dramatized when as often, old mansions were replaced or rebuilt, a process seen with William III at Hampton Court.[5] Classical designs came to inform English architecture, an aspect of

4 T. Castle, *Masquerade and Civilisation: the Carnivalesque in Eighteenth-Century English Culture and Fiction* (London, 1986).

5 J.R. Jones, "The Building Works and Court Style of William and Mary," in *Journal of Garden History*, 8 (1988): pp. 1–13.

a redefinition of taste and style that reordered fashion and acceptability. In the 1690s and 1700s, William Blathwayt, a prominent Whig, had his Tudor house at Dyrham Park totally transformed, the east front being the responsibility of William Talman, the Comptroller of the Royal Works. A serious fire at Wilton in 1705 led to rebuilding in which the Tudor Great Hall was replaced with a rectangular Classical-style structure. In the 1720s, the Tudor Lyme Park, Cheshire was transformed by the Venetian architect Giacomo Leoni, who in 1716 was responsible for an English edition of the first book of Palladio's *Quattro Libri*.

Although drawing in part on Palladio, Palladianism and the classical themes it encapsulated were presented—notably by Richard, 3rd Earl of Burlington, who was responsible for Chiswick House, and his protégé, the architect Colen Campbell—as a distinctly British style in contrast to the Baroque of Wren, Vanbrugh, and Nicholas Hawksmoor. The latter was criticized as less purely classical, and thus less worthy of emulation. Campbell's works include Wanstead House, which was praised by Defoe. The tightly-controlled symmetry of Palladianism was an architectural language that worked at a number of scales, and outer symmetry lent itself to the symmetry of interior layout and rooms. The classical interests of patrons and painters combined in the depiction of Classical landscapes and stories, rendering the heroes of ancient Rome as suitable companions for the portraits of modern aristocrats.

So it was with the grounds. Gardens were created and continued in the formal geometric patterns that characterized continental designs. They were an opportunity for ostentation and display, and there was a clear segregation between gardens and the surrounding estate. Many gardens of the period maintained earlier layouts. For example, a drawing by Margaret Weld of 1721 reveals that Lulworth Castle still retained its sixteenth-century formal gardens, with their extensive parterres, the statuary at the center, and with neatly-regimented and clipped trees in formal lines and blocs. Others reflected newly-fashionable geometric layouts. Formal gardens of the period include the Dutch-style water area at Westbury Court, the French-style creation at Dunham Massey, and Charles Bridgeman's masterpiece of the geometric at Eastbury.[6]

6 P. Willis, *Charles Bridgeman and the English Landscape Garden* (Newcastle, 2002). The gardens at Hampton Court laid out under William III have recently been returned to their original form.

A key figure was Henry Wise (1653–1738) who was superintendent of the royal gardens to William III, Anne and George I, and a protégé of George London, who had in turn been influenced by André Le Nôtre (1613–1700), the French gardener employed by Charles II. London and Wise, described by Joseph Addison in the *Spectator* of 6 September 1712 as "the heroic poets" of gardening (an instructive comparison from another genre), worked in accord with French and Dutch influences, although they were not slavish emulators and instead showed an ability to respond to the possibilities of particular sites. Aside from their work on the royal gardens—especially Hampton Court and Kensington—the partners were responsible for some of the leading gardens of the period, including Wanstead and Melbourne. The gardens of the latter were remodeled between 1704 and 1711, with Wise's plan including a water feature and other fashionable components of the formal garden.

Dutch and French influences were very much seen in the use of water in many gardens, but also contributed to a more general favoring of geometric layouts. The water features themselves were straight-edged and part of the geometric pattern. "Canals" or long straight-edged ponds appeared in many grounds, for example Ickworth in the 1700s. Charles Bridgeman introduced an important innovation, the "ha-ha" (a term first used in 1712), which is a ditch, sunk from view, placed to create a boundary between garden and parkland that did not interrupt the prospect but did prevent animals from entering the garden. In contrast to the short horizons of the Dutch style, this contributed to the stress on long vistas, joining house to park.

The common theme was symmetrical formality. At Chiswick, the grounds included straight alleys converging on a round-point.[7] The aerial perspective plan for Castle Howard in *Vitruvius Britannicus* included two obelisks and a temple-style structure in the grounds; in the event, one obelisk was erected as was a Temple of the Four Winds designed by Vanbrugh, and a Mausoleum designed by Nicholas Hawksmoor.

Sir John Brownlow who built Belton House, judging from the plate in *Vitruvius Britannicus,* created a state-of-the-art landscape at the same time

7 J. Harris, *The Palladian Revival: Lord Burlington, His Villa and Garden at Chiswick* (New Haven, 1994).

in 1685, with formal parterres, symmetrical patterns of walks—some centered on *rond points*, or ponds with straight boundaries— plentiful statues, topiary trees, and an obelisk; all enclosed within a five-mile wall.

Defoe's style of directness was more explicit than those of the Baroque or classical, and looked back rather to Dissenting spiritual biography, among them John Bunyan's being most prominent. Defoe's novelistic emphasis on an awareness of sin as the basis for approval matches his criticism of the *Tatler* and the *Spectator* for relying on humor as a means to manners, a criticism most clearly expressed in the *Review* on 14 August 1711:

> The *Tatler* and *Spectator*, that happy favourite of the times, has pleased you all; indeed you were ashamed not to be pleased with so much beauty, strength, and clearness; so much wit, so gentlemanly reproofs, and such neat touches at the vulgar errors of the times: But alas! Are we to be laughed out of our dear brutality? Our vices are too deep rooted to be weeded out with a light hand; the soft-touches, the fineness of a clean turn, nay, the keenest satire, dressed up in, and couched under gentle and genteel expressions, has no effect here; that gentleman that has all the art of pleasing, may yet complain of the few converts he has made, considering the expense of wit that he has laid out upon them.

The term convert is particularly apt for Defoe. He focuses on moral improvement but with an important role for entertainment. "Advice from the Scandal Club," which appears in the *Review* from February 1704 until May 1705, is described in that paper on 2 March 1710 in terms of worthy admonition:

> When first this paper appeared in the world, I erected a court of justice, for the censuring and exposing vice, and for a due discouragement of the scandalous manners of the age … recorded in the vast journals of our scandal club.

The extent to which books were reprinted (and plays staged anew) captures the difficulty of arguing in terms of clearly delimited periods. So also can this be said in regards to terms of styles and cultural spheres. Rather than thinking in terms of clear divisions between popular and élite culture, and/or oral and written, it is more appropriate not only to consider gradations in literacy levels— instead of a crude dualism of literacy and illiteracy—but also to emphasize cultural gradations within a world that encompassed differing groups and forms. Moreover, instead of thinking in terms of competing styles and influences, it is necessary to emphasize their coexistence, even though public criticisms of existing styles were part of the establishment of an identity for newer styles. Furthermore, in so far as specific styles are concerned, it is better to write in terms of stylistic tendencies rather than suggest that distinct uniformities can be discerned. In a comparable fashion, alongside critics who saw a moneyed interest challenging landed society and its associated culture, as well as the speculation associated with financial assets appearing to challenge reality and value, social divisions were permeable and status was open to negotiation and adjustment.

Defoe as writer was clearly a significant cultural figure, but he was not a prime writer of cultural matters in so far as the latter can be isolated. Certainly, although he was a wide ranging as well as prolific pamphleteer, he focused far more on economic than cultural matters. The debate on what could be judged irreligious or sacrilegious in lay culture did not agitate him. After 1688, there was no future for Dryden who had converted to Catholicism in 1685, but without a comparable exclusion from the new order, High Churchmen and Non-Jurors critical of the Williamite regime also regarded both it—and society as a whole—as licentious and dissolute.

In particular, there was criticism of the alleged profanity and immorality of the stage, for example by the Non-Juror cleric Jeremy Collier in his pamphlet, *A Short View of the Immorality and Profaneness of the English Stage* (1698). This criticism led in 1699 to government pressure on London playhouses and on Congreve and Vanbrugh, forcing some alterations in their plays. William Congreve (1670–1729) had made his name with a number of comedies, notably *The Old Bachelor* (1693), *The Double Dealer* (1693), *Love for Love* (1695), and *The Way of the World* (1700), studies of social values with a strong accent on relations between the sexes. Witty dialogue was ably used to depict character in mannered works, based firmly in the fashionable society of contemporary England; and Congreve dwelt much on the role that marital practices offered for intrigue and deceit. In 1712, the

Society for Promoting Christian Knowledge asked Collier to write a pamphlet discouraging the teaching of lewd songs and the composing of music to profane ballads. In contrast, Colley Cibber's play *The Non-Juror* (1717) was a popular version of Molière's *Tartuffe*, which, in its attack on Non-Jurors, struck a chord with Whig audiences. Thomas Herring, later an archbishop, condemned John Gay's *Beggar's Opera* (1728) for immorality. This was an aspect of the wide-ranging "culture-wars" of the period.

The popularity of devotional verse and religious poetry was clear in publications, including biblical texts on boards in churches. Thomas Newcomb, a cleric, published in 1723 his longest work, *The Last Judgment of Men and Angels: A Poem in Twelve Books, after the Manner of Milton*. Printers competed for the right to publish Bibles because they sold well, as did translations of the psalms. The printing of chantry sermons also became common.[8]

The same can be said for such works within Dissenter culture, as seen in new editions of *The Pilgrim's Progress*, as well as accounts of the pious such as the *Brief Account of… his Life and Profession* (1707, reprinted 1720) by a Seventh Day Baptist, Joseph Davis.

Defoe's strong moral stance meant that he did not favor another type of theatre, the social gatherings that were to be seen as important to the "politeness" of eighteenth-century Britain. For Defoe, the settings and content of culture repeatedly took a moral tone. This was shown in his attitude toward the social fluidity offered by assemblies, which provided a means of behavior that troubled moralists. One of Defoe's standard methods was that of contrast, for nuance was not generally his forte in the *Tour*. Thus, the praise of society in Maidstone becomes a way to challenge the fashion for assemblies:

> This neighbourhood of persons of figure and quality, makes Maidstone a very agreeable place to live in, and where a man of letters, and of manners, will always find suitable society, both to divert and improve himself; so that here is, what is not often found, namely, a town of very great business and trade, and yet full of gentry, of mirth, and of good company. It is to be

8 J. Farooq, *Preaching in Eighteenth-Century London* (Woodbridge, 2003).

> recorded here for the honour of the gentry in this part of England; that though they are as sociable and entertaining as any people are, or can be desired to be, and as much famed for good manners, and good humour; yet the new mode of forming assemblies so much, and so fatally now in vogue, in other parts of England, could never prevail here; and that though there was an attempt made by some loose persons, and the gentlemen, and ladies, did for a little while appear there; yet they generally disliked the practice, soon declined to give their company, as to a thing scandalous, and so it dropped of course.

Writing of York in the *Tour*, Defoe observes:

> the keeping up assemblies among the younger gentry was first set up here, a thing other writers recommend mightily as the character of a good country, and of a pleasant place; but which I look upon with a different view, and esteem it as a plan laid for the ruin of the nation's morals, and which, in time, threatens us with too much success that way.[9]

In *Moll Flanders*, Bath is "a place of gallantry … where men find a mistress sometimes, but very rarely look for a wife." This is an instance of what had already begun since the Restoration on spa visitors but was to become a more sustained attack by writers on Bath in particular. With *Roxana* and with his accounts of assemblies in the *Tour*, Defoe hints at the nature of sexuality in circles beyond those of the poor that were bluntly recorded though bastardy prosecutions. *Roxana* provides a depiction of dangerous moral possibilities—notably for propositioning, assertion, and disguise—of more private assemblies.

The suppression of material is a matter that helps direct attention to the lives suggested by Defoe for his fictional characters: The manuscript diary of John Thomlinson contains the thoughts of a young cleric in his search for a wife and living. Extracts were published in 1910, but the edition removed all the passages that contained anything

9 *Tour*, 9.

then deemed vulgar,[10] including the following entries from 1717 to 1721:

> Sir John Brownlow's Lady[11] abused other women with her clitoris etc.... Daniel Burgess[12] one rainy day complained in the pulpit of the absence of the ladies, saying they were afraid of spoiling their fine clothes etc and so indulged themselves in bed – he wished he was with them, he would fuck them into devotion....
>
> I have tried one woman and did not like her. I was to try another shortly for some overtures had been made etc., and if I found her answer the description etc I intended to attack her briskly and reduce her by storm etc....
>
> Cousin Clarke said that Mr Repington was clapped and yet he lies with Sarah etc....
>
> Arthur Grey condemned for burglary – his plea was that he got in drink and had a mind to see if Mr Burnet[13] was not in bed with her, and he knew he would use him roughly if he was there and therefore to took pistol – it was proved by all the servants that he often stayed till morn and then one of the servants had called to let him out. She is niece to the Duke of Atholl.

Thomlinson's diary entries were often extracts from the letters he wrote to his brother, and part of a world of shared male sexuality.

Differently, there was satire directed against the moral authority of members of the élite as with *Terrae Filius* (1713), an attack on the authorities of the University of Oxford including Dr Bernard Gardiner, the Vice-Chancellor, printing a poem attributed to his "nag," Mr Ball:

> "Since I" said Bag "your nag have been
> Han't I gone through both thick and thin;

10 J.C. Hodgson (ed.), *Six North Country Diaries* (1910), p. 64.
11 His first cousin, Eleanor, 1691–1730.
12 London Presbyterian cleric (1645–1713), whose meeting house was attacked in the Sacheverell riots.
13 Thomas Burnet, a notorious rake, third son of Gilbert, Bishop of Salisbury.

F—d handsome, ugly, rich and poor,
Did I e're fail those twenty years
Except of Mr Fulk's stairs?"

The author, John Willes, later a MP and Chief Justice of Common Pleas, was a notorious womanizer.

In 1717, George I felt able to use the standard pun of mounting women and horses when responding to the presentation of a woman at court, telling her husband that if he "connoissoit aussi bien en cheavaux qu'en femmes il ne pourroit manquer d'etre bien monté."[14]

The "culture-wars" of the period included the tension between cosmopolitanism and nationalism. A number of writers discussed culture in these terms. Gerard Langbaine's *Account of the English Dramatic Poets* (1691) offers a tabular ranking that sought to establish a national dramatic heritage, and onoe free of borrowings from French romances. Jonathan Richardson's *Essay on the Theory of Painting* (1715) argues that English painters could equal old Italian masters. Cultural nationalism took many forms, including consumption, as in a pressure to wear British rather than foreign clothes. More generally, consumerism involved the tension over such nationalism. Defoe praised British as opposed to foreign horses.[15] The "Glorious Revolution" ended the monopoly of the London Guild of Distillers in 1690 and was followed by a major rise in the distillation of gin that was seen as a patriotic alternative to French brandy, on the import of which restrictions were imposed. Gin production in London existed before William came to the throne, but became very much more popular thereafter, and a deadly Gin Craze followed in the early eighteenth century, one that was brutally depicted by Hogarth.

Very differently, the presentation of London was in part a cultural project of greatness. The naval role was celebrated in the Royal Hospital for Seamen, for which the Tudor palace at Greenwich had been rebuilt in accordance with a decision by Charles II. Executed by Christopher Wren,

14 Friedrich Wilhelm von den Schulenberg to Friedrich Wilhelm von Görtz, 12 Feb. 1717, Darmstadt, Staatsarchiv, Gräflich Görtzisches Archiv, F23, 153/6 f. 14.

15 *Tour*, 8.

who was also responsible for the Royal Hospital in Chelsea for ex-servicemen, the result was a masterpiece of English Baroque architecture. In 1708, James Thornhill was commissioned to paint the Great Hall, and by 1712 he had provided a triumphant ceiling work proclaiming British power. William and Anne were shown bringing Peace and Liberty to Britain and Europe. The subsequent painting at the end of the hall made reference to naval success and power, a list of naval victories appearing as part of the group portrait of the Hanoverian royal family, the depiction of cornucopia in the painting underlining the idea that victory led to material plenty.

The extent to which London was changing, while yet retaining traditional features, was captured in Marco Ricci's painting *A View of the Mall from St James's Park* of about 1710. The Mall was a walk where fashionable society went to see and be seen, to intrigue, to flirt, and to proposition. The park contained three avenues for pedestrians, and in the 1700s Queen Anne's gardener, Henry Wise, planted 350 limes to provide shade. In his painting, Ricci has Wren's St. Paul's in the distance and shows London society on display, but this is also a world with cattle grazing in order to provide the city with milk. Elizabeth Cromwell had kept cattle there. The large number of women depicted in Ricci's painting reflected the extent to which many public places were not segregated. An additional take on the scene may be provided by Bird Cage Walk in the park being a major center for homosexual sex, and by Roxana's nearby role in decadent parties.

There was a series of settings for cultural activity that were intended as accessible. The most significant remained churches. In his *An Essay on Criticism* (1711), Alexander Pope notes:

> As some to church repair,
> Not for the doctrine, but the music there.

Henry Purcell, organist of Westminster Abbey in 1680–95, and the composer of a large number of anthems and hymns, had a considerable influence on the next generation of English musicians, although it was superseded in terms of style by that of Handel. John Weldon (1676–1736), another successful composer of much sacred and secular music, was organist of New College, Oxford, and later in the Chapel Royal, St. Bride's Fleet Street, and St. Martin's-in-the-Fields. Maurice Greene (*c.* 1696–1755), the son of a London vicar, who was educated by Richard Brind, the organist of St. Paul's Cathedral, succeeded the latter after being organist of two other London churches, before becoming organist and composer to the Chapel Royal in 1727 and Master of the King's Band of Music eight years later. Noted as an organist, his works include numerous anthems.

The continued popularity of the Three Choirs Festival and the meetings of the cathedral choirs of Gloucester, Hereford, and Worcester, is one legacy of the period,[16] and also a testimony to the collective and sociable nature of an important cultural strand. The Festival technically began in 1724, when it rotated between the three cathedrals, but in 1719 there were advertisements for choral events, and in Worcester a festival prior to 1709.

A theme of the period was the growth of a public, entrepreneurial culture defined by the market, a culture that had flowered in the Elizabethan and Jacobean theatre, but then been hit hard by politics. This was a culture that was of the vernacular, which was Defoe's forte, and also using genres that were not closely attuned to the classics. In contrast, Pope translated Homer into heroic couplets.

Public concerts became more frequent, including those outside churches. Those organized by John Banister in 1672 were the first of these to be advertised. The role of advertising was enhanced by the expansion of the press from the 1690s, and this in turn helped create the sense that music performed for, and paid by, the public was normal. Henry Playford, who succeeded his father as an active publisher of music, in order to broaden his position in the music market founded a tri-weekly concert in 1699 at a London coffeehouse where his music could also be sold, and established a club for music practice. In his preface to the fourth edition of *The Second Book of the Pleasant Musical Companion* published in 1701, Playford links improvement and sociability, both key themes in cultural activity and ethos:

> The design therefore, as it is for a general diversion, so it is intended for a general instruction, that the persons who give themselves the liberty of an evening's entertainment with their

16 W. Shaw, *The Three Choirs Festival: The Official History of the Meetings of the Three Choirs of Gloucester, Hereford and Worcester, c. 1713–1953* (Worcester, 1954).

> friends, may exchange the expense they shall be at in being sociable, with the knowledge they shall acquire from it.

Such activity was far from limited to the capital. In *Moll Flanders*, there is mention of the "little country opera-house" at Bury St. Edmunds, where Moll is able to pickpocket a gold watch. Yet she prefers the opportunities of London.

Meanwhile in London, spatial differentiation was becoming more apparent with the development of the West End, which was very different, for example, from that of Shadwell in the late seventeenth century. This differentiation was also a cultural one, captured repeatedly in plays across the period that portray a rivalry between citizens and gentlemen. The former could be criticized for greed or praised for industry and honesty; and the latter praised for nobility or criticized as vicious seducers especially eager for the wives of merchants. The Whig playwright Nicholas Rowe, in *The Tragedy of Jane Shore* (1714), presents a city merchant acting an honorable part in opposition to a nasty nobleman. London recorded and propagated these tensions, and each of these images contributed to the impression it created, both for its citizens and further afield.

The role of the middling orders has recently been repeatedly presented as the driving force of eighteenth-century English culture. From this perspective, the forcing house of public demand provided the essential pressure for cultural modernization and for the definition of taste. This is an account of a conflation of consumerism and the public sphere through which taste is defined, imagination organized and encouraged, and culture developed.[17] Such an assessment is linked to a portrayal of the English Enlightenment as an inclusive movement, sustained by a vibrant and unconstrained world of newspapers, coffee houses, and other public meeting houses.[18]

Aside from the degree to which the evidence is largely urban and therefore unrepresentative, the problem with this account is that polite consumerism can act as a universal solvent, apparently banishing analytical

17 J. Brewer, *The Pleasures of the Imagination: English Culture in the Eighteenth Century* (London, 1997).

18 R. Porter, *Enlightenment: Britain and the Creation of the Modern World* (London, 2000).

problems. One relates to the definition of the middling orders and their culture. In practice, much "middling" culture exhibited a "trickle down" effect, in both form and culture, from élite culture. Secondly, divisions affected every aspect of life, including such cultural dimensions as music and the patronage of painters, but that is not a theme that is adequately worked out if the emphasis is on consumerism. Social and regional divisions are underplayed in such an emphasis, as those largely derived from politics and religion.

Thirdly, gender has to be considered. As both producers and consumers of culture, women shared in the same cultural world as men, but there were also important differences in access and presentation. Thus, in conversation pieces—the group portraiture that presented relationships—men took the more prominent roles and also commissioned the paintings.

Fiction was part of this process. Many women were active writers, but some are obscure, for example the dramatist Mary Pix (1666–*c.*1720), whose plays include the comedy *The Beau Defeated* (1700) and Penelope Aubion (*c.*1679–1731), the author of romantic novels, including *The Life and Adventures of the Lady Lucy*. Successful writers included not only Eliza Haywood but also Susannah Centlivre, who produced social comedies such as *the Busy Body* (1709), *The Wonder! A Woman Keeps a Secret* (1714), and *A Bold Stroke for a Wife* (1718).

Fiction served for contemporaries to present accounts of truth. Thus, fiction as history underlined the cultural salience of the latter. Moreover, Providence does not arise solely in terms of the individual salvation discussed in Defoe's novels, for historical works readily found Providence the key defender of nationhood, and history-writing thus an appropriate way to assert nationalism. In his dedication of volume two of his history of England to George I, Laurence Echard, a clergyman, presents the Glorious Revolution as "wonderful and providential." He also writes:

> England in an especial manner has been such a mighty and distinct scene of action, in the latter ages of the world, that during the compass of this History, there appears a greater variety of changes, governments and establishments; and there seems to have been more visible and signal instances of judgements and punishments, mercies and deliverances from above,

> then perhaps can be paralleled in any other part of the Western world.

The text of this book was very clear that "Divine Providence" played a key role, not least due to the lapsed nature of mankind as a consequence of Adam's Fall.[19] This lapsed nature made divine support even more necessary, a point valid for nations as well as individuals, in this-time as well as all-time. The Restoration of Stuart monarchy in 1660 was described accordingly as "the most free and exalted expression of a delivered and overjoyed nation, triumphantly restored, without one drop of blood, by the All-merciful and powerful Hand of Heaven."[20] With it, episcopacy, an important buttress of monarchy, was restored. National history and identity, mutually dependent, could not be separated from Providence. The perfectibility of society is not at the behest of humans, and the emphasis on Providence, as it is understood in the period, inherently cuts across any idea of a solution for Humanity as a whole. Millenarian thought is different in its prospectus.

Echard was a moderate Tory, and the Whigs added a powerful theme of human intervention in history in the shape of the balance of power and its application. This interpretation permitted a representation of England in terms of moderation, which was to be a standard theme in the self-presentation of English distinctiveness. Indeed, a key source was that of the supposed middle way, or *via media*, in Church matters between radical Protestantism and Catholicism. This account drew on classical ideas of moderation. In political terms, there was a standard Aristotelian tension between royal prerogatives and popular privileges, a tension that, at its best, produced a balance that guaranteed liberty. The Saxon *witan* and the post-1688 Parliament were presented as the prime instances of this balance, and there was a ready reading—both forward and back–from one to the other.

The understanding of a revolution as a return to past circumstances, and ideally to a past golden age that had been lost as a consequence of usurpations of some kind, was a significant variant on the progressivism or improvability with which Whig thought is associated. The account of

19 Echard, *History*, II, 1.
20 *Ibid.*, II, 910.

1688–9 as a Glorious Revolution made it possible to reconcile both views and sets of images, and this reconciliation helped Whiggism function as a potent and resonant ideology with the Revolution Settlement as a later version of Magna Carta (1215). Although, Whiggism always contained ideological, policy, and factional divisions, which created problems for those hoping to hold consistent views. Multiple themes, interpretations, and echoes—much like identities—are significant. They could be located in terms of a lasting struggle, or simply placed alongside in an accumulative fashion.

Thus, alongside the classical linkage to the Whig ideas referred to in the previous paragraph, comes the religious drive that Defoe felt personally, even as a kind of animus. This was seen in the *Tour* in his description of the remains of Melrose Abbey, a description that scarcely prefigures the later fashion, even cult, for such places:

> … 'tis easy to know it was a most magnificent place in those days. But the Reformation has triumphed over all these things, and the pomp and glory of Popery is sunk now into the primitive simplicity of the true Christian profession; nor can any Protestant mourn the loss of these seminaries of superstition, upon any principles that agree, either with his own profession, or with the Christian pattern prescribed in the scriptures. So I leave Melrose with a singular satisfaction, at seeing what it now is, much more than that of remembering what it once was.[21]

His religious stance gave depth to Defoe's offer of a form of cultural nationalism in *Robinson Crusoe*. Moreover, the social location of his protagonists is also instructive in that they are not at the peak of society. Roxana gets there, only to discover that it is sinful and empty.

The setting of repentance and virtue found among the middling orders and necessary for ordinary people was seen not only with Defoe, but also in George Lillo's play, *The London Merchant* (1731), in which a weak apprentice murders the hero merchant and then undergoes an exemplary repentance. This popular work represents a major change in tragedy in that

21 *Tour*, 12.

it was written in a prose idiom and given a bourgeois setting and values. It was indicative of the cultural importance of London that this play made Lillo's name while the court masque he wrote in 1733 for the marriage of the Princess Royal and William IV of Orange was unperformed because of the postponement of the marriage. As Fielding notes in the prologue to Lillo's tragedy *Fatal Curiosity* (1750), a prologue also suited to Defoe's novels:

> No fustian hero rages here tonight
> No armies fall, to fix a tyrant's right:
> From lower life we draw our scene's distress:
> Let not your equals move your pity less.

As a related but different point, it is simply inaccurate to argue that from: "Defoe to Austen, the predominant theme of eighteenth-century fiction is money.... [I]ts presence is as associated with happiness as its absence is with limited choice."[22] Defoe in practice saw money as an element in wider stories, whether of national greatness or of personal redemption, not least creating the niches in which a good life could be pursued.

Money was also the necessary means of cultural interchange, and indeed of the social grounding that writers sought and that Defoe eventually obtained for his family. This was particularly so for authors, but also for all other artists. Thus, Samuel Carpenter, a Yorkshire mason, received £84 10s in 1705 for carving the ornate capitals in the Hall at Castle Howard, while in August 1717, Robert Walpole's account book recorded £86 "paid to Mr [Jonathan] Richardson painter for drawing your Honors and Sir Charles Turner and brothers pictures," and the following April £13 was "paid for two pictures at Mr Graffier's auction."[23]

There was also in the *Tour* an aesthetic placement in terms of the landscape values of the period, one in which Defoe very much corresponds to those of most of his contemporaries. Defoe did not match the sensibility

22 J. Feather, "The Power of Print: Word and Image in eighteenth-century England," in J. Black (ed.), *Culture and Society in Britain, 1660–1800* (Manchester, 1997), p. 63.

23 BL. Add. 74062.

of Matthias Read (1669–1747), a Londoner who in 1690 settled in Whitehaven, which Sir John Lowther (1642–1706), who owned nearby coal pits, developed as a port. Aside from painting many of the Cumbrian country houses for their owners, Read was also one of the first native painters of English landscape, painting Cumbrian mountains and skies. In doing so, he became the only notable painter of the Lake District prior to the late eighteenth century.[24]

In Wales, in contrast, Defoe refers to "a ridge of horrid rocks and precipices."[25] He adds of the Lake District:

> Nor were these hills high and formidable only, but they had a kind of an unhospitable terror in them. Here were no rich pleasant valleys between them, as among the Alps; no lead mines and veins of rich ore, as in the Peak; no coal pits, as in the hills about Halifax ... but all barren and wild, of no use or advantage either to man or beast.[26]

In that section, Defoe refers several times to the frightful character of the mountains. He argues a cultural as well as artistic character to landscape, and this was one that drew on culture as well as topography. Thus, of northern Ayrshire in lowland Scotland:

> we thought ourselves in England again. Here we saw no more a Galloway, where you have neither hedge or tree, but about the gentlemen's houses; whereas here you have beautiful enclosures, pleasant pastures, and grass grounds, and consequently store of cattle well fed and provided.[27]

Highland Scotland is described with some harshness, both in terms of the "hideous desert mountains" and with reference to a "horrible

24 M.E. Burkett and D. Sloss, *Read's Point of View: Paintings of the Cumbrian Countryside* (Bowness, 1995).
25 *Tour*, 6.
26 *Tour*, 10.
27 *Tour*, 12.

ignorance."[28] Defoe's preference for well-cultivated land was readily apparent, as was the norm. Attitudes to towns, in contrast, were more ambivalent, for Defoe and even more so for other writers. At the same time, through the towns there was the articulation, indeed circulation, of a national culture that benefited writers who wrote for money. Entrepreneurs played a major role in this, acting as impresarios—for example, John Heidegger and John Rich. Writers perforce were part of this world, but also frequently criticized it. Far less critical than Pope or Swift, Defoe was able to benefit from the opportunities offered.[29]

28 *Tour*, 13.

29 P. Rogers, *Literature and Popular Culture in Eighteenth-Century England* (Brighton, 1985) and *Eighteenth-Century Encounters. Studies in Literature and Society in the Age of Walpole* (Brighton, 1985).

8. From Restoration to Revolution, 1660–88

> "On 29 May 1660, Charles II entered London with a triumph of … horse and foot, brandishing their swords and shouting with inexpressible joy; the way strewed with flowers, the bells ringing, the streets hung with tapestry, fountains running with wine; the mayor, aldermen and all the companies in their liveries, chains of gold, banners; lords and nobles, everyone clad in cloth of silver, gold and velvet; the windows and balconies all set with ladies, trumpets, music and myriads flocking the streets …. I stood in the Strand and beheld it and blessed God. And all this was done without one drop of blood … it was the Lord's doing."

John Evelyn was sure in his values, but the Restoration of monarchy in the person of Charles II in 1660 was no triumph for Dissenters such as Defoe. More generally, Charles' reign (1660–85) was important for his writing, not only because it provided the frame of reference for his life and that of his readers, but also because some of his writing is set in the reign, *Moll Flanders* allegedly being written in 1683. To understand all three, it is therefore necessary to address the reign, while also noting that, alongside major changes during the reign, there were very different views held by contemporaries. Indeed, they lived in a world that was established and contested in terms of the oft-expressed memories of the past. As a young man, Colonel Jack loves "to talk with seamen and soldiers" about the Third Anglo-Dutch War (1672–4), and by extension of other conflicts including:

> the wars in Oliver's time, the death of King Charles the first [1649], and the like.
>
> By this means, as young as I was, I was a kind of an historian,

> and though I had read no books, and never had any books to read, yet I could give a tolerable account of what had been done, and of what was then a doing in the world, especially in those things that our own people were concerned in.

Restored Monarchy

The Restoration Settlement brought Charles II to the thrones of England, Ireland, and Scotland. He was an appropriate figure to preside over the reconciliation and, still more, the stabilization required after the 1640s and 1650s. Able and determined in his rights, Charles was nevertheless flexible, and in some respects, not least his major turns in fortune, provided a counterpart to such novelistic characters as Colonel Jack. Charles's ambition was essentially modest, consisting in the preservation of his position rather than centering consistently on any creation of a strong monarchy. He lacked the autocratic manner and potent means of his cousin, Louis XIV of France, who assumed personal power in 1661. If there were to be a royalist reaction, it would not be led by Charles, although it was claimed that he told his trusted advisers in 1669 that he planned an autocracy. Charles's charm was also a definite asset and even if he was not trusted by all—and was seen as a tyrant and a rake by some—he was able to avoid the reputations and fates of his father, Charles I, and his brother, James II and VII.

In 1660, Oliver Cromwell's corpse was exhumed and hanged at Tyburn, the traditional place of execution for common criminals. Yet, apart from those who had signed Charles I's death warrant and a few others, parliamentarians and Cromwellians were pardoned by the new regime. This would have included Robinson Crusoe's fictional eldest brother, a Cromwellian Lieutenant-Colonel who, however, had already been killed fighting the Spaniards in 1659 at a time when England was allied with France. The Spaniards were heavily defeated by an Anglo-French army at the battle of the Dunes in 1658, and it is to this event which Defoe is probably referring.

Alongside a benign account of forgiveness should be presented the reality of the removal of those who were distrusted, or had simply kept the wrong side—for example John Chaffin Junior, who was dismissed as

Postmaster of Sherborne in 1661.[1] Some Dissenting preachers like Vavasor Powell spent most of the 1660s in prison, where he died in 1670, but most did not.

Royal powers under the Restoration were to be fewer than they had been with Charles I in 1640, but greater than in late 1641, during which time Charles was under heavy political pressure from Parliament, let alone later in the 1640s. Charles II was given a reasonable peacetime income and control over the army, but the controversial prerogative of taxation and jurisdictional institutions of the 1630s—for example ship money and Star Chamber—were not restored. There was to be no substantial landed estate under Crown control that might enable the monarch to maintain his financial independence. Proposals advanced in the 1650s for the reform of Parliament, the law, and the universities were certainly not welcome in the conservative atmosphere of the 1660s. Indeed, Bradford, Leeds, and Manchester lost their recently-granted parliamentary seats.

The monarch might again reign by divine right, and a very different right from the providentialism claimed by Cromwell, but he was nevertheless to rule thanks to Parliament—this was intended to be a parliamentary monarchy. The loss of prerogative powers and the need for parliamentary taxation ensured that Charles would also rule through Parliament. This was shown in 1661–2 when his hopes of a broadly-based established Church incorporating as many Protestants as possible—with toleration for the rest—were rejected by the "Cavalier Parliament" (1661–79); this followed upon the failure in the Savoy Conference of 1661 to produce agreement between Anglicans and Presbyterians. The Corporation Act (1661) obliged town officials to conform to an Anglicanism that clearly differentiated itself from Dissent, while the Test Acts (1673, 1678) excluded Catholics from office and Parliament, and Dissenters from office. Ideological uniformity was pursued in a new repression.

Thanks to the Act of Uniformity of 1662, Presbyterian clergy were ejected from their parishes, and worship with five or more people was forbidden unless according to Anglican rites. One hundred and thirty ministers lost their livings in Wales, and in England the Baptist preacher John

1 P. Drake, "Captain John Chaffin of Sherborne," in *Notes and Queries for Somerset and Dorset*, 32, 325 (March 1987): p. 578.

Bunyan was convicted of preaching without licence to unlawful assemblies and began writing *The Pilgrim's Progress* in prison, where he was held from 1660 until 1672 and again in 1676–7. Nevertheless, much of the legislation was undermined when Puritan gentry evaded it: gentry JPs often colluded in this evasion. Ejected Puritan clergy were frequently employed by Puritan gentry as private chaplains and tutors, the gentry ignoring the law which could lead to imprisonment. Moreover, there was a reduced role for Convocation and the clerical Parliaments of the Archdioceses of Canterbury and York, which after the Restoration lost their power to tax the clergy.

Control over the world of print was more readily reimposed. Under legislation of 1662, printing was strictly limited to the master printers of the Stationers Company of London and the university printers. Only twenty of the former were permitted, and vacancies were filled by the authority of the Archbishop of Canterbury and the Bishop of London, who were troubled enough by the dissemination of heterodox opinions not to support a relaxation in the control of printing.

Fear as well as revenge conditioned the Restoration Settlement. A sense of precariousness, especially fears about republican conspiracies that indeed existed, led to Treason and Militia Acts. The fortifications of towns that had supported Parliament in the Civil War, such as Gloucester and Northampton, were "slighted" so that they would not be defensible again. In 1661, an attempt by "Fifth Monarchists" led by Thomas Venner, a millenarian cooper, to seize the City on behalf of "King Jesus" was defeated by the city's forces. They were supported by troops under George Monck, the army commander in Scotland, whose occupation of London in 1660 had been instrumental in the Restoration. By 1661, Monck was Duke of Albemarle. He would later be in charge of London during the Great Plague of 1665, maintain order during the Great Fire of 1666, and be buried in Westminster Abbey in 1670. This was an aspect of a new governing order that struck some as involving betrayal as much as compromise.

In Ireland, the Cromwellian land settlement on behalf of Protestants and at the cost of Catholics was put into only mild reversal, whereas in Scotland, Parliament, episcopacy, and aristocratic power and influence were all restored. However, about a third of the Scottish parish ministers were unwilling to accept the new religious settlement. Presbyterian conventicles acted as centers of defiance, and government attempts to suppress them led to unsuccessful rebellions notably in 1679. Relying on military force, John, Duke of Lauderdale, the Secretary for Scottish Affairs, maintained royal power.

Charles was unhappy with the religious settlement and with attempts to restrict his freedom of manoeuvre. In 1667, he emphasized his determination that Parliament should not be able to do so.[2] Attempts to restrict this freedom became more serious as a result of his apparent Catholic leanings. Charles's morality was also a matter of comment, as with a lampoon of 1681 "At the Royal Coffee House," in which 24 French dancing girls at Whitehall performed naked before Charles. He was the ruler on whom the fictional King Bolloximian of *Sodom: or, the Quintessence of Debauchery* (1684, possibly by John, 2nd Earl of Rochester), was modelled:

> Thus in the zenith of my lust I reign;
> I eat to survive and survive to eat again
> … And with my prick I'll govern all the land.

A more favorable account was offered by John Dryden in his comic *The Kind Keeper; Or, Mr Limberham* (1677), which was written at the suggestion of Charles, who had made him Poet Laureate in 1668, and related to the "keeping" women activities of both monarch and writer.[3] Defoe's *Roxana* has references in its decadent Court life to the fashion for masquerades under George I (r. 1714–27), but more clearly drew on the far more overt vice at Court during Charles's reign. The reference to "the Queen not affecting to be very much in public" was to Catherine of Braganza, Charles's wife. George's wife never came to Britain as she was under house arrest in Germany for adultery. Already, in *A Journal of the Plague Year*, Defoe links the immorality of the Court to the nation's problems. Noting that God had preserved the Court when it retired to Oxford, Defoe added:

> for which I cannot say that I ever saw they showed any great token of thankfulness, and hardly anything of reformation,

2 Henri, Marquis de Rouvigny, French envoy, to Louis XIV, 3 Oct. 1667, AE. CP. Ang. 89 f. 114.

3 J. Winn, *John Dryden and His World* (New Haven, 1987).

> though they did not want being told that their crying vices might without breach of charity be said to have gone too far in bringing that terrible judgment upon the whole nation.

The Restoration had seen a new Bear Garden built at Southwark after the Puritan prohibition of bull- and bear-baiting was lifted, while the maypoles destroyed under Cromwell were replaced. These steps were widely popular, but not the sin associated with the Court. This sin could be associated with religious and political attitudes held by and around Charles—for example, the role of his mistress, the Duchess of Portsmouth, in supporting the French interest.[4]

If vice and corruption at Court were bad enough to many, an alleged Catholic as ruler was totally unacceptable. In a culture that knew little of religious toleration, such a king appeared to imperil national independence, the Church, and society. George Larkin's pro-government *Publick Occurrences Truly Stated* refers to "the confiding coffee-houses, where the grave men puff out sedition." Anti-popery and fear of arbitrary government were as important in the second half of the seventeenth century as in the first. Yet, as later with George III, it would be unwise to exaggerate the king's unpopularity. Indeed, at a sacral and mystical level, tens of thousands of people sought Charles's physical touch to treat the King's Evil (*scrofula*), evidence of faith in, and demand for, the curative powers of kingship. So also did the exiled Stuarts after 1689.

Failure in the Second Anglo-Dutch War (1665–7), including an humiliating attack on the English fleet in the Medway (1667), was followed by the Secret Treaty of Dover with the most powerful Catholic monarch, Louis XIV (1670). Charles, in broad terms, promised to declare his conversion to Catholicism and to restore the religion to England. The two monarchs were to unite in attacking the Dutch—the leading Protestant power—as they indeed did in 1672. This was the real Popish Plot. Suspicion about Charles's intentions helped not only to bedevil the rest of his reign, but also to ensure that his successor—his Catholic brother, James II (VII of Scotland, 1685–8)—came to the throne in an atmosphere in which suspicion concerning Catholics had been heightened and crucially linked to

4 Notes by Lord Treasurer Danby, undated, BL. Add. 28042.

Louis XIV. The latter's moves against Protestants in France, culminating in the revocation of the Edict of Nantes (1685), were an apparent warning that Catholic rulers could not be trusted and would always be bitterly anti-Protestant. Public criticism, both of the Third Anglo-Dutch War (1672–4) and of moves against parliamentary scrutiny led to the conviction that only a Parliament with independence and power could protect the nation from French universal dominance and from a French style of government in Britain, and a definition of nationalism must be established accordingly.[5]

The Popish Plot

The Third Anglo-Dutch War (1672–4) was unsuccessful and expensive, and it led to the fall of Charles's ministry—the Cabal—while in the more partisan politics access to the king was restricted by Charles.[6] There was a sense of distrust, notwithstanding of a government dependent on Parliament,[7] and one Charles resisted when telling the Commons in 1677 that he would not allow the infringement of his prerogative powers in foreign policy because to do so would effectively be to end his sovereignty. Yet such political storms could be mastered by the adept Charles, always ready to sacrifice ministers to secure his own position, but the Popish Plot crisis of 1678 was an attack on Charles at his weakest points. Although he was the father of at least fourteen male bastards—most prominently James, Duke of Monmouth—succession was a major problem for Charles. There were no legitimate children by his marriage to the Portuguese princess, Catherine of Braganza (who had brought Bombay and Tangier as her dowry in 1661), so his Catholic brother James, Duke of York, was his heir. The Popish Plot stemmed from false claims made by the adventurer, Titus Oates, of the existence of a Catholic plot to assassinate Charles and replace him with James. This was an aspect of the process by which politics was understood and pursued through wild conspiracy stories, which in part saw an

5 S.C.A. Pincus, "From Butterbox to Wooden Shoes: The Shift in English popular sentiment from anti-Dutch to anti-French in the 1670s," in *Historical Journal*, 38 (1995): p. 361.

6 B. Weiser, *Charles II and the Politics of Access* (Woodbridge, 2003).

7 Courtin to Louis XIV, 1 Oct. 1676, AE. CP. Ang. 120 fol. 26.

overlap of fact and fiction. The murder of Sir Edmund Berry Godfrey, the magistrate who took the evidence of the plot, and the discovery of suspicious letters in the possession of James's former private secretary, Edward Coleman, inflamed suspicions and led to politics by orchestrated paranoia. What followed was a series of show-trials in which Catholics were convicted and then executed, but which only fed paranoia. In its issue of 19 August 1679, the recently launched *Domestic Intelligence* reports:

> There is great lamentation both in France and Flanders for the death of those saints and martyrs as they call them lately deservedly executed for treason, of whom divers [various] legends [accounts] are printed … it appears that they have great hopes, yet once again to enslave us, and to convert us by the infallible arguments of fire and faggot.

Three days later, the paper reported the persecution of Protestants in France, but noted that a panic that the Catholics would try to burn all the ships of the Medway was groundless.

The revelation by political rivals that Charles II's leading minister, Lord Treasurer Danby, had been negotiating with Louis XIV, fanned the flames. Danby fell from office, being sent to the Tower of London in 1679, and Court power collapsed. The legacy of the Popish Plot continued with later references in print, as with the account in the *Weekly Journal or, British Gazetteer* of 2 May 1724, of the 1679 trial of Catholic barrister, Richard Langhorne, for treason.

The Exclusion Crisis

The Popish Plot became an attempt to use Parliament to exclude James from the succession and to weaken Charles's government—thus named the Exclusion Crisis of 1679–81. Its leading advocate, Anthony, Earl of Shaftesbury, created what has been seen as the first English political party, the "Whigs." This was an abusive term referring to Scottish Presbyterian rebels that was originally used by their opponents, though the party should rather be seen as a faction held together by informal ties, ambition, and ideology—as well as personal and family connections—and not by party discipline and central control. The Whigs looked to the same groups and tendencies that had opposed Charles I: Whig common councillors tended to represent parishes that had a strong Nonconformist tendency, one looking back to Puritanism. Following a pattern that in many respects went back to the Reformation, the differing religio-political groups were based in specific places and neighborhoods. Defoe indeed in his novels shows a very clear grasp of London's topography, not least in his criminal protagonists escaping pursuit. A French diplomat had reported in 1676 that London led the kingdom.[8] London spread news, being the center of newspaper activity and postal services.

Mistrust of the Court wrecked the possible success of an alternative to Exclusion in the shape of the limitation of James's power. Anti-Catholicism helped create a crisis that the Whigs could exploit, and royal powers were weakened, as with the Habeas Corpus Act of 1679 that made imprisonment without trial difficult. This legal principle was to be important to English political culture and to Britain's bequest to the world of liberal values.

The Whigs, however, suffered during the Exclusion Crisis from the determination of most people to avoid rebellion and a repetition of the chaos of the Civil War, the damage of which was still being repaired—for example, by the Myddeltons at Chirk Castle and by the citizens of Worcester. The chances of Exclusion were also limited by the strength of Charles's position in the House of Lords and the king's right to summon and dissolve Parliament as he thought fit, both of which blocked Exclusion in a legal fashion; firstly, by the lack of a generally agreed alternative to James, and secondly by Charles's fixed determination. With Scotland and Ireland securely under control after the Covenanter rising of 1679 in Scotland was suppressed, Charles II would not face a crisis comparable to that of 1638–42 when both had rebelled. In addition, he avoided foolish moves such as his father's attempt to arrest the Five Members of the House of Commons.

In reaction to the Whigs, the "Tories" developed as a conservative and loyalist grouping, supporters of the king and the Church of England. The

8 Honoré Courtin to Simon, Marquis de Pomponne, French foreign minister, 9 July 1676, AE. CP. Ang. 119 fols 22–3.

association of London with the Whigs, even though there were also many Tories there,[9] led Charles to summon the new Parliament to Oxford in 1681, which returned to the geographical politics of the Civil War. Whig failure to secure Exclusion that year led to a reaction that was eased by Charles's negotiation of 1681 of a subsidy from Louis XIV that enabled him to do without Parliament for the rest of his reign. Although there was little overall violence then or prior, Tory crowds turned out in force in London in 1681, burning effigies of Jack Presbyter and of the Whig leader, Anthony, 1st Earl of Shaftesbury, who had earlier been in the Tower of London in 1677–8. Shaftesbury had been taught by Locke at Oxford. He was to be lacerated in 1681 in *Absalom and Achitophel* by Dryden, a writer as politically committed as the very different Defoe was to be. The work went through three editions in 1681.

The reaction was based on Tory-Anglican support, which helped keep London quiescent in 1683–5 and ensured demonstrations against Dissenters, in Bristol and Norwich as well.[10] Whig office-holders were purged in the reaction, Sir John Hotham for example being excluded from the list of East Riding JPs, and Whig leaders fled or were compromised in the Rye House Plot (1683), an alleged conspiracy to assassinate Charles and James. This led to executions and the creation of Whig martyrs and encouraged the attacks on Whig strongholds, an aspect of the highly partisan nature of urban politics.[11] Corporation charters—for example that of London—were remodelled in order to increase Crown influence, and Dissenters were persecuted. The Whig newspapers were suppressed. In Scotland, the Test Act of 1681 obliged all ministers and office-holders to repudiate Covenants. James was based in Edinburgh in 1679–82, and Holyrood Palace in Edinburgh was rebuilt as a Court center in the northern kingdom. Wales was especially badly affected by the culling of the magistracy and lord lieutenancies.

9 T. Harris, *London Crowds in the Reign of Charles II* (Cambridge, 1987).

10 T. Harris, "Was the Tory Reaction Popular?: Attitudes of Londoners towards the Persecution of Dissent, 1681–6," in *London Journal*, 13 (1988): pp. 116–17.

11 P. Halliday, *Dismembering the Body Politics: Partisan Politics in English Towns, 1650–1730* (1998).

James II and VII, 1685-8

Thanks to the reaction against the Exclusion Crisis, James II (James VII in Scotland) was able to succeed his brother with little difficulty (1685). Although he struck the French envoy as showing resolution and focus on rapid results,[12] James was initially emollient and promised to protect the Church of England. His situation was strengthened that year by the defeat of rebellions in England and Scotland. Charles II's most charismatic bastard, James, Duke of Monmouth, had pressed a claim to be Charles's heir during the Exclusion Crisis, arguing that Charles had really married his mother, Lucy Walter, for which his "evidence" was highly problematic. Monmouth landed at Lyme Regis in June 1685 and drew on opposition to James. That month, Katherine Hall, the wife of a London malt factor, was accused by her servant, Thomas Tothall, of saying that "the late King [Charles II] was a black bastard and that the Duke of York, his present Majesty, was a duke of Devils."

The questioning of captives after Monmouth's total defeat at Sedgemoor led James to tell the French envoy that the Monmouth conspiracy had been carried out in concert with Huguenot refugees who sought also to lead to rebellion in France, and that William of Orange was involved. And, if the envoy found this report very vague,[13] it was symptomatic of an enduring sense of conspiracy. Like Cromwell, victory gave James a conviction of divine approval, and the rebellion led him to increase his army. However, Parliament was unhappy about this and especially with his appointment of Catholic officers. In response, James prorogued the English and Scottish Parliaments and they never met again during his reign. With less constraint, he then moved toward a Catholicizing of the government, which made him unpopular. Indeed, James's more dogmatic and inflexible stance squandered the legacy left him. The changes necessary to establish full religious and civil equality for Catholics entailed a destruction of the privileges of the Church of England, a policy of appointing Catholics, the insistent use of prerogative action, and preparations for a packed Parliament—all of which led to anger and suspicion. Ninety-seven parliamentary

12 Barillon to Louis XIV, 7, 10 May 1685, AE. CP. Ang. 155 f. 9, 16.
13 Barillon to Louis XIV, 10, 13 Sept. 1685, AE. CP. Ang. 156 fols 40–1, 46.

boroughs were purged, with Catholics and Dissenters installed as members of corporations, while Catholics were made Lords Lieutenant. The purpose was to gerrymander the boroughs to produce a Commons willing to back James.

The dismissal of William, 9th Earl of Derby, as Lord Lieutenant in both Cheshire and Lancashire was a break with local patronage structures and assumptions of hierarchy, as were the extensive purges of JPs. The political culture of the period assumed deference in return for good kingship, expectations of political behavior that involved a measure of contractualism. Spurning these boundaries, James set out to create a new constituency of political support. Furthermore, James took steps to develop the army into a professional institution answerable only to the king and thus a means to power, a move that was quite unpopular.[14]

And yet there was no revolution in the British Isles after Monmouth's failure.[15] Unlike in 1638–42, the Stuart monarchy was now strong enough to survive domestic challenges, and there was no breakdown of order in Scotland and Ireland. However, James helped ensure that opposition to his policies for autocracy and Catholicization drew together much of the political nation. There was not time for him to put in place the various measures necessary to impose a new order, not least of which were new appointments.[16]

London played a major role in this opposition, as James's attempt to use the formal levers of power repeatedly clashed with a strongly-held sense of loyalty to national and Protestant liberties and local interests. In 1685, to the disquiet of some ministers, Henry Compton, who had backed the Huguenots, was suspended as Bishop of London for refusing to suspend John Sharp, Rector of St. Giles-in-the-Fields, who had criticized Catholicism from the pulpit.[17] In the winter of 1687–8 the questions about favoring tolerance for Catholics—which the king put to all parliamentary candidates and magistrates—were also put to members of the London

14 Barillon to Louis XIV, 16 Sept. 1687, AE. CP. Ang. 162 f. 164.
15 Barillon to Louis XIV, 6 Oct. 1687, AE. CP. Ang. 162 f. 190.
16 Barillon to Louis XIV, 2 July, 25 Aug. 1687, AE. CP. Ang. 162 f. 61, 130.
17 Barillon to Louis XIV, 7 Jan., 4 July 1686, AE. CP. Ang. 158 f. 29, 159 f. 19–20.

Livery Companies, 3,500 of whom were expelled for failing to agree. Meanwhile, Catholic schools were founded in London, a Benedictine house was established in Clerkenwell and a convent in York, and Catholic priests sought to proselytize, all this only contributing to a sense of menace.

The birth of a Prince of Wales on 10 June 1688 was a major shock to those unhappy with James's policies. "It could not have been more public if he had been born in Charing Cross," noted the future Bishop Atterbury, a Tory. Nevertheless, unhappy critics like William Lloyd spread the rumor that a baby had been smuggled into the Queen's bed in a warming pan. Hitherto, James had had no surviving children from his fifteen-year long second Catholic marriage to Mary of Modena, a marriage supported by Louis XIV.[18] In contrast, after the death of his son in 1677, James had two daughters, Mary and Anne, living from his Protestant first marriage. Mary, whom James had failed to convert,[19] was married to her first cousin and James's nephew, William III of Orange, who was the leading Dutch political figure and a Protestant. It had been expected that they would succeed James, and that his changes would therefore be temporary, as had been those of Mary Tudor when she was succeeded by Elizabeth I in 1558. Anne married the Protestant Prince George of Denmark in 1683.

However, a male Catholic heir threatened to make James's changes permanent, ensuring a very different historical resonance to that of Mary Tudor. Separately, on 30 June, in an enormously popular verdict, Archbishop Sancroft of Canterbury and six bishops were acquitted on charges of sedition for refusing to read James's order that the Declaration of Indulgence granting all Christians full equality of religious practice be read from all pulpits. The Declaration challenged the position of the Church of England. Celebrations included a large number of bonfires. The importance of public opinion was emphasized by the extent to which both James' supporters and his opponents published tracts and books about such episodes, although the government also sought to control opinion by forbidding

18 Marquise Campana de Cavelli, *Ls Derniers Stuarts à Saint-Germain en Laye* (Paris, 1871), p. 1–22.

19 Barillon to Charles Marquis de Croissy, Foreign Minister, 26 Jan. 1688, AE. CP. Ang. 165 f. 61.

newspapers in coffee houses.[20] The acquittal was to be memorialized as part of the national tradition in the frescoes that were painted when the Houses of Parliament were rebuilt following the devastating fire of 1834.

The "Glorious Revolution" of 1688

The more volatile and threatening situation led seven politicians to invite William to intervene in order to protect Protestantism and traditional liberties. Motivated rather by a wish to keep the British Isles out of Louis XIV's camp—and not to invade France as was reported[21]—William of Orange had already resolved to invade Britain. In many respects, however, his invasion was a gamble and dependent on whether Louis decided to attack the Dutch, as opposed to advancing into the Empire (Germany), as well as on the policies of other powers, the winds in the North Sea and English Channel, and the response of the English fleet and army to the invasion.

After his initial attempt, indeed, had been thwarted by storms—leading to comments in the Hague that Heaven had shown its displeasure[22]—William landed at Torbay on 5 November 1688 with a substantial army (as well as a printing press) as he expected a difficult campaign. Yet, he was still heavily outnumbered. Nevertheless, William benefited from a collapse of will on the part of James, who had an army twice the size of William's own. James had been a brave commander earlier in his life, but in the face of very contradictory reports about support[23] he suffered from a collapse of resolve and a series of debilitating nose-bleeds, and failed to lead his army into battle. There was also a haemorrhage of support, culminating with the flight of Lieutenant-General John Churchill from James's camp at Salisbury to William's side, and that of Princess Anne from London. As James retreated on London, his army collapsed:

20 Sir John Lowther of Whitehaven to Sir John Lowther of Lowther, 13 Oct. 1688, Beinecke, Osborn Files, Lowther.

21 Sir Robert Holmes, Governor of the Isle of Wight, to Preston, 5, 6 Nov. 1688, BL. Preston papers 1688, fols 17, 26.

22 D'Avaux, French envoy in The Hague, to Gravel, his counterpart in Berlin, 19 Oct., 2 Nov. 1688, AE. CP. Hollande 157 f. 259, 267; James II to George, Lord Dartmouth, 20 Oct. 1688, BL. Add. 18447 f. 96.

23 Barillon to Croissy, 25 Nov. 1688, AE. CP. Ang. 167 f. 106.

> Our retreat from Sarum [Salisbury] was sudden and to confess the truth with some uncommon precipitation, our intelligence generally false, our leaders gone over to the enemy, and their men would have followed them if they could.[24]

More mundanely, the French in addition noted insufficient care for forage.[25] James and his diplomats had sought action from France, including warships in the English Channel and a diversionary attack on the Dutch on the Continent, but without success.

In turn, William refused to halt his march on London in order to allow negotiations to proceed, as the Tory leaders, who were less unfavorable to James than were the Whigs, would have preferred.

Despite initially intending to stay, James fled the capital, throwing the Great Seal of England into the Thames. Fear of the London mob—which was already attacking Catholic houses and (diplomatic) chapels—and of anarchy led the Archbishop of Canterbury and leading peers to take control of the city. Throughout Britain there was a shift in the local distribution of power with many Lords Lieutenant abandoning James,[26] while many of those who had backed him were purged, especially if Catholics. Some fled abroad, such as William, 1st Marquess of Powis. In Warwickshire, a Protestant mob sacked Coughton Court, the seat of the Catholic Throckmortons. Those forced into exile under Charles or James, such as Sir John Hotham, returned and gained posts, in his case as Governor of Hull, a fortified port of key strategic consequence.

Captured and returned to London, where his presence obstructed the creation of a new political and constitutional order, James was finally driven abroad by Dutch pressure. The report in the *London Courant* of William's arrival at St. James's Palace linked demonstrations of support with the ideology of the new order. The Prince arrived:

24 Barillon to Sir John Lowther of Lowther, 1 Dec. 1688, Beinecke, Osborn Files, Lowther.

25 Barillon to Croissy, 1 Dec. 1688, AE. CP. Ang. 167 f. 136.

26 V.L. Stater, *Noble Government. The Stuart Lord Lieutenancy and the Transformation of English Politics* (Athens, Ga, 1994).

> attended by a great number of persons of quality in coaches and on horseback, while multitudes of people of different ranks crowded the highways, echoing their joy from all hands in the loudest acclamations of welcome, which was more entirely testified by the cheerfulness and serenity that sat in all peoples countenances, to whom either true religion or liberty are of any value, all such ascribing their deliverance from popery and slavery to the courage and conduct of his Illustrious Highness, next to the providence and power of the Almighty. Nor were the exterior testimonies of ringing of bells, bonfires at night etc. wanting to testify a general satisfaction at the coming of His Highness.

Public spaces were very differently and more lastingly altered when statues of James were pulled down in Newcastle and Gloucester, while the staff of authority on his statue in Whitehall was broken. At the same time, the scepter was broken out of the hand of Mary Tudor in the Royal Exchange, a very public demonstration of change.[27]

A vacuum of power had been created within the context of a Dutch occupation that drew on considerable British support. Most people did not want any breach in the hereditary succession, and William had initially claimed that he had no designs on the Crown. Indeed, in early October 1688, the Austrian envoy had suggested that such a move would cause a lengthy civil war. However, as the situation developed favorably for him, especially when James had been driven into exile, William made it clear that he sought the throne after all. This was achieved in 1689 by declaring it vacant (which was a travesty as James had been driven out) and inviting William and Mary to occupy it as joint monarchs, which was a novelty. All Catholics were debarred from the succession, which settled the position of James's baby son.

Defoe was not only a partisan political commentator of events at the time, but also shows, in his memorialization of the country's history, a willingness to make partisan points and an ability to do so that reflected his reading of politics and his skill in references that hit home. This is evident

27 N. Smith, *The Royal Image and the English People* (Aldershot, 2001).

in terms of a political nationalism as well as the cultural vision he otherwise offered. Thus, Defoe refers in the *Tour* to seeing the Norfolk seat of Edward, Earl of Orford, a member of the Whig "Junto" of ministers who had defeated the French fleet in 1692 at Barfleur:

> a victory equal in glory to, and infinitely more glorious to the English nation in particular than that at Blenheim, and above all more to the particular advantage of the Confederacy [Alliance] because it so broke the heart of the naval power of France, that they have not fully recovered it to this day.[28]

That Defoe was accurate did not make his point less politically acute, although he does not note the shorter-term aspect—namely, that Jacobite hopes had also been blasted in 1692. What this would then mean for Defoe was as yet unclear, but his prospects had been transformed by James's removal.

28 *Tour*, 1.

9. A New Political World, 1689-1731

In a speech of 1710 supporting the impeachment of the Tory High-Churchman Henry Sacheverell, Robert Walpole, an important Whig leader in the Commons, declares

> The doctrine of unlimited, unconditional passive obedience [to a monarch] was first invented to support arbitrary and despotic power .... What then can be the designs of preaching this doctrine now, unasked, unsought for, in Her Majesty's reign, where the law is the only rule and measure of the power of the Crown, and of the obedience of the people.[1]

Moreover, Benjamin Hoadly, a Whig cleric, argued that year that "without the authority of the Parliament, no law is of force."[2]

The Revolution Settlement was to be seen subsequently, not least by Walpole and Hoadly, as a decisive break with autocratic practices. The creation of the modern political system, first parliamentary government and then democratization, has for long seemed to be the major theme in British history. Due to the Whig myth of history, and the concept of political Darwinism (that the most appropriate wins out), this process was automatically associated with progress. The years beginning with 1688 could be readily understood within such a schema. It was the period of the establishment of parliamentary government thanks to the "Glorious Revolution."

Ministers and diplomats (many of whom were in Parliament) were so conscious of parliamentary and popular scrutiny that they felt it necessary

1 BL. Add. 9131 fol. 8; J. Israel (ed.), *The Anglo-Dutch Moment: Essays on the Glorious Revolution and its World Impact* (Cambridge, 1991).

2 B. Hoadly, *The Original and Institution of Civil Government* (London, 1710), edited by William Gibson (London, 2009), p. 106.

"to prevent all appearances of grounds for complaint at home though never so unreasonable."[3]

All turning points invite qualification and the search for continuities. Nevertheless, eighteenth-century Britain really began in 1688. The "Glorious Revolution" of that year led to constitutional change, set a new political agenda, and transformed the relationship between the parts of the British Isles. It was to be the central point of reference in subsequent discussion of the political system, and played a crucial role in the public ideology of the state for over a century, such that most commentators were or became Whiggish around the time of the Glorious Revolution.

The events of 1688–9 have to be understood not only in terms of their future significance, but also as a consequence of the divisions, tensions, and fears of seventeenth-century British politics, especially those of the 1670s and 1680s.[4] As mentioned earlier, the political culture of the period assumed deference in return for good kingship, expectations of political behavior that involved a measure of contractualism. James rejected these boundaries, but there was no clear and prudent political course for those who were disenchanted, and with Parliament prorogued there was no institutional expression of national discontent that could instigate a change in policy and recreate the consensus between crown and social elite that was the hallmark of early-modern government.[5] This helped explain the scale of the change from 1688 onward.

Scotland from Revolution to Union

In Scotland, James's position collapsed in December 1688. The Convention of the Estates that met in Edinburgh the following March was dominated by supporters of William, and on 4 April 1689 the Crown of Scotland was declared forfeit—William and Mary being proclaimed joint sovereigns a week later. Catholics were excluded from the Scottish throne and from public office. The contractual nature of the Revolution Settlement, the extent

3 William, Lord Cadogan to James, 2nd Earl of Stair, 4 Dec. 1716, NAS. GD. 135/141/6.
4 T. Harris, *Politics under the Later Stuarts 1660–1715* (Harlow, 1993).
5 J. Miller, *James II* (2nd ed., New Haven, 2000).

to which the Crown had been obtained by William and Mary on conditions, was far more apparent in Scotland than in England. The offer of the Scottish crown to William and Mary was made contingent upon their acceptance of the Claim of Right issued by the Scottish Convention, which stated that James VII had forfeited the crown by his policies and that no Catholic could become ruler of Scotland or hold public office. The degree of radicalism in the Scottish constitutional settlement reflected different political circumstances to those in England. These included the far greater impact of William III's wishes in England.

James II and VII was determined to regain his thrones, and the "Glorious Revolution" launched Jacobitism—as the cause of the exiled Stuarts came to be known from the Latin for James—*Jacobus*. Initially, James controlled most of Ireland and had armed support in Scotland. This situation harkened back to the last period of Stuart dispossession, the British Civil Wars, and Interregnum (1639–60). This had all ended with the "Restoration" of Stuart monarchy in the shape of Charles II, which gave hope to the Jacobites.

James's standard was raised in Scotland in April 1689 by John Graham of Claverhouse, who was backed by the Episcopalians, the supporters of a Scottish Church controlled by bishops, just as it was in England. On 27 July, at the battle of Killiecrankie, which was mentioned by Defoe in his *Tour*, Claverhouse's Highlanders[6] defeated their opponents but their leader was killed and the cause did not thrive under his mediocre successors. Nevertheless, despite defeats at Dunkeld and Cromdale, the Jacobites carried on the struggle and it took two years and a negotiated settlement before peace of a sort could be achieved. Most of the Highland chiefs swore allegiance to William in late 1691.

England might have dominated the British Isles onward from 1691, but a sense of separate identity and national privileges continued to be important in Ireland and Scotland, though not in Wales. This sense of separation was accentuated at the ecclesiastical level, as in 1689 the Scottish Parliament abolished Episcopacy and in 1690 a Presbyterian Church was established there. As a result, the Union of 1707 between England (and Wales) and Scotland led to the creation of a multi-confessional state. Scotland also had a distinctive legal system.

6 The army included an Irish battalion.

Welsh, Irish, and Scots sought to benefit from links with England, Scots coming to play a major role in the expansion of empire, and not least through service in war. This process had begun in the seventeenth century, especially under William III. On the eve of the parliamentary union, Scots held ten percent of the regimental colonelcies in the British army, and between 1714 and 1763 this increased to twenty percent.

Protestantism, war with France, and the benefits of empire—it has been argued[7]—helped to create a British nationhood, which developed alongside the still strong senses of English, Scottish, and Irish identity. It is, however, difficult to determine the extent of the sense of British nationhood as it is not easy to demonstrate the everyday attitudes of the majority of the population. Although "Britain" pre-dated 1707, not least as a result of the personal Union of the English and Scottish Crowns in 1603, British nationhood was imposed by legislation and it is unclear what it meant, and how important it was, for many.

Jacobitism, and the strategic threat to England posed by an autonomous or independent Scotland and Ireland, pushed together those politicians in the three kingdoms who were in favor of the Revolution Settlement. Indeed the Union of 1707 between England and Scotland arose essentially from English concern about the possible hazards posed by an autonomous, if not independent, Scotland when Anne eventually died. There was some support for Union in Scotland, though its passage through the Scottish Parliament in 1706 ultimately depended on successful political management, corruption, self-interest, and the determination not to be shut out from the English and colonial market.

Defoe was employed to further the Union, although the complexities of politics were such that his support for it led him in part to take a different stance in Scottish politics and confessional alignments to those that he adopted for England. Defoe both reported to ministers in London on the situation of Scotland and acted in favour of the Union, not least by producing pamphlets as part of a broader attempt to influence opinion. The situation in Scotland was understandably febrile and characterized by an active level of debate, much in print.[8] This entailed attempts to define

7 L. Colley, *Britons. Forging the Nation 1707–1837* (New Haven, 1992).

8 J. Robertson (ed.), *A Union for Empire: Political Thought and the Union of 1707* (Cambridge, 1995); K. Bowie, *Scottish Public Opinion and the Anglo-Scottish Union, 1699–1707* (Woodbridge, 2007).

public opinion in ways that supported the arguments. These captured broader arguments across Britain concerning the nature of public politics after the "Glorious Revolution" and were an important aspect of defining the Revolution Settlement, as with the pro-Union pamphlet, *A Seasonable Warning* (1706), which has been attributed to Defoe[9]:

> … the multitude of petitions or noise of people are not sufficient to make the Parliament delay their proceedings unless they be found to come from men of more interest in the nation, and of more capacity to judge what is to be done, or can give better reasons against a Union, than has been debated in Parliament, and fully answered to the satisfaction of the greatest and wisest part thereof. I think no good nor wise man will much value or regard the noise and clamour of a mob which is ordinarily made up of a company of rude, ignorant and desperate fellows, mad women and boys, with huzzas in the streets, till they plunder the houses of honest people, and scruple not sometimes to commit the horridest murders.[10]

The Scottish economy was in a poor state, and this had been emphasized by the failure of the Darien Scheme to establish a Scottish commercial entrepot near Panama. Conversely, the strengthening pull of the London market had a growing effect on the Scottish economy, while in wartime the English navy helped provide useful protection for Scottish trade in the face of French privateers.[11] The civil war of 1689–91 had underlined the divisions in Scottish society and indicated the difficulty of independence from England. The powerful leadership of the Presbyterian Church accepted the union as a political necessity. There was no good Protestant alternative—

9 For a criticism of this attribution, P.N. Furbank and W.R. Owens, *Defoe De-Attributions: A Critique of J.R. Moore's Checklist* (London, 1994), p. 26.

10 [Defoe], *A Seasonable Warning or the Pope and King of France Unmasked* (Edinburgh, 1706), p. 13. For a psychoanalytic reading of Defoe's political rhetoric in this period, L.J.D. Kennedy, "Defoe's political rhetoric, 1697–1707" (PhD, King's College London, 1997).

11 James, 1st Duke of Montrose to 3rd Earl of Loudoun, 19 June 1706, HL. Lo. 11667.

the refusal of the exiled Stuarts to convert to Protestantism lessened Scottish options.[12] Yet, Scottish doubts were also slighted. This attitude can be seen in the letters sent by Defoe's patron Harley, for example to George Stepney, envoy in Vienna:

> The Parliament of Scotland go on with the articles of Union, though the Opposition makes them drive heavily, but the ferment of the mob and the kirk, their two governors, seems to abate and some of them return to their senses, and if the ministers and Parliament there stand firm, their opposers will dwindle to nothing or be very inconsiderable.[13]

This was to be an incorporating, not a confederal, union. In 1708, the new Parliament of Great Britain abolished the Scottish Privy Council—the principal executive agency for Scotland—and thus ensured that there would be one British Privy Council sitting in London. The governmental implications for England were less important because it was the more populous and wealthier of the two states and dominated the new British political system. However, a Union was crucial to the political geography of Britain over the following century. An independent or autonomous Scotland would have provided the French with opportunities for intervention. The prospect of Franco-Scottish alliance had been a threat for centuries and its removal was crucial to the geopolitics of the British state. Furthermore, Scotland now contributed powerfully to the resources of this state. Without Scottish troops, the British army would have been much less successful. Thus, the Union had a compound effect on the growth of British power.

In the *Tour*, Defoe reflects at length on the Union, offering his capacity to engage with a variety of perspectives. At the local level, as Defoe notes in the introduction to the third volume of the *Tour*, Union meant that the "marches or borders" were now peaceful and developing, as, more specifically, with agricultural enclosure. However, as he correctly pointed out, as

12 C.A. Whatley, *"Bought and Sold for English Gold": Explaining the Union of 1707* (Edinburgh, 1994); J. Robertson (ed.), *A Union for Empire: Political Thought and the British Union of 1707* (Cambridge, 1995).

13 Harley to Stepney, 29 Nov. 1706, BL. Add. 7059 f. 116.

a whole it took a while for the Scottish economy to derive the possible benefit from the Union.[14]

War for Ireland

The decisive battles in 1689–91 were fought in Ireland, the Williamite conquest of which demonstrated the ability of a powerful and well-led military force to overcome a largely hostile population. Ireland was more accessible than Scotland to the major French naval base of Brest. James's supporters controlled most of Ireland in 1689, although Derry—fearing Catholic massacre— resisted a siege and was relieved by the English fleet that July. The following month, William III's forces, mostly Danes and Dutch, landed and occupied Belfast and Carrickfergus. Naval power thus offered William military flexibility and prevented James from controlling the entirety of Ireland.

Arriving in Ireland in June 1690, William marched on Dublin to find the outnumbered Jacobite and French army (21,000 men to 35–40,000) drawn up on the south bank of the River Boyne. Louis XIV's failure to attach the importance to Ireland that William did was crucial in terms of the resources available to the combatants. Having beaten the Jacobites at the Boyne on 1 July—and after which James fled Ireland—William easily took Dublin, though he failed to capture Limerick the following month. John Churchill, then Earl of Marlborough, captured Cork (September) and Kinsale (October). On 12 July 1691, Major-General Hugh Mackay (who had been defeated at Killiecrankie in 1689) turned the Jacobite flank at the last major battle in Aughrim by leading his cavalry across a bog on which he had laid hurdles—and here the Jacobite force broke, their infantry suffering heavy casualties in the rout. Galway fell and the Jacobite position collapsed with the capitulation of Limerick on 3 October. The war had done much damage. For example, the east town of Athlone was burnt in 1690, while the besieged west town was badly damaged in 1691 after receiving 12,000 cannon shots and 600 mortar bombs from William's artillery.

Ireland was then subjected to an Anglican ascendancy. The Catholics

14 C. Whatley, *Scottish Society 1707–1830. Beyond Jacobitism, towards industrialisation* (Manchester, 2000).

held twenty-two percent of the land in 1688 but only fourteen percent of the land in 1703, and five percent in 1778. Catholics were prevented from freely acquiring or bequeathing land or property and were disfranchised and debarred from all political, military, and legal offices, and likewise from Parliament. The culture of power in Ireland became thoroughly and often aggressively Protestant.

The "Glorious Revolution" led to English domination of the British Isles, albeit domination that was helped by and shared with important sections of the Irish and Scottish population, Irish Anglicans, and more significantly with Scottish Presbyterians. The alternative had been glimpsed in 1689 when James II's Parliament in Dublin had rejected much of the authority of the Westminster Parliament. This path, however, had been blocked by defeat, although in uncertainty and at times crisis a febrile atmosphere were readily glimpsed there. In June 1714, and as a clear challenge to the view that this was an age of stability, shortly before the death of Queen Anne, Alan Brodrick, the Speaker of the Irish House of Commons, writes from Dublin to his elder brother Thomas, a Whig MP in London:

> The resentments, apprehensions, and fears which may be observed among people are not to be expressed: I do not take on me to say how well grounded they are, but am convinced the hopes of the Papists and apprehensions of most of the Protestants with whom I converse were never greater in my memory. Hardly a night passes in which there is not something done either to alarm or disquiet the minds of men; I wrote formerly that at one end of the town in one night there were great numbers of Protestants' doors marked with letter H: which some fancy was intended as if they deserved hanging, others that the dwellers were for the house of Hanover. Last night Sir John King's and Mr Gore's houses in Capel Street had these words wrote on their doors, King James the third in spite of the Whigs. Others had a gallows painted on them with these words A fart for all Whigs; and indeed the haughty air the Papists give themselves, and their more than ordinary numbers in town give considering people very anxious thoughts.

Alan Brodrick adds a reference to the hostility of at least some Church of England supporters to Dissenters as well as Catholics, a situation that put the former in a difficult position and that created the context in which Defoe had to operate:

> Lord A—this day said in Lucas coffee house that there was no difference between Papists and Presbyterians,' that being jumbled and mixed together they would make an excellent salad for the Devil.[15]

There was some support in Ireland for Union with England. Union had been considered by English ministers in 1697 and the Irish Parliament petitioned for it in 1703. Union, however, had little to offer to English politicians, and, although Irish resources and personnel were important to British imperialism,[16] Ireland was treated with scant consideration. Indeed, Defoe does not devote the work or attention he was to show to the Scottish equivalent. The Westminster Parliament's Declaratory Act of 1720 states its supremacy over that of Dublin. Protectionist legislation in Westminster hindered Irish exports, while the granting of Irish lands and pensions to favored courtiers accentuated the problem of absentee landowners and revenue-holders, with a consequent loss of money to the country.

In Ireland, a sense of exploitation was exacerbated by particular steps. For example, in 1722, a Wolverhampton ironmaster, William Wood, purchased a patent to mint copper coins for Ireland, a move that led to bitter complaints; constitutional and political weakness were seen as leading to economic problems. As a result of the agitation, Walpole's government was obliged to cancel the patent in 1725—Walpole having been lacerated by Jonathan Swift in his *Drapier's Letters*.

Thereafter, greater care was taken of Irish sensitivities, but the relationship with England was still far from equal. The Irish Parliament was compelled to pay the cost of quartering a large part of the army in Ireland to support the Anglo-Irish establishment and hide the size of the army from

15 Alan to Thomas Brodrick, 24 June 1714, Guildford, Surrey Record Office, Brodrick Mss 1248/3, f. 187.

16 D. Akenson, *If the Irish Ran the World: Montserrat, 1630–1730* (Liverpool, 1997).

English public opinion. Long-standing politico-religious grievances were to help exacerbate Irish disaffection in the 1790s.

Ireland retained its Parliament until the Act of Union of 1800, and in the face of criticism of the Dublin and London administration[17] the need to manage this Parliament obliged London politicians to devise strategies that included winning over Irish "undertakers," the key politicians in the Dublin Parliament. Issues as much as patronage were at stake. The preservation of this Parliament enabled Ireland's Protestant politicians to retain a measure of importance and independence.[18] However, when in 1755, William, Marquess of Hartington and the Lord Lieutenant of Ireland, writes, "This country is divided into two parties both party near equal, each struggling for the superiority,"[19] he is referring to factionalism within the political élite, rather than to any really widespread political alignments.

Although possibly over 80, or even 90, percent of its population used Welsh as the medium of communication, Wales lacked centralizing institutions, or distinctive social, ecclesiastical, and legal arrangements. In part because resistance to the "Glorious Revolution" was perfunctory (unlike in Ireland or Scotland), there was no attempt to transform Welsh politics and society. The Catholic William, 1st Marquess of Powis, fled into exile with James, and his estates were granted to Dutch followers of William who were made Duke of Portland and Earl of Rochford, but the estates were restored to the 2nd Marquess in 1722. The suppression of the Council of Wales and the Marches in 1689 was scarcely comparable to developments in Scotland and Ireland, and did not lead to any sense of loss. This was important to the stability of Wales over the following century, a stability that was only to be disrupted subsequently by the pressures of industrialization and social change.

The Politics of William III

In William's reign, a Tory-Whig polarity was confused by a Country-Court opposition. However, in the late 1690s the Country Whigs were largely

17 Archbishop Boulter to Newcastle, 19 Mar. 1730, NA. SP. 63/392 f. 76.

18 R.E. Burns, *Irish Parliamentary Politics in the Eighteenth Century. II 1730–1760* (Washington, 1990).

19 Hartington to Newcastle, 30 July 1755, BL. Add. 32857 fol. 462.

absorbed by the Tories, such that a Whig-Tory division was central to Anne's reign. Nevertheless, the identity, nature, and aspirations of political groupings were far from constant, and the terms used by contemporaries were far from uniform in meaning, let alone consistent.

However, the very existence of a government tended to produce one rough distinction—that between those who supported the ministry of the day, and those who opposed it, irrespective of how divided these two groups might be. Toryism repeatedly found it difficult to cope with the consequences of the Revolution Settlement. Division was the key problem: some Tories were prepared to accept that the legally constituted authority was now that of William III, but others, for whom he was a source of unwelcome transformation and a new Cromwell,[20] sought his overthrow. This tension in Toryism remained strong until the collapse of Jacobitism in 1746, but did not prevent the development of a constitutional Tory parliamentary politics opposed to those of the Whigs.

The 1690s saw increased party organization, in part because of more elections and of parliamentary sessions becoming more frequent, and in part because royal attempts to govern without relying on an individual party were abandoned. William tried to do so, but onward from late 1693 he came to rely increasingly on the Whigs, and by the following summer a largely Whig government was in power. Moreover, by the late 1690s, the leading Whig ministers—the so-called Junto—held frequent meetings in order to maintain party consistency in government. Separate to the constitutional changes, this was a limitation on the king's freedom of manoeuvre.

Yet, the extent to which William was able to impose his views indicated his political importance as the arbitrator both of court factionalism and of the overlapping ministerial struggle for influence.[21] This role was not really compromised by the emergence of political parties because, within themselves, they lacked the structure and ethos necessary to provide clear leadership and streamlined policy. Furthermore, the established position of the monarchy remained significant, and was strengthened by the clarity of

20 C. Rose, *England in the 1690s: Revolution, Religion and War* (Oxford, 1999).
21 A. Marshall, *The age of faction. Court politics, 1660–1702* (Manchester, 1999), pp. 154–83.

Anne's succession in comparison to that of William and Mary. The continued role of the monarch as arbitrator was demonstrated by Anne's central importance in the struggle for primacy within the Tory ministry between Bolingbroke and Harley in 1714.

In hindsight, the "Glorious Revolution" was frequently seen as essentially conservative, especially in comparison with the social disruption of the Civil Wars and because it eventually led, under George I and George II, to a government by the "Old Corps Whigs" who were to be criticized by radical politicians. However, irrespective of the specific intentions of those who took part and co-operated, it really was a revolution, especially to Tories and High Churchmen. Parallels between Cromwell and William III were made. Furthermore, the breach in the succession, and also the strains of the Nine Years' War (1688–97) with Louis XIV, "that Monster of Monsters,"[22] provided occasion and cause for bitter debate about the role of Providence.[23] The "Glorious Revolution" indeed led to a crisis over the nature of authority in Church and State, a crisis made urgent by the need to define as well as sell and contest the new order.[24]

William lacked the freedom earlier given James by peace. The war with France did not become the war of religion Louis XIV had called for when appealing to Catholic support,[25] and William was part of a major European league. Nevertheless, the war proved very difficult. Between 1691 and 1697, the army and the navy each cost an annual average of £2.5 million. Taxation rose greatly in the 1690s as a result of the need to support war. The Land Tax, introduced in 1692, was followed by tax on salt (1694), seaborne coal (1695), and malt and leather (1697). The regressive character of such excises is captured by the *Manufacturer* of 25 April 1720, when it complains that "for the poor ... not a pound of candles, or a bushel of coals they burn; not a peck of salt they eat, or a pot of beer they drink" was untaxed. War,

22 Anon., *A Most Pleasant, but True Description of the Old and New Jacobites* (London, 1691), p. 8.
23 C. Rose, *England in the 1690s. Revolution, Religion and War* (Oxford, 1999).
24 T. Claydon, *William III and the Godly Revolution* (Cambridge, 1996).
25 Louis to Rebenac, French envoy in Spain, 3 Nov. 1688, AE. CP. Espagne 75, f. 158–9.

and notably French privateering,[26] also hit trade, making it more difficult to finance huge external remittances. This led to expedients, such as the clipping of the coinage, and to serious financial crises,[27] particularly in 1694 and 1696. Contributing to the sense of crisis, William was a poor communicator and an indifferent manager of domestic politics, and his conduct in the war resulted in serious criticism, which escalated in response to his post-war diplomacy.

The costs of the war forced a parliamentary monarchy on William. Whereas Parliament had not met for most of the period 1682–8, elections became more frequent. By limiting the royal power to dissolve, suspend or prolong Parliament, the Triennial Act of 1694 ensured regular meetings of the Westminster Parliament and, by limiting their life-span to a maximum of three years, required regular elections. There were ten elections between 1695 and 1715, and this rate helped to encourage a sense of volatility.[28]

The war also led to a reorganization of public finances that introduced significant principles of openness and parliamentary responsibility. The funded national debt, based on the Bank of England (founded in 1694) was guaranteed by Parliament. Michael Godfrey suggested in 1694 that the Bank would lay a "foundation of trade, security, and greatness."[29] With its central role in public finances, the Bank provided a key junction between government and capital, and one in which London acted as the focus for—and anchor of—national financial activity, although that was not a solution without problems.[30] Defoe reflected this, not only in his political commen-

26 Robert Yate, Master of the Society of Merchants to Sir Richard Hart and Sir John Knight, Bristol's MPs, 23 Nov. 1692, enclosing list of ships taken belonging to the port of Bristol from December 1691 to September 1692, Wardens of Society of Merchant Adventurers to Lords of the Admiralty, 18 Oct. 1693, Bristol Library, Southwell papers, vol. 3.

27 D.W. Jones, *War and Economy in the Age of William III and Marlborough* (Oxford, 1988).

28 W.A. Speck, *Tory and Whig: the Struggle in the Constituencies 1701–15* (1970); G. Holmes, *British Politics in the Age of Anne* (2nd ed., 1987).

29 M. Godfrey, *A Brief Account of the Intended Bank of England* (London, 1694), p. 18.

30 Robert Henley to William Blathwayt, no date, Bristol, Southwell papers, vol. 3.

tary, but also when Roxana is urged by a Dutch merchant in Paris to lodge her wealth in the Bank of England "in the most secure manner in the world."

The Revolution Settlement not only suited powerful London interests but also helped ensure the definition and potency of the self-image of the city as a modern commercial center. However, moral and paternalistic attitudes toward wealth clashed with the reality of new money. Indeed, in 1696, as an alternative to the Bank of England, there was a politically pointed (and unsuccessful) attempt to found a Land Bank using landed wealth as a credit source.

In a political situation in which conventions of behavior were slowly adapting to the consequences of annual parliamentary sessions—and thus to an enhanced role for parliamentary leadership and management—William, however, continued not only to follow his own views, but also to underrate the importance of political management. The consequent political crisis was encapsulated in the title of the Act of Settlement of 1701, "an Act for further limitation of the Crown and for better securing the rights and liberties of the subject." William's lack of interest in Parliament's views had led to bitter political divisions that weakened his international position. "Here are horrible cabals on all sides," observes Edward, 1st Earl of Jersey, in November 1697.[31]

This was especially true regarding the size of the army, an issue that had been politically charged for decades. Critics were concerned not so much about foreign policy as about the possible consequences of a large army for domestic politics. On 2 December 1697, at the opening of the session, William told Parliament that the maintenance of a standing force was essential. Nine days later, in open defiance, the Commons decided to disband all land forces that had been raised since 1680. As a result, the English establishment was cut to 10,000 men. A year later, the Commons decided to reduce the English establishment to 7,000 and its Irish counterpart to 12,000, and to restrict them to native troops, thus ensuring that Dutch regiments would have to return to the United Provinces and dealing a blow to William that he tried without success to reverse. In contrast, the Dutch

31 Jersey to Richard Hill, 26 Nov. 1697, London, Greater London Record Office, Acc. 510/71.

army was kept at 45,500. There was little doubt where William's views were more influential. This was of consequence for Dissenters given they looked more to the United Netherlands than other groups in England.

In 1698, the French envoy, Camillle, Count of Tallard, presented a volatile situation: a two-party system, the Whigs opposed to royal authority and the Tories unhappy about the Glorious Revolution, a monarch facing much parliamentary opposition and who found it difficult to assemble ministers upon whom he could rely, "un movement perpetuel" in the political sphere, and a kingdom short of money.[32] Furthermore, in another sign of parliamentary assertiveness, in 1701 the leading Whig ministers were attacked for their alleged responsibility in signing the Partition Treaties with France, crucial measures taken to further William's international policy. The previous year, as a sign of the extent to which publicity was seen as a political lever—via the press and Parliament—Charles, 1st Duke of Manchester in his diplomatic report from Paris about Jacobite intrigues notes:

> The same persons say there is going to the press a book wherein they asperse all the ministry; and others who they think had any hand in the late treaty concerning the succession of Spain. There are to be 3000 copies, and not dispersed till a little before the meeting of the Parliament in England that there may not be time to answer it.[33]

Needs must is a theme Defoe very much advanced: these attacks produced a greater degree of accommodation toward Parliament on the part of the Crown, as relations with France deteriorated in 1701–2,[34] although ministers could still express anger about "the parties" striving "to outdo one another."[35] On 18 March 1701, William sent Parliament a report on the

32 Tallard to Louis XIV, 17 Sept. 1698, AE. CP. Ang. 177 fols 76–7.
33 Manchester to Blathwayt, 26 July 1700, Beinecke, Manchester Box.
34 Vernon, Secretary of State, to Alexander Stanhope, envoy in The Hague, 9 Jan. 1701, Maidstone, Kent Archive Office, U1590 053/10; Tallard to Louis XIV, 2 Ap. 1701, AE. CP. Ang. 191 f. 125.
35 Blathwayt to George Stepney, 11 Mar. 1701, Beinecke, Blathwayt Box 21.

negotiations at The Hague, giving as his reason his "gracious intention to acquaint you, from time to time, with the state and progress of those negotiations." He knew he needed parliamentary support, not least for the expansion of the army. In 1702, in contrast to the declaration of war with the Dutch in 1672, the declaration of war on France was again made by royal authority, but also in clear response to the addresses and resolutions of both Houses of Parliament, a pattern in some respects matching that of the constitutional settlement of the Crown in 1689.

There had been, and continued to be, commitment to a process of consultation and review whereby the monarch retained the initiative over foreign and military policy. In a situation that posed problems for writers such as Defoe, Parliament could debate and fund proposals and investigate outcomes, but it did not make policy. The somewhat uncertain use of royal authority under William gave way to a more managed approach under Anne and George I. The role of the monarch also became more defined. For example, whereas in 1689 the independence of the judiciary was in practice established, under the Act of Settlement judges were now removable only after Parliament had played a role. Meanwhile, the politics of both nation and localities both adapted to circumstances and sought to change them. Politics in localities, including London, saw Whig-Tory divides that were linked to socio-economic differences, religious tensions, and national politics.[36]

Divisions could lead to violence. In Norfolk in 1698, Sir Henry Hobart of Blickling Hall, a firm Whig, was killed in a duel with his Tory neighbor, Oliver Le Neve, which arose from election-time allegations. Hobart had alleged that Le Neve had accused him of discreditable conduct at the battle of the Boyne in 1690, and that this had affected the 1698 election. Le Neve fled the country.

More seriously, Jacobite conspiracies continued, and some were serious—notably the attempt to assassinate William III, especially in 1696—and the government showed vigilance in order to keep an eye on Jacobite messages and plots, arresting in 1693 at Harwich a woman with a box in the false bottom of which were near 100 letters. There were also measures

36 Gary de Krey, *A Fractured Society: The Politics of London in the First Age of Party, 1688–1715* (Oxford, 1985).

against Jacobite printing presses.[37] These measures were part of the intimidation, pressure, and violence affecting the press as a whole, a situation that in turn was to affect Defoe.

Politics under Anne

Anne (1702–14) has been re-evaluated as an able and independent monarch, less dependent on her courtiers than had been hitherto believed.[38] Intelligent in politics, Anne was able to learn from her mistakes, not least in maintaining her autonomy in the face of ministers and favorites, and in particular refusing to permit the politicians to control court patronage. As she had no significant domestic program of change, despite her deep-felt piety, she was a relatively uncontroversial figure, and indeed political criticism in her reign was centered on ministers, not monarch. Anne followed William in sustaining the Grand Alliance created to fight Louis. Amidst an atmosphere of distrust caused by Louis XIV's acceptance in 1700 of the will of the last Habsburg king of Spain, which left his dominions to Louis' second grandson, Philip V, attempts to settle Anglo-French differences broke down. Moreover, in 1701 Louis's recognition of James II and VII's son as ruler of Britain played a significant role in the deterioration of relations.

In the War of the Spanish Succession, in which Britain was involved between May 1702 and 1713, troops under John Churchill—who was onward from 1704 1st Duke of Marlborough, and in 1702 described as "Grand Vizier"[39]—drove the French from Germany and the Low Countries. Other forces, however, were eventually defeated in Spain. Marlborough won major victories at Blenheim (1704), Ramillies (1706), and Oudenaarde (1708) but was less successful at Malplaquet (1709). Under Marlborough, the British army reached a peak of success that it was not to repeat in Europe for another century, although this was not a topic that interested Defoe. Marlborough was also skillful in holding the anti-French coalition together.

37 John Ellis to Stepney, 10 Mar. 1702, BL. Add. 7074 f. 99.

38 A. Gregg, *Queen Anne* (1980).7

39 James Vernon to Blathwayt, 2, 6 June 1693, Beinecke, Blathwayt Box, 19.

This posed problems but so did domestic politics. Anne's accession had led to the rise of "the Church party,"[40] However, this group lost royal support in part as a result of the managerial difficulties they posed, not least their consistent and vocal attacks on Dissent, as well as their hostile attitude toward Marlborough. He and his close ally Sidney Godolphin, the Lord Treasurer, were instead moderate Tories who became disenchanted with much of the Tory party and allied with the Whigs to dominate politics; although, in turn, Marlborough and Godolphin found it increasingly difficult to restrain Whig efforts to increase their power.

The public followed the news with great attention. The *Observator* of 10 June 1702 comments on the public's interest in the war:

> 'Tis an easy matter to pull down pallisades, to attack half-moons, bastions, and counterscarps, in the coffee-houses of London and Westminster, and to bomb citadels and castles with quart bottles of wine in a tavern, where there is seen no smoke but that of tobacco, nor no shot felt but when the reckoning comes to be paid.

Because it challenged constitutional and social convention, such commentary was politically and socially subversive, or at least potentially so. In Delarivier Manley's novel, *Secret History of Queen Zarah and the Zarazians* (1705):

> apprentice boys assume the air of statesmen before they have learned the mystery of trade. Mechanics of the meanest rank plead for a liberty to abuse their betters, and turn out ministers of state with the same freedom that they smoke tobacco. Carmen and cobblers over coffee draw up articles of peace and war and make partition treaties.

Like William at the end of the Nine Years' War, Anne realized that a compromise peace would have to be negotiated. A sense of being led astray

40 Stephen Evans to Thomas Pitt, 1 Aug. 1702, Captain Harrison to Pitt, 14 Feb. 1703, BL. Add. 22852 f. 10, 75.

to allies in a "tedious war"[41] became increasingly common, not least in government circles.[42] Anne's awareness in 1709–10 that the war was unpopular, and that the vital war goals had already been obtained, played a major role in weakening the ministry that wanted to fight on. In addition, at court the Marlborough interest was under pressure, not least because Anne had long wearied of her megalomaniac would-be favorite—namely, his wife Sarah, Duchess of Marlborough. Now, without the support of the Crown, the Whigs fared badly in the 1710 election.

Conversely, Anne supported their Tory successors—Robert Harley, Defoe's patron and soon to be Earl of Oxford, and Henry St John the soon to be Viscount Bolingbroke—in their contentious tasks of negotiating peace with France, and she was willing to create Tory peers in order to ensure that the peace preliminaries passed through the Lords in the face of Whig opposition. In 1706, Harley reflects:

> It is plain if the Allies will be but true to themselves, France may be reduced to reason, but there is no security against that Crown, but taking away the power to do hurt.[43]

What that might mean, and at what cost, however, were both unclear and affected by the contingencies of war and domestic politics, and the perceptions of them no less. Defoe, who was receiving a quarterly payment of £100 from the secret service funds,[44] advanced the Tory view on the developing international crisis in 1711. He argues, in *The Felonious Treaty* (1711) and the *Review*, that the possibility that the Austrian and Spanish Habsburg inheritances would be combined to present a new threat to the European System as well as to Protestantism, and that Britain should not press forward to achieve this combination. The Peace of Utrecht of 1713 brought French recognition of a failure to dominate Europe and of the Protestant

41 Charles Davenant to son Henry, 15 Mar. 1706, BL. Add. 4291 f. 64.

42 Robert Harley, Secretary of State for the Northern Department, to George Stepney, envoy in Vienna, 4 June 1706, BL. Add. 7059 f. 101, 199.

43 Harley to Stepney, 28 Sept. 1706, BL. Add. 7059 f. 110.

44 J.A. Downie, "Secret Service Payments to Daniel Defoe, 1710–1714," in *Review of English Studies*, 30 (1979): pp. 437–41.

Succession in Britain. Wartime gains—Gibraltar, Minorca, and Nova Scotia—were formally ceded to Britain, and she also gained the right to (controlled) trade with the Spanish New World. The peace was popular, in London "the mob" broke the windows of those who did not illuminate them to express their pleasure.[45] Yet, the establishment of a Bourbon on the Spanish throne was to prove a key element in what was to be a continuing Whig critique of the peace.[46]

In office, the Tories turned on the Whigs and their supporters, legislating against the Dissenters, with the Occasional Conformity Act of 1711 and the Schism Act of 1714. There was also a general attack on the financial administration of the Godolphin ministry in the 1700s. The Tory Commission of Public Accounts was partisan, but their findings were not necessarily untrue. What they said about Marlborough's corruption was accurate. One of the most active younger Whigs, Robert Walpole, a Norfolk gentleman landowner, was accused of receiving bribes whilst making forage contracts for the army in Scotland in 1709–10. In 1712, he was expelled from the Commons and committed to the Tower of London, a sign of the acute partisanship of politics. On the other hand, he was not executed.

Party politics and ministerial instability since 1688 had revealed the grave limitations of the "Glorious Revolution." A parliamentary monarchy could not simply be legislated into existence. It required the development of conventions and patterns of political behavior that would permit a constructive resolution of contrary opinions within a system where there was no single source of dominant power, and also the establishment of a measure of cohesion among those "of the same side."[47] The slowness of the development of these patterns was particularly serious as Britain was at war for much of the period and Jacobitism was a significant force. The Revolution Settlement had created the constitutional basis for an effective parliamentary monarchy, with parliamentary control over the finances of the state—the aim of many of the critics of Charles II—but the instability of

45 Warre to Birch, 8 May 1713, BL. Add. 46546 f. 62.

46 Anon., *The Woeful Treaty: or the Unhappy Peace. An Ode* (3rd ed., London, 1716).

47 James Craggs, Whig MP, to Thomas, Duke of Newcastle, 15 July 1714, BL. Add. 32686 f. 16.

the ministries of the period suggests that the political environment within which such a monarchy could be effective had not yet been secured.

Defoe was criticized at the time for adopting different political stances in pursuit of his own profit, as when *Judas Discovered* (1713) refers to Defoe as "a thorough-paced, true-bred hypocrite, an High-Churchman one day, and a rank Whig the next." Subsequent scholarship has further probed his many inconsistencies, both real and apparent, although Defoe's clear opposition to the Schism Act includes his suggestions of means whereby Dissenters might evade it.[48]

Rather than emphasizing inconsistency, it is more appropriate to see Defoe as motivated by goals that were difficult to advance in the face of the many political changes of the period, and therefore evasive of simple definition, like so many politicians and churchmen of the day. Given his need to make money, these changes were particularly problematic for him, but the money was not his singular goal. It was not so much Defoe who was the source of inconsistency, rather the environment in which he had to adapt. The difficulties this created appear to have helped Defoe to turn to the opportunities—personal and political—offered through writing fiction.[49] To a degree, there was a parallel to Dryden's more pronounced adaptation to his political redundancy after the "Glorious Revolution."[50]

The Succession of 1714

By the reign of George III (1760–1820), great-grandson of George I, there was no question about who should be king; only speculation about his powers. The situation had been very different earlier in the eighteenth century. The principal political threats to the Protestant succession and the Whig system were seen as coming from Jacobitism until mid-century, and from France. James II and VII was succeeded in 1701 as the claimant to the throne by the "warming-pan baby" of 1688, now "James III and VIII."

48 [Defoe], *The Schism Act Explained* (London, 1614) and *The Family Instructor* (London, 1715); r. Stevens, *Protestant Pluralism. The Reception of the Toleration Act, 1689–1720* (Woodbridge, 2018), pp. 98–100.

49 G. Sill, *Defoe and the Idea of Fiction* (London, 1984).

50 D. Bywaters, *Dryden in Revolutionary England* (Berkeley, 1991).

Although the latter's attempt to invade Scotland with French support in 1708 was totally unsuccessful[51]—an attempt discussed by Defoe in the *Tour*—his claim was a threat to the Hanoverian succession. Indeed, that attempt stirred alarm: "we were on the brink of being destroyed."[52] Separately, there was concern that Tory ministers might ensure a Jacobite succession.[53]

The childless William III had been succeeded by his sister-in-law, Anne, none of whose many children survived to adulthood. Under the Act of Settlement (1701), she was to be succeeded by the German house of Hanover, descendants of James I's daughter, Elizabeth. The Act of Security passed by the Scottish Parliament, however, directly contradicted the settling of the crown on Hanover and this led to the Union of England and Scotland and the thrust of the Act of Settlement upon Scotland by incorporation.

The unexpectedly peaceful accession of George I in 1714 was a major disappointment for James, for the threat of a Jacobite rebellion or succession had been taken seriously. In the *Review* of 30 September 1712, Defoe refers to "the growth and increase of Jacobitism at home." On 11 November, he followed up bluntly:

> I have stated the case of the succession with what clearness I can; I have told you where your danger lies, and from what cause it proceeds. If what I saw is just, I care not how much my noise offends you, for I write to please none of you, but to waken you.

A week later, Defoe continues: "Nobody would be willinger than I to forward anything that would secure us against the Pretender." In 1713, Defoe produced a satire on Jacobitism, *Reasons Against the Succession of the House of Hanover*, a work that includes a lot of historical information and

51 J. Gibson, *Playing the Scottish Card: The Franco-Jacobite Invasion of 1708* (Edinburgh, 1988).
52 David, 4th Earl of Norhesk to "My dear Lord," 1 Ap. 1708, HL. Lo. 7885.
53 Marlborough to Jean de Robethon, adviser to the future George I, 8, 22 July; Galke to Robethon, 10 July 1713, HL. HM. 44710 f. 62–3, 79–80, 93.

argument, not least on the folly of letting Mary Tudor become Queen in 1553. In it, Defoe also satirizes passive obedience.[54]

In 1714, largely as a result of inadequate Jacobite preparations and a refusal of several possible backers, British and foreign, to provide support, this potential danger was avoided. Defoe and other earlier commentators were of course unaware that this would be the situation. Edmund Gibson, Archdeacon of Surrey and Whig cleric, reflects on 10 August 1714:

> Unless the next post brings us word that the disturbances in Scotland and Ireland are very great, we shall reckon the Pretender's game entirely at an end, the King of France being too wise to hazard a new war, for the sake of an enterprise so unpromising as a descent upon us is like to be, without very great distractions among ourselves.[55]

The French government emphasized in its explanations to Catholic clerics not only James's lack of popularity but also Louis's recent treaty obligations to Britain under the Peace of Utrecht, and the British government was informed of the latter.[56]

Despite reports that George I would try to rule through all parties,[57] partisan politics came to the fore. George indeed told his first Privy Council that he wished for the repeal of the Occasional Conformity and Schism Acts. In 1715, as part of the Whigs fixing control with the new reign, Walpole was appointed chairman of the Committee of Secrecy established to punish those who had plotted to restore "James III and VIII." Walpole drew up the resulting report and was responsible for the impeachment of Bolingbroke and other leading Tories. A Riot Act was passed in 1715 in

54 Defoe, *Reasons*, p. 13.

55 Gibson to Nicolson, Bishop of Carlisle, Bod. Add. A. 269 p. 34.

56 Jean-Baptiste, Marquis de Torcy, French Foreign Minister, to Cardinal Alessandro Albani, 23 Aug., Torcy to Cardinal Filippo Gualtieri, 25 Aug., Louis XIV to Cardinal de la Tremoille, 27 Aug. 1714, AE. CP. Rome 538 f. 219, 228–9, 245; Matthew Prior, envoy in Paris, to George I, 23 Aug., Prior to Thomas, 1st Earl of Strafford, First Lord of the Admiralty, 20 Aug. 1714, NA. SP. 78/159 f. 94, 124.

57 Iberville, French envoy, to Louis XIV, 11 Sept. 1714, AE. CP. Ang. 265 f. 43.

order to deal with Jacobite disturbances, making rioting and riotous assemblies felonies, but the army was handicapped by the lack of clarity over its position under the Act. In response to George's appearance as so heavily committed to the Whigs and, indeed, as having waged a "cruel war on the Tories,"[58] there was a revival not only of Jacobite schemes but also of interest from foreign powers in how best to respond.[59]

George's support for the Whigs, who did well in the 1715 general election, alienated the Tories, whom he regarded as sympathetic to Jacobitism. Sir John Perceval, a Whig politician, observes:

> Put the case in the most favourable manner for the Tories, and allow they are not really in the interest of the Pretender, yet they must own they are not so zealous and determined against him as those his Majesty now employs.[60]

George saw the danger of being a prisoner of a Whig ministry but it was difficult to operate a mixed Whig-Tory ministry. George's replacement of Anne's Tory ministers by a Whig ascendancy left the Tories no option in government service. Tories were excluded from most senior posts in government—namely, the armed forces, the judiciary, and the Church—and their role in county government was lessened. The Tories while very numerous also suffered from being very divided.[61]

The '15

In 1715, the Jacobites planned three risings. "James III and VIII" was to copy William III by landing in the south-west of England, where there was to be the major rebellion, followed by a march on London. There were also

58 Count of Iberville, French envoy to Jerome, Count of Pontchartrain, French Minister of the Marine, Paris, AN. AM. AE. Correspondance Consulaire Londres, B1 760.

59 Count of Monteleon, Spanish envoy, to Pontchartrain, 2 Aug. 1715, Paris, AN. Am. B7 265.

60 Perceval to his brother Philip Perceval, 26 Jan. 1715, BL. Add. 47028 f. 6.

61 Charles d'Iberville, French envoy, to Jean, Marquis de Torcy, French Foreign Minister, 25 Dec. 1714, AE. CP. Ang. 260 fols 261–2, 266.

to be risings in the Highlands and the Border counties, the latter including the north of England. The likely popular response is unclear. Edward Southwell, a senior civil servant and recent MP, who was also a Fellow of the Royal Society and commissioned Vanbrugh to be architect for his new house, reported that Somerset and Gloucestershire were: "like to all Wales, perfectly indolent which gets the better the King or the Rebels, so as to toss cross or pile."[62] The latter was a reference to a popular game (on which gambling could be based) in which coins were tossed in order to see if heads or tails came up.

A prompt government response proved crucial. The rising in the South-West was nipped in the bud in September 1715 as a result of prompt action on the basis of intelligence, and Jacobite indecision. Across the country, Lords Lieutenant were ordered to call up the militia. Vigilance was demanded. Thus, Charles, 2nd Viscount Townshend, one of the two Secretaries of State, writes on 21 September to Charles, 1st Duke of Manchester, the Lord Lieutenant of Huntingdonshire, and a keen Whig:

> As your lordship will receive an Order in Council to enforce more strongly the putting in execution the laws concerning Papists, Non-Jurors and other disaffected persons, I am directed by the King particularly to recommend the due and punctual execution of that order on your part to your Lordship's immediate care and application. His Majesty looks upon the seizing and securing in this critical juncture all such persons as are described in the said Order in Council, to be a matter of the most important consequence to the peace and welfare of this kingdom; and therefore His Majesty will take your Lordship's exact and faithful discharge of these his commands as a great mark of your true zeal and loyalty towards him.[63]

That was the voice of power, a power in fright. On 6 September, John, Earl of Mar, had raised the Stuart standard at Braemar, launching a serious

62 John, Lord Perceval to —, 1 Nov. 1715, BL. Add. 47028 f. 97.

63 Townshend to Manchester, 19, 21 Sept. 1715, Beinecke, Manchester corresp. Vol. 15.

challenge to the newly-established Hanoverian regime. Perth was seized and the royal forces under John, 2nd Duke of Argyll, were heavily outnumbered. Argyll was grandson of the Earl executed in 1685 for rebelling against James II and VII. Indecision on Mar's part—combined with the need to have his raw recruits trained—to wait for the Western clans to arrive, and to await the arrival of the experienced Duke of Berwick to lead the army (who did not come), allowed the loss of valuable campaigning time. Mar might have attacked Argyll sooner, such that Scotland could have been a base for assisting the risings in the Borders and the north of England. Instead, he did not march on Edinburgh until November. On 13 November, Mar fought Argyll at Sheriffmuir, north of Stirling. Unaware of the dispositions of the other, each general drew up his forces so that their right wings overlapped the other's left. The left wings of both armies were defeated, but, let down by Glengarry (the remaining senior chief who did not want to attack), Mar failed to exploit his greatly superior numbers. The indecisive battle, which was reported in Venice as a Jacobite triumph,[64] was in practice a victory for Argyll, as Mar needed a triumph in order to both hold his army together and to help the Jacobites in the borders.

Rising there in October, the Jacobites had decided that Dumfries, Newcastle, and Carlisle were too strong to attack, and had instead resolved to invade Lancashire, an area with many Catholics whom they hoped to raise. However, aside from being poorly led, the dependence on Catholic support weakened the appeal of the rising. There were maybe about 1,500 active English Jacobites in the '15. The Cumberland posse offered no resistance, and on 9–10 November the Jacobites entered Preston, but it was to prove as unfortunate for them as it had been for the invading Scots in August 1648. Yet the defence of Preston was effective on 12 November, most attacks were repelled with loss to the enemy. Thomas Forster failed to defend the line of the Ribble against advancing government troops, and instead of attacking the besiegers or trying to fight their way out, the Jacobites allowed their enemies to surround the town on the 13th. In Defoe's novel, this failure disillusioned Colonel Jack who then fled the town. The weak Forster unconditionally surrendered on 14 November. Archbishop

64 Cunningham, British envoy in Venice, to Pringle, 13 Dec. 1715, NA. SP. 99/61 f. 90.

Wake and the bishops ordered declarations for George I to be read in all churches.

Meanwhile, in France, where Louis XIV had died prior to the rising, the new government did not act—as had been feared—on behalf of the Jacobites. Nevertheless, British warships, diplomats and spies urgently kept watch on French moves as well as those of the Jacobites in French ports.[65]

"James III and VIII" arrived at Peterhead on 22 December and Scone, where his coronation was planned for 8 January 1716. Yet, freed of concern about England, where support for the Jacobite cause was "patchy at best"[66] and the battle of Preston marked the end of the Jacobite rising, Argyll had now been provided with a far larger army, including 5,000 Dutch troops. Despite the bitterness of the winter and a Jacobite scorched-earth policy, Argyll marched on Perth on 21 January. The Jacobites were badly affected by low morale and desertion, and James abandoned Perth. The army retreated to Montrose, but rather than defending it James and Mar sailed for France on 4 February, and their abandoned army dispersed. Reports that James had been captured by a British frigate were inaccurate.[67]

Justice was tempered with mercy, and there were far fewer executions of the defeated than in 1685 or 1746. Many of those who surrendered at Preston were transported to the colonies. In Scotland, alongside exiles after the suppression of the '15, there was a measure of *rapprochement* between the Scottish élite and the new regime. Indeed, when large-scale rebellion broke out again in 1745, the effective neutralization of many Jacobites active in the '15 denied the movement of the public support from influential members of the élite it so badly needed.

George I as Party Monarch

The failure of the '15 lent fresh energy to the purge of Tories, although being an opposition group in Parliament did not mean coming from the

65 Lieutenant William Rowley RN, to Josiah Burchett, Secretary of the Admiralty, reporting from Le Havre, 2, 3, Dec. 1715, Commodore Swanton to Burchett, 27 Mar. 1716, NA. SP. 42/14 fols 372–4, 42/15 f. 193.

66 J. Oates, *Anti-Jacobitism and the English People, 1714–1746* (Abingdon, 2022), p. 249.

67 Report from Brink, French agent in Hamburg, 2 Mar. 1716, AN. AM. B7 267.

ranks of the socially excluded. Thus, among the MPs for Oxfordshire, Sir Robert Jenkinson (MP 1710–17) was a baronet, the son of an MP, and had houses in Walcot, Oxfordshire, and Hawkesbury in Gloucestershire; his brother Robert (1717–27) succeeded to the baronetcy, the country houses, and the seat in Parliament; and the father of Henry Perrot (1721–40) was nicknamed "Golden Perrot" on account of his wealth. Many constituencies were under the control of the local élite, the Norths of Croxton providing MPs for Banbury. In contrast, purges of JPs ensured that by 1719, the Tories had only minority status in the Commissioners of the Peace.

Separate from the purge of the Tories, Jacobitism continued but remained weak. In June 1716, on George I's birthday, there were Jacobite shouts of "No Cromwell" in the streets of London, as well as the oak leaves that commemorated the restoration of Charles II.[68] John, Lord Egmont, provided an instructive commentary from London the following month, one that casts light on the difficulties commentators faced in reconciling the episodes of the moment with longer-term situations and developments:

> I am sorry to own the civil spirit among the people is very little better than ever, and the army is necessary to contain them. But France is in a miserable condition, and our King respected abroad.... I think there is nothing to apprehend for the public of very bad consequence, and when I reflect that scarce any new line came to the throne without some uneasiness and disturbance at first which afterwards died away and the government more firmly fixed than before, I entertain few uneasy thoughts other than what so unaccountable and unworthy behaviour of Church of England men must give a man of any religion.[69]

Meanwhile, Jacobitism continued to display the politics of failure, although concerns about Jacobite activity continued, leading in 1718 to requests for the dispatch of troops to the North-East, with George Liddell, a

68 Newsletter, 1 June 1716, papers of Prince-Bishop Ernest Augustus, brother of George I, Osnabrück, Staatsarchiv, 196 II f. 346.
69 Egmont to Charles Dering, 30 July 1716, BL. Add. 47028 fols 160–1.

key figure in the coal trade that interested Defoe, being particularly insistent.[70]

War with Spain onward from 1718 made the situation more serious. In 1719, there was a pro-Jacobite Spanish invasion of Scotland, but most of the force was dispersed by storms, and the very small Spanish force—allied with a larger (yet still small) Highland army—was defeated at the battle of Glenshiel by an Anglo-Dutch army. Three years later, the Atterbury Plot, a plan to seize London, was blocked by prompt government action, including the creation of a large army camp in Hyde Park.

Having defeated the Tories and Jacobites in 1714–15, the Whigs had divided, in large part due to rivalry among the Whig leaders.[71] Hanover's close involvement in the Great Northern War of 1700–21, which at this stage was a struggle to partition Charles XII of Sweden's Baltic empire, meant that George I expected commitment to Hanoverian interests from his British ministers and treated differences of opinion over foreign policy as tests of loyalty. Matters were made worse by tensions between George I and his son, George, Prince of Wales and later George II, and among the Whig elite, and by the relationship between the two. Whig unity had ebbed as soon as the dangers posed by Toryism and Jacobitism had receded.

The ministry split openly in the spring of 1717 with Walpole, then First Lord of the Treasury, and his brother-in-law, Charles, 2nd Viscount Townshend, opposing George's anti-Swedish policy that was supported by Charles, 3rd Earl of Sunderland, and James Stanhope. This helped drive George further into support of the latter. Townshend was dismissed, being replaced as a Secretary of State by Sunderland, while Walpole resigned. The two men tried co-operating with the Tories in order to thwart the ministry, which helped block ministerial plans to introduce legislation favorable to the Dissenters in the 1718 session. Walpole's co-operation with the Tories raised the always fluid and uncertain confluence of principled stands with the political tactics of the moment and threw light on the difficulties confronting opposition.

70 Liddell to William Cotesworth, 2 Mar., 6, 18 Ap., Liddell to Sir Henry Liddell, 5 Ap. 1718, Gateshead, Public Library, Cotesworth Mss CP/1 nos 19, 33, 37, 32.

71 W.A. Speck, "The Whig Schism Under George I," in *Huntington Library Quarterly*, 60 (1977): pp. 171–9.

Indeed, the political crisis of 1718 foreshadowed the developments of the subsequent quarter-century, the "Age of Walpole." An alliance between the Tories and government Whigs was impossible due to differences over foreign policy and ecclesiastical issues. In foreign policy, most Whigs sought to limit the personal role and Hanoverian aspirations of George I and George II. However, they were more willing to comply with the monarch's wishes than the Tories. The Tories, drawing on an anti-cosmopolitan or xenophobic approach to abroad, harped incessantly on the theme of British resources being used to help Hanover, specifically to make territorial gains. The breakdown in relations with Charles XII of Sweden, largely as a result of Hanoverian expansionism at the expense of Sweden's German possessions, led Charles to support Jacobite plotting, notably in 1717.

Having produced the critical *History of the Wars, of his Present Majesty, Charles XII, King of Sweden* (1715)—one in which the king appeared bellicose and unstable—Defoe wrote about this crisis in relations, a crisis that for Britain spanned foreign policy, national politics, and domestic stability. *The Case of the War in Italy Stated* (1718), a defence of action against Spain, has also been attributed to Defoe. The pamphlet presents Spanish expansionism as a threat to British trade, and argued that war with Spain was not on behalf of Austria but rather to protect Britain, including its colonies and the freedom of trade upon which its industry rested.

Walpole's inability to use the Tories to force himself back into office in 1718 prefigured the failure from 1726 against him as first minister of the more famous "Patriot" platform of Henry, Viscount Bolingbroke, and William Pulteney, which was as unoriginal as it was unsuccessful. Forced to oppose foreign policy, and thus to anger the king, the opposition Whigs of the late 1720s and 1730 reaped only failure from their Tory alliance.

While Walpole's success in influencing governmental legislative policy in 1718 did not take him into office, it did challenge the cohesion and confidence of the ministry. Walpole made it clear that a Whig government could not necessarily expect, much less command, the support of Whig parliamentarians, a lesson that his own years in office were to show that he had learned well. His years in opposition revealed that Walpole's political skills were not simply dependent on his deployment of the fruits of patronage. He was also an effective parliamentarian—as speaker, leader, organizer, and tactician.

In 1720, Walpole returned to office. He benefited from the tension between George I's German confidants, and Stanhope and Sunderland, and from a reconciliation between George and the Prince of Wales, which he helped broker. Breaking with the Tories, Walpole began to steer government business through the Commons.

He was helped by the drama of life in the shape of the bursting of the South Sea Bubble and the subsequent political fall-out. The rise in the shares of this finance company had been seen as a way to private wealth and public stability: it was presented as a way to help pay off the national debt. The collapse of the Company's stock that September ruined the finances and hopes of many, and led to accusations of fraud against the directors and the ministers close to them. Some of the latter had indeed been rewarded with large amounts of stock, and several had been implicated in the very dubious financial practices of the directors. As Bank of England and East India Company stock also fell heavily, there was a danger of a widespread financial collapse.

The South Sea Crash led to considerable public anger, including a spike in publications, and to lurid suggestions for the public shaming of:

> a knot of private persons, who have dared to abuse the king's authority, and the credit of the nation, for enriching themselves by the ruin of thousands of families … having some public mark of infamy.… What think you of having a gallows erected before all their houses, and at the chief seats of their several estates, not to be removed but by Act of Parliament.[72]

The idea, however, that kings reign "by justice, as well as mercy," while attractive did not describe the reality of bias and connections in the society of the period, one that Defoe successfully analyzes.[73]

Walpole played a central role in producing a plan involving the rescheduling of the inflated debts of the Company and a writing down of its capital. There were many losers, but fewer and far less than had seemed

72 Charles Whitworth, envoy in Berlin, to Delafaye, 31 Dec. 1720, NA. SP. 90/12.

73 *Ibid.*, 28 Jan. 1721, 90/13.

likely prior to the restructuring. Wapole helped restore confidence both in the financial system, and in the government's financial activity, probity, and prospects.

Although criticized for defending ministerial colleagues implicated in the Company, Walpole greatly benefited from their problems. In April 1721, he became First Lord of the Treasury, while Townshend became a Secretary of State again. Walpole faced difficulties aplenty, not least among them Sunderland's continued role at Court, but he was now as clearly the dominant figure in the ministry as he had been in the Commons since his return to office in 1720. Defoe did not have the relationship with Walpole that he had had with Harley, who had been a bitter rival of Walpole.

The 1720s and 1730s were bleak years for the Stuart cause, although conspiracies and reports of plots were frequent, and government archives are full of such reports.[74] The venal, but able, Walpole followed policies that were less aggressive and objectionable to the Tories than the Stanhope-Sunderland ministry of 1717–20. Moreover, the Whiggism now to the fore lacked the radicalism and radical potential earlier seen in the movement, and notably so in the 1680s, particularly the early 1680s, and then differently when in power during 1717–19. Instead, there was an emphasis on continuity and on the legitimacy of the newly-constructed order.[75]

Walpole was also adroit, resisting opponents outside government and supplanting rivals within, until his fall and enforced retirement in 1742. Once in office, Walpole swiftly rose to dominate politics. The parliamentary opposition had negotiated with Sunderland in 1721 as he sought to outmanoeuvre Walpole. The failure of these negotiations led instead, in the autumn of 1721, to a regrouping by the opposition that produced an alliance between the Tories and a group of dissident Whigs led by Earl Cowper and the Duke of Wharton—all part of the incessant inconsistency of political manoeuvrings. In November 1721, this group began a bitter parliamentary assault on the ministry. There was little hope that the government could be defeated in Parliament, but the opposition hoped to discredit

74 For example B. Creet to Newcastle, 28 Sept. 1727, NA. SP. 36/3.

75 P. Hammond, "The King's Two Bodies: Representations of Charles II," in J. Black and J. Gregory (eds), *Culture, Politics and Society in Britain, 1660–1800* (Manchester, 1991), p. 42.

it in the eyes of the electorate. Thanks largely to Walpole's skill in presenting the ministerial case in the Commons and in managing government patronage, the opposition failed.

Within government, a struggle between Walpole and Sunderland for dominance that involved ministerial patronage ended when Sunderland suddenly died of pleurisy on 19 April 1722; Stanhope had suddenly died the previous year. Their former adherents were removed from office, although the process took several years. Such sudden deaths were aspects of the inherent unpredictability of politics, one that ensured that circumstances were never consistent.

Walpole was invaluable to George I and George II (1727–60) as government manager and principal spokesman in the House of Commons, and as a skilful manager of the state's finances. He also played a key role in the successful elections of 1722, 1727, and 1734. Aside from his policies, Walpole was adept in parliamentary management and in his control of government patronage. He helped to provide valuable continuity and experience to the combination of limited monarchy with parliamentary sovereignty.

In the first session after the 1722 general election, Walpole displayed his mastery of the Commons. On 26 October, there was a majority of 71 on a motion to increase the size of the army. The following August, Walpole congratulated himself on the flourishing condition of public credit and of having accurately predicted to George I the price of stocks, adding, "I think it is plain we shall have the whole supply of next year at 3 per cent … and I flatter myself that the next session of Parliament will bring to discredit to those that have the honour to serve the king in his revenue."[76]

The failure to appoint William Pulteney Secretary of State led him to go into opposition in 1725, creating an articulate and active opposition Whig group. Walpole, however, still enjoyed substantial majorities in Commons divisions—for example, 262 to 89 against an opposition motion of 9 February 1726 for an inquiry into the national debt, and 251 to 85 on the Address on 17 January 1727.

Aware of opposition within the ministry, Walpole was conscious of the need to maintain royal support. His relations with George, Prince of Wales,

76 Walpole to Townshend, 30 Aug. 1723, NA. SP. 43/4 fol. 292.

was not particularly good, and it was expected that the Prince's Treasurer, Spencer Compton, Speaker of the Commons, would replace Walpole. However the accession of a new monarch in 1727 meant that Parliament had to be summoned, the Civil List (annual grant paid to the Crown by Parliament) settled, and elections held for a new Parliament. With his proven track record as a parliamentary manager, Walpole was needed for these purposes, and he also benefited from the support of Queen Caroline, the wife to George II. Walpole secured an enlarged Civil List from Parliament, and made full use of patronage interest to increase the government majority in the Commons. This helped secure his position and he remained first minister until 1742, and therefore for the remainder of Defoe's life.

A different occasion from 1727, but also one of recognition for the future, was Newton's funeral in Westminster Abbey. A very grand—indeed majestic—affair, it is described by the visiting Voltaire as that "of a king who had done well by his subjects."

Defoe died against a background of international crisis that was to prompt renewed fears of French invasion, fears that were to revive in 1733. At the same time, the domestic situation was more stable, and the ministry well-established. Yet, the continued role of contingency was to be abruptly demonstrated in 1744–5, first with a major, storm-wracked, French invasion attempt, and then by the most serious of the Jacobite risings. Defoe's age might be one of growing national power, prosperity, and stability, but it was also shot through with uncertainty. That provided the context and topics for his writings, both factual and fictional.

10. The Press and Polemics

Like Dickens, a journalist before he was a novelist, Defoe—who lived at a time when journalism was emerging as a practice—was significant in the 1700s as part of Robert Harley's propaganda world. Harley had some characteristics in common with Defoe, both men being pious, resourceful, moderate, and opposed to corruption.[1] The *Review*, which Defoe edited from 1704 to 1711, might have relatively low circulation figures, but the measure of a paper's political significance was not simply that of its circulation. Like other papers, there was more to the *Review* than politics.[2] Thus, "Anti-Venereal Pills" were advertised in it in 1709. Yet, it was a political paper and reflected the norms of such works. For example, the importance of foreign news in the politically-sensitive debates over foreign policy that occupied Defoe's political lifetime, the partisan nature of most of the political press, and the pervading reality of newspaper rivalry all helped to make accuracy a subject of insult and controversy. Indeed, the initial title of Defoe's *Review* was *A Weekly Review of the Affairs of France: Purged from the Errors and Partiality of News-Writers and Petty-Statesmen, of all Sides*.

Essay papers, such as the *Review*, *Spectator*, and *Tatler*, were very different in their frequency to debate by pamphlet. As such, they reflected the grounding in Defoe's thirties of the move toward a consistent press that had occurred earlier in the seventeenth century. By 1622, newsbooks, which appeared weekly, were appearing in a numbered sequence. This helped create a sense of location in time: news was placed in an ordering, and later items in this sequence qualified what had gone before and therefore clarified

1 B.W. Hill, *Robert Harley Speaker, Secretary of State and Premier Minister* (New Haven, 1988).

2 J. Evans, "The Review," in A. Sullivan (ed.), *British Magazines: The Augustan Age and the Age of Johnson, 1698–1788* (Greenwood Press, 1983): 289–95.

the accuracy of fears based on earlier reports. Location in this ordering also contributed to a sense of the enduring character of news and thus of newsbooks as important to the establishment and configuration of historical memory and awareness, which was a background to Defoe's use of history. The news became a means of public speech.

Inherently, however, this process proved a contentious matter as there were contradictory reports, but this was also caused by politics. The development of the press was therefore intercut with regulation. In 1632, as a result of a complaint from a Spanish diplomat, there was government prohibition of *corantos*, newsbooks or newspapers, only for the collapse of royal authority in 1641 to lead to an explosion of publications. In turn, Parliamentary victory and Cromwellian takeover ensured that in 1649, 1652, and 1655 most of the press was banned and a licensing system restored. This approach was supported by commentators who saw a free press as part of a world of disorder. In his *Leviathan* (1651), Thomas Hobbes presses the need to control public opinion.

Indeed, in *A Journal of the Plague Year*, there is discussion of reports of whence the plague originated in 1665, Defoe following by saying:

> We had no such thing as printed newspapers in those days to spread rumours and reports of things, and to improve them by the invention of men, as I have lived to see practised since.

This might be read ironically, even as an in-joke, while anyway there was then the *Gazette*, but the latter was not like the unlicensed newspapers that were to come.

Control over the press broke down during the Exclusion Crisis of 1679–81. This provided an opportunity for the opposition Whigs. While Defoe was not positioned at this stage to take a role in this assault on the government of Charles II and the prospect of a Catholic monarchy, others used pamphlets and newspapers to elaborate and spread anxieties.[3] By the end of 1679, more papers were being published than at any time since 1649. The establishment of the Penny Post for London in 1680 facilitated

3 J. Raymond, *Pamphlets and Pamphleteering in Early Modern Britain* (Cambridge, 2003).

the transmission of information and the distribution of publications. The Whigs produced a mass of propaganda. The first unlicensed newspaper made clear its didactic nature in its title, *The Weekly Pacquet of Advice from Rome ... in the process of which, the Papists arguments are answered, their fallacies detected, their cruelties registered, their treasons and seditious principles observed.* In response to the spread of unlicensed newspapers, the circulation of the *Gazette* fell greatly.[4]

A Tory press was founded in response to opposition publications, but Charles II wished not to conduct a propaganda war, rather to terminate it. A resumption of royal control over the press was an aspect of the strengthening of royal authority as the Exclusion Crisis was brought to a close. The judiciary supported the power of the royal prerogative to control the press, and prosecutions for seditious libel were launched. Chief Justice Scroggs directed that juries were only competent to determine whether the defendants had published the libel; judges alone could decide whether it was seditious, a ruling that greatly limited the role of juries. Certain of government support, officials of the Stationers Company and of the Secretaries of State enforced the law against illegal printers. The Company dealt with Richard Baldwin, the Whig publisher of the *Protestant Courant* in 1682. In 1685, James II had Parliament renew the Licensing Act.

The ministerial success in stamping out Whig newspapers in the early 1680s contrasted with the situation the following century. Contrasting circumstances were important. The press in the 1680s was newer, smaller, confined to London, with a less-developed distributive network and smaller financial resources, and without the loyalties of a long-established readership. However, the key contrast was that in government attitudes. No eighteenth-century ministry sought to control the press with the thoroughness and vigor of Charles II and James II. The Civil War, the Popish Plot, and the Exclusion Crisis all engendered a fear and a desire for action in ministerial circles that had different consequences to the subsequent situations. Ministries became more accustomed to the expression of various opinions—often antagonistic—in the

4 J. Childs, "The Sales of Government Gazettes During the Exclusion Crisis, 1678–81," in *English Historical Review* 102 (1987): p. 105.

press, and also responded to circumstances. The press, both newspapers and newsletters, was indeed used by the royal family for the purposes of gaining information.[5]

The system of press control was greatly weakened when William III (of Orange) seized power in the "Glorious Revolution" of 1688–9. William brought a mobile printing press with him when he invaded in 1688: he knew the importance of the press. As a consequence of the "Glorious Revolution," it is possible to link the rise of press freedom to the end of Stuart authoritarianism. Nevertheless, once in control, William moved to revive the machinery of press control. The "Glorious Revolution" had led to the appearance of newspapers, many short-lived but all of them favorable to William. However, the revival led to attacks on unlicensed works—for example, Richard Baldwin finding himself in trouble with both Secretaries of State and Parliament in 1690–1, despite his Whig credentials. Very differently, in the early 1690s, Defoe was one of those active in the *Athenian Mercury*, which answered readers' ostensible questions on social, cultural, religious, and emotional issues.[6]

Because the existing system for the supervision of printing was felt to be inadequate, plans were drawn up to prepare a new regulatory act, only for them to be killed by parliamentary divisions and a lack of parliamentary time. As a result, the Licensing Acts lapsed in 1695. Linked to this, it is readily apparent that newspaper development might have gone on a number of different paths in England. No one path was inevitable. Instead, the key context explaining English distinctiveness was that of politics. This provided the context for the independent initiative of entrepreneurs, and thus for a press focused on free market and liberal principles.

Moreover, much of the discussion of political issues in the English press, and particularly by the late-seventeenth century, was handled in pragmatic terms, with detailed, specific instances, reasons, and means of cause and effect each playing a major role in the discussion. At the same time, the context was generally that of moral factors presented in terms of Chris-

5 James, Duke of York, to Colonel George Legge, 4 Feb. 1681, BL. Add. 18447 fol. 25.

6 G. McEwan, *The Oracle of the Coffee House: John Dunton's Athenian Mercury* (San Marino, CA, 1972).

tian values, while religious partisanship was also an important filter of information.

The development of a relatively unregulated press in England after the lapsing of the Licensing Act in 1695 helped lead to a form of political culture, and one very different to that of earlier times, one in which, in a newly uncensored context, there was an expectation of news and thus of novelty, if not change. A major increase in the press followed, including in 1702 with the launch of the *Daily Courant*, the first English daily (weekday) newspaper. This development was an instance of the extent to which the political and social power of print technology, as with other information technologies, depended on particular conjunctures. The most specific in the 1690s was the massive interest in foreign news linked to the Nine Years' War, in which England participated from 1689 to 1697. This war was crucially important to the survival of the new political order. This helped the *Gazette*, the official newspaper founded in 1665, to achieve considerable sales, but it also was part of a system of news management, and from 1695 it had to engage with legitimate independent newspapers that added to and complicated an already highly-active world of print.[7]

In England, the result was the development of what has been termed a "public sphere" in which printed opinion played a major role.[8] This is an exaggeration as many were not comprehended in such a sphere. Instead it was more an "élite and some others sphere."

Newspaper readership certainly developed after the lapse of the Licensing Act. Despite attempts in 1697, 1698, 1702, 1704, and 1712 to revive a licensing system—attempts that drew on members of both political parties—the press, nevertheless, remained free of pre-publication supervision, even though Customs officers confiscated unwelcome "printed papers" as they arrived into the country.[9] Moreover, there were many specific attempts to influence publication on particular issues or by individual titles. For

7 N. Glaisyer, "The Most Universal Intelligencers": The circulation of the *London Gazette* in the 1690s," in *Media History* 23 (2017): pp. 256–80.

8 P. Lake and S. Pincus (eds.), *The Politics of the Public Sphere in Early Modern England* (Manchester, 2007); E.L. Furdell, *Publishing and Medicine in Early Modern England* (Rochester, NY, 2002).

9 Report from Customhouse London, 24 Mar. 1730, NA. SP. 36/18 f. 80.

example, anger with "the madness and folly of the press" led to frequent legal action in 1711.[10]

Earlier, the end of control over the number of printers by the Stationers' Company meant that this number increased. Moreover, many moved out of London to seek work, which was to be crucial for the development of the provincial press. Hitherto, printing had been limited to Cambridge and Oxford, but other cities now followed, such as Exeter in 1698. Newspapers at this juncture were mostly founded and controlled by their printers who were key entrepreneurs as befitted a small-scale production system requiring only modest investment. Crucially, this usually involved general-purpose printers choosing to try their hands at a newspaper as well.

As it was clear that the new situation was not going to be similar to previous lapses in the licensing system, there was thus a sounder basis for investment. A spate of new titles rapidly followed the lapse, including on 17 May 1695 the *Post Boy, an Historical Account of the Public Transactions of this Nation*, a triweekly that was published in London on Tuesdays, Thursdays, and Saturdays when the post left London. This enabled the new papers to meet both metropolitan and provincial demand and to establish their claims as a national voice. One of the leading newspapers in the second quarter of the eighteenth century was a triweekly, the *London Evening Post*. In 1722, Thomas Townshend, then seeking election at Winchelsea, was sent "a *London Journal* to amuse you."[11] The press certainly spread news around the country. Thus, a London report of 21 May 1723 published in the *Northampton Mercury* of 27 May reports the arguments in the Lords for and against taxation of the estates of Catholics and Non-Jurors. Benjamin Griffin's play, *Whig and Tory. A Comedy* (1720), shows Sir John Indolent's house in Norfolk, with Sir John reading pamphlets that came from London and had been sent by his bookseller.

The industry grew rapidly. The annual sale of newspapers in England was about 2.5 million in 1713. Increases in sales did not mean guaranteed

10 George Tilson, Under-Secretary for the Northern Department, to John Chetwynd, envoy in Turin, 16, 19 Oct., 16 Nov. 1711, Stafford, Staffordshire County Record Office, D649/8/7.

11 Stephen Poyntz to Thomas Townshend, 27 Oct. 1722, Beinecke, Osborn Shelves c.201.

profitability, particularly in England where anybody could start a newspaper, and it was relatively simple for printers—many of whom were in practice "jobbing"[12]—to test a market by doing so, especially where no widespread distribution network was required. This lack of specialization reflected the absence of any need for specific equipment or trained staff for newspaper production (although, thanks to the 1712 Stamp Act, later the First Stamp Act, devised by Harley, there was a need for a supply of stamped paper), thus the relatively limited investment required when founding a paper. This contributed to a highly competitive atmosphere and a large number of failures. By raising prices and depressing demand, Stamp Duty indeed may have served to create market saturation at certain junctures.

Newspapers were different to other forms of printed news or commentary—such as pamphlets—because they were regular and frequent. Defoe was expert in both, which was an aspect of his more general range. Pamphlets could be seen as a way "to put people on the right way of reasoning" against newspaper "scribblers," obliging "Ministers as usual" to "wade through a great deal of dirt and scandal."[13] Yet it was by no means clear that pamphlets necessarily had the advantage. Separately, the extent to which pamphlets could be variously judged, as in "plausible enough for to deceive a populace; but not much of solid argument ..."or "pulled to pieces; though they will last and appear judicious, when the other pamphlet is forgotten,"[14] underlined the difficulty of assessing impact and influence, and the number of criteria that might be employed in doing so.

In contrast to pamphlets, newspapers offered a predictable sequence of communication for which the only real counterpart was the weekly sermon. The English newspaper world saw qualitative and rapid quantitative growth, but also—and more so than elsewhere—a diversification of type with the foundation of the first daily in 1702, the *Daily Courant,* and the first

12 J. Raven, *Publishing Business in Eighteenth-Century England* (Woodbridge, 2014).

13 Tilson to Waldegrave, 9, 27 Jan. 1730, Chewton.

14 Tilson to Waldegrave, 13, 17 Feb. 1730, Chewton, of *Observations Examined* and *Observations* respectively.

provincial paper, probably the *Norwich Post* in 1701, although possibly *Farley's Exeter Post-man* the previous December.[15] The first paper published in the North-East was the *Newcastle Gazette* of 1710. The first evening paper was the *Evening Post* in 1706. This diversification contributed to a sense of dynamism. At the same time, both the *Daily Courant* and the *Evening Post* were published in London. Diversification was more limited elsewhere as provincial papers were weeklies.

There was also a marked growth in the number of titles. There were twelve London newspapers by 1712—when the revenue-raising First Stamp Act put several out of business—and about twenty-four English provincial papers by 1723. Some cities, such as Bristol, Exeter, Newcastle, Norwich, and York, acquired more than one title, and these competed with each other, both commercially and politically.

As Britain was at war in 1689–97, 1702–13, and 1718–20, much of the press coverage related to foreign affairs. Thus, the *Stamford Post* of 30 June 1712 advertised *Dutch Alliances*, a critique of the War of the Spanish Succession, while that paper also informed its readers of regional views on the international situation, as in the issue of 17 July 1712 when it printed Addresses from the towns in Newark, Northampton, and Cambridge. This fascination with foreign policy encouraged an interest in secret histories, and that stirred anticipation for Defoe's novelistic writings. Indeed, the rise of the press was a factor in that of the novel.[16] Separately, the average number of advertisements per week (one issue) for the *York Mercury* in 1720 was thirty-two.

The influence of the press was, and remains, a matter of contention, which indeed helps explain the difficulty of assessing Defoe's role in the matter.[17] Most politicians did not match Harley's activity in this sphere,[18] and Godolphin in particular was not a great inspirer of printed propaganda. Yet, as one party sponsored a paper, another felt it necessary to reply.

15 I. Maxted, *Bibliography of British Newspapers, Devon and Cornwall* (London, 1991), p. 40.

16 L.J. Davis, *Factual Fictions: The Origins of the English Novel* (New York, 1983); M. McKeon, *The Origins of the English Novel, 1600–1740* (Baltimore, 1987).

17 J.A. Downie, "Stating facts right about Defoe's *Review*," in *Prose Studies* 16 (1993): 8–22.

18 Downie, *Robert Harley and the Press* (Cambridge, 1979).

Indeed, subsidies played a key role in launching and sustaining newspapers.[19] Moreover, the personal political role of some writers, such as the Whig Richard Steele, may have encouraged greater political commitment to the press. Yet it is unclear how many politicians shared the belief expressed in June 1711 that "it is possible to scribble these men [of the ministry] down." Queen Anne herself could see opposition literature as evidence simply "that it was party and faction that was discontented and not the nation,"[20] while, once out of office and being persecuted by the Whig writers, Harley could write "News is a Trade."[21]

Defoe both benefited financially from writing political works—not least for the *Review*[22]—and sought the opportunity to disseminate his views. This could lead him into difficulties as the room for manoeuvre was affected not only by political cross-currents but also by the continuing legal penalties that remained after the lapse of the Licensing Act. Not least among these penalties was the punishment of the pillory as a punishment for seditious libel, which remained possible until 1837 although very rarely used, added to the disruption produced by arrests, trials, imprisonment, and fines. Defoe himself fell into considerable legal difficulties from his ironical *The Shortest Way with the Dissenters* (1702). This treatment in turn became a point of reference about Defoe, as in 1708 with the criticism of another pamphlet, *Advice to the Electors of Great Britain*, probably by Arthur Maynwaring: "though he may think himself as much above the shameful punishment of the pillory, as he exceeds that author in art and malice."[23] Pope was to pigeonhole Defoe in terms of "Earless on high, stood pillory'd D—."[24]

19 Downie, "Periodicals and politics in the reign of Queen Anne," in Myers and Harris (eds.), *Serials and their Readers* (Winchester, 1993), p. 58.

20 H. Snyder, "Arthur Maynwaring and the Whig Press, 1710–1712," in P. Haas et al. (eds.), *Literatur als Kritik des Lebens* (Heidelberg, 1975), p. 127; P. Roberts (ed.), *Diary of Sir David Hamilton* (Oxford, 1975).

21 Harley, "Meditations in the Tower," 3 Jan. 1716, BL. Loan 29/38.

22 Downie, "Periodicals and Politics in the Reign of Queen Anne," in R. Myers and M. Harris (eds.), *Serials and their Readers, 1620–1914* (Newcastle, 1993), pp. 47–8, 57.

23 *Scandal Displayed* (London, 1708), p. 1.

24 T. Ross, *Writing in Public: Literature and the Liberty of the Press in Eighteenth-Century Britain* (Baltimore, 2018); T. Keymer, *Poetics of the Pillory: English*

In the meanwhile, Defoe as a political writer had been "pinched" politically by the contrasts between his links with Harley and many of the key policies of the Tory ministry of 1710–14. The latter were often better expressed by Swift's *Examiner*. Swift there had a bite that Defoe's more prolific *Review* lacked, and Swift was able to outmanoeuvre Defoe as a form of spokesman for the Tory government.[25] Defoe and Swift held different attitudes, but as part of a much wider and far more complex mosaic of political, religious, and personal commitments and rivalries.[26]

There were contrasting tones and styles in coverage, and contention concerning what should be included. The *Examiner*'s leading opponent, Arthur Maynwaring's Whig *Medley*, argued that the Tories were foolish to let the *Examiner* deal in descriptions and images, but as people frequently think in images they were indeed an effective means of persuasion. The *Examiner*'s strategy marginalized its opponents by stressing the values of homogeneity—a seamless, organic society—and of unanimity of opinion and action, and by presenting itself as above party.[27]

The divided nature of the press and the implications of the "Glorious Revolution" for divisiveness are captured in the first issue of the *Monitor*, that of 22 April 1714:

> one of the methods by which the distractions of the present times have been brought to such a height has been the unprecedented liberty of the press, whereby printed pamphlets and daily papers appear in all parts of the nation; in which such provocations are given such indecencies and such expressions as no age can show the like.... It is one of the unhappinesses attending a free constitution that a pernicious liberty cannot be easily

Literature and Seditious Libel, 1660–1820 (Oxford, 2019). See also review of the latter by Alan Downie in *Review of English Studies* 72 (2021): pp. 188–90.

25 H.J. Müllenbrock, "Swift as a Political Essayist: The Strained Medium," in R.H. Rodino and H.J. Real (eds.), *Reading Swift* (Munich, 1993), p. 158.

26 Z. Jamoussi, *The Snare in the Constitution: Defoe and Swift on Liberty* (Newcastle, 2009).

27 F.H. Ellis (ed.), *Swift vs Mainwaring:* The Examiner *and* The Medley (Oxford, 1985).

> restrained and that no laws can be made to remedy it, but what shall one way or another clash with the general fund of liberty which we all desire to preserve. And therefore this evil is borne to prevent falling into a greater, that of an arbitrary administration.

The press wars continued in the reign of George I and George II. Launched in December 1716, Nathaniel Mist's *Weekly Journal: or, Saturday's Post* repeatedly met trouble in a fashion that throws light on the difficulties that Defoe encountered, most obviously in his *Shortest Way with the Dissenters.* In 1717, Mist, a Jacobite, was tried for printing a trial without permission, and was arrested twice for printing seditious libels. In 1718, he was arrested on the complaint of the Russian envoy for his comment on the death of Alexis, son and heir of Peter the Great—who was supposedly murdered by his father—while, in the same year, Mist was arrested (in a coffee-house) and questioned for an attack on foreign policy. In 1720, Mist was tried for arguing that the persecuted Protestants in the Palatine were not seriously mistreated. This led to Mist standing twice in the pillory, paying a fine, spending 1721 in prison and giving surety for good behavior for seven years. More arrests, fines, and imprisonment followed in 1720, 1723, 1724, 1725, and 1727, but Mist did not have to flee abroad until 1728 when he changed the title to *Fog's Weekly Journal.*[28]

Defoe's role in the secret pay of the government can be difficult to fathom, but it was not restricted to writing for Mist. In 1720–6, Defoe was probably the main contributor to *Applebee's Original Weekly Journal*, a leading London newspaper, although this attribution has been challenged.[29]

Religious animosities remained significant. On 23 January 1720, Fran-

28 J. Black, "An Underrated journalist: Nathaniel Mist and the Opposition press during the Whig ascendancy," in *British Journal for Eighteenth-Century Studies* 10 (1987): pp. 27–41; P. Rogers, "Nathaniel Mist, Daniel Defoe, and the Perils of Publishing," in *The Library* 10 (2009): pp. 298–313.

29 J.D. Alsop, "New Light on Nathaniel Mist and Daniel Defoe," in *Papers of the Bibliographical Society of America* 75 (1981): pp. 57–60; Maximilian Novak, "Daniel Defoe and *Applebee's Original Weekly Journal*: An Attempt at Re-Attribution," 45 (2012): pp. 585–608.

cis Clifton, in the last issue of his *Weekly Medley*, refers to his attempt to lay "open all the vile aims of Presbyterian and Whiggish principles." In turn, in 1721–2, emerged Thomas Gordon, the writer of Cato's Letters in the anti-ministerial *London Journal* and a Whig and a Dissenter, whose views on Tories and religious topics offended Mist.[30]

Alongside the trickle-down practice of news—which resulted from and encouraged the "scissors-and-paste" technique of reporting—there was another aspect of "reactive" news-construction, namely the extent to which most newspapers relied on contributions from interested readers. This process of response helped ensure a measure of differentiation between individual titles. Most pieces were anonymous. Many were sent in as poems. G.C. from Enfield, anonymous or pseudonymous as was the norm, applauded the return of John, Duke of Marlborough, to military command after George I replaced Anne's Tory ministry in 1714. The *Flying-Post: or The Postmaster*, a leading London Whig newspaper, in its issue of 2 November carries his contribution:

These following lines are wrote by a lover of loyalty, courage, conduct, and the present ministry, and a soldier's friend.

I need not sing what is already known,
Of what bright jewels sparkle in the crown;
How lately sullied, now it will appear
Which were the true, and which the false ones were,
Marlborough's return unto the soldiers sight,
Welcome to all their eyes as wished for light;
Renowned for Council, and for courage great,
And merit only made him fortunate..
Louis in earnest never would have mourned
Great Anne's death, had Marlborough not returned:
He loyal, true, and trusty ever was,
And, now for rightful George his sword he draws,
The same his courage, and the same his cause.
Louis 'tis thought, laughed in his sleeve to see,
Mardyke imposed on our late ministry.

30 *Weekly Journal*, 15, 22 April, 13 May, 9 September 1721, 13 October 1722.

The times are changed, no more his laughing day,
Great George now reigns, and Marlborough doth obey.

Nine days later, the same newspaper illustrates the national sway of partisan poetry when it publishes an article from Frome in Somerset—a woollen-cloth manufacturing center—criticizing the strength of Tory sentiment in nearby Bristol. The piece ended with a description of an hypocrite:

Among the beasts that range the hills and woods,
Or scaly fish that shame the liquide floods;
The treacherous crocodile the worst appears,
That aims at mischief with deluding tears:
So if mankind in various forms we view,
The hypocrites appear a dreadful crew;
Who, juggler-like, surprise us with delight,
Yet cast a cheat upon our easy sight,
If in the state these double gamesters play,
Their thoughts are different to whate'er they say;
In boasting words their loyalty reveal,
Yet the false traitor in their hearts conceal;
A thousand different tongues their conscience keeps,
And every tongue a different language speaks;
So artificial glasses fall, or rise,
As fair, or cloudy weather rules the skys.

"A New Ballad to an Old Tune" follows in the issue of 26 February 1715, offering an account of politics and the struggle between George I and "James III and VIII," the Stuart Pretender, which ended with the Pope making the latter a cardinal (which did not occur, although James's younger son, Henry, "Henry IX," later becomes one). The advertisements also recorded not only the role of songs, but also the extent to which political partisanship overlapped with the world of print. Readers of this Whig newspaper would have known what to expect from the following, advertised in the issues of 24 March, 14 April, and 23 April 1715:

> *Political Merriment: or Truths Told to Some Tune*; being a collection of above 150 of the choicest songs and poems that were composed and writ during the four last years of the late reign, many of which never before appeared in print.
>
> *Perkin's Cabal....* A satirical poem on [the Earl of] O[xfor]d....
>
> A key to the Lock; or a treatise proving beyond all contradiction, the dangerous tendency of a late poem, entitled, *The Rape of the Lock* [by Alexander Pope], to government and religion. By Esdras Barnivelt.

Facetious notices also played a role, as with the paper's suggestion on 30 January 1714 that Swift, author of *The Tale of a Tub*, was both an opportunist and a Jacobite:

> The newest edition of the *T—le of a T—b*, so long reprinted and modestly laid by in sheets, will be published very swiftly by that famous hand who has boasted in one of the former editions, that he was wrote fourscore and eleven pamphlets under three reigns, and for the service of six and thirty factions, subscriptions are carried on in Italy, France, Lorraine [seat of the Jacobite court] and Lancashire [an area with many Catholics], and as soon as the books are ready to be delivered out to subscribers, notice will be given in the *Examiner* of London [Swift's newspaper], and at Pasquin's statue in Rome.

Tone was a key aspect of difference between newspapers, and as both a distinctive aspect of literature and of part of the more general world of writers. In the *Tour*, Defoe visits Ross-on-Wye, and refers to the fame of:

> a monstrous fat woman, who they would have had me gone to see. But I had enough of the relation, and so I suppose will the reader, for they told me she was more than three yards about

> her waist; that when she sat down, she was obliged to have a small stool placed before her, to rest her belly on, and the like.[31]

On 19 September 1719, the *Weekly Medley* disparages Mist's *Weekly Journal: or Saturday's Post* by referring to Mist's "vast success among the lower class of readers"; itself an instructive distinction among the literate. Mist preferred to regard his popularity as due to tone and not to a particular social appeal. In his issue of 6 February 1720, Mist identifies a major section of his market in a letter from Timothy Trifle: "To me it is not one farthing matter who you are for, what king, what church, what party: it is enough that you write the *Journal*, where we expect something to please us or displease us, make us laugh, or make us frown." "Daniel Foe" sat alongside Mawson[32] and Mist as those to whom Pope was told he owed "great thanks" in the account of preparations for a Guy Fawkes procession in London in the *Weekly Journal: or British Gazetteer* of 25 October 1718. This reflected both Defoe's writing for Mist, a difficult employer—the extent to which there were considerable cross-currents in newspaper and political tensions, with the Whig-Tory divide matched by the Whig Split—and with Defoe's ability to work undercover as an agent for the Whig ministry in order to affect the content of the *Weekly Journal*.[33] Ministerial and other comments on publications make it clear that readers were able to detect whether writings had life in them,[34] and this played to the advantage of experienced and skilful writers such as Defoe.

Political impartiality, general utility, and the satisfaction of their readers were the general goals pronounced by newspapers, whether new or well-established, provincial, or metropolitan; yet claims for impartiality frequently disguised pronounced political allegiances. Moreover, there could

31 *Tour*, 6.

32 Mawson's *Weekly Journal* was Jacobite in its sympathies.

33 Defoe to Delafaye, 26 Ap. 1718, G. Healey (ed.), *The Letters of Daniel Defoe* (1955), pp. 450–4; government documents of autumn 1718 on press; P.N. Furbank and W.R. Owens, "Defoe and 'Sir Andrew Politick'," in *British Journal for Eighteenth-Century Studies*, 17 (1994): pp. 27–39; NA. SP. 35/13, 31-6; Backscheider, *Defoe*, pp. 430–6.

34 Townshend to Stanhope, 15 Sept. 1716, Maidstone, Kent Archive Office U1590 0145/30.

be direct political intervention, notably through subsidies. Major politicians could and would also write for the press. In 1729, John, 1st Earl of Egmont, a Whig politician, notes in his diary:

> *The British Journal* of this day, or *Censor*, pretended to be writ by one Roger Manby, Esq., but published by a writer for Sir Robert Walpole, and supposed to be dictated by him on extraordinary occasions, contains a clear succinct account of the grounds of the present disagreement among the princes of Europe, and deserves to be kept and read more than once.[35]

It was understandable that Defoe, who had demonstrated his entrepreneurialism as a merchant, should seek new entrepreneurial opportunities in the political world and repeatedly find this access through his writing. Being a reporter of information for Harley overlapped readily with the role of seeking to affect public attitudes. Informed political comment was necessary to both. Writing, and with rapid pace, was crucial. In doing so, Defoe presented himself as engaging with a political system as well as society in flux, the two joined by the significance of the same public opinion that writers sought to influence. Thus, on 18 October 1712 in the *Review*, Defoe sees Jacobitism as a threat precisely because it could influence the public mood:

> These are the artifices of the Jacobite party over the whole kingdom, and by these methods they prevail but too much over the common people … [if] the interest of the Pretender becomes popular, I speak it plainly, I'll not give a farthing for your Protestant Succession.

The world of print in which Defoe was so active encouraged contention and a linked sense of governmental accountability, both in the parliamentary context and outside it. The *London Journal* observes on 21 December 1728, "Liberty has made us a kingdom of politicians." The *Craftsman* on 28 November 1730 encourages electors to press their MPs "according to

35 HMC, *Egmont III*, pp. 323–4.

ancient and laudable custom" to take a particular line on a contentious issue. From the perspective of government, this could be an "Inquisition, which plagued our offices."[36] Moreover, from espionage—notably postal interceptions and deciphering—the government was aware that foreign diplomats read and used publications and were concerned about the state of the press and pamphlet conflicts over public opinion.[37]

As a reminder that tone very often did not match the requirements of politeness, we might note that a 1722 work by Swift went through many editions:

> The benefit of farting explain'd : or, the fundament-all cause of the distempers incident to the fair sex. Inquir'd into: Proving à Posteriori most of the Disordures in tail'd on, them are owing to Flatulencies not seasonably vented. Wrote in Spanish, by Don Fart-Inhando Puff-Indorst Professor of Bumbast in the University of Craccow. And translated into English at the request and for the use of the Lady Damp-Fart, of Her-Fart-Shire.
> "A Fart, tho' wholesome does not fail,
> If barr'd of Passage by the Tail,
> To fly back to the Head again,
> And by its Fumes disturb the Brain:
> Thus Gun-Powder confin'd, you know Sir,
> Grows stronger, as 'tis ram'd the closer;
> But, if in open Air it fires,
> In harmless Smoke its Force expires."
> The thirteenth edition, with additions, revis'd by a College of Phyzz-icians, and approved by several Ladies of Quality.

36 Tilson to Sir Charles Hotham, 13 Mar. 1730, Hull, University Library, Hotham papers DDHo 3/1.

37 Count Gortz, Swedish minister to Count Gyllenborg, Swedish envoy in London, 27 Oct., Baron Petkum, Holstein envoy, to Baron Sparre, Swedish diplomat, 1 Oct. 1716, NA. SP. 107/1B f. 197, 92.

11. Defoe's Foreign Worlds

> ... doubtless peace, abstracted from such circumstances, and which are accidents to it, is in itself infinitely preferable to war, and especially to a wealthy, trading nation, such as we (without boasting) may allow ourselves to be.... [A] lingering, doubtful state of negotiation, being a suspense between peace and war, is like an ague, which comes now hot, then cold, intermitting and periodical; now shaking with cold, then burning with heat; sometimes exhausting by a tedious sweat, at other times giving intervals of health; one while threatening with death and then flattering with the hopes of life; that the poor patient may be said to be neither dead nor alive, but between both.

Defoe, *Reasons for a War, in order to establish the tranquillity and commerce of Europe* (1729), pp. 4, 7

Defoe was an industrious and important commentator on one of Britain's major changes, the shift toward world power, a change he wished to further and to help formulate. In 1660, England was in the shadow of France and a bitter rival of the Dutch. Indeed, Defoe's lengthy discussion in the *Tour* of the defences in the Thames estuary reflect the three Anglo-Dutch wars between 1652 and 1674 and, in particular, the successful and highly damaging Dutch raid on the English naval anchorage and base at Chatham. In 1683, with the Turks besieging Vienna and coming close to success there, Christendom itself appeared to be under threat. Defoe later recalled that he had written on the issue "having read the history of the cruelty and perfidious dealings of the Turks in their wars, and how they rooted out the name of the Christian religion in above threescore and ten kingdoms."[1]

1 Defoe, *An Appeal to Honour and Justice* (London, 1715), p. 51.

In contrast, by Defoe's death in 1731, Britain, as the state could now properly be called following the Union of 1707, had enjoyed over three decades as the world's leading naval power, was a major force in European international relations, and was an important imperial state, notably in North America. In addition, and here Defoe played a major role especially with *Robinson Crusoe*, the British global perspective had widened and deepened. There was far greater engagement with trans-oceanic trade, with the commercial opportunities presented by Spanish America, and with the possibilities of distant waters in the southern hemisphere. Furthermore, after the Restoration, this English version of mercantilism played a central role in the development of the state, and of political and governmental practices.[2]

Defoe played an active role in the discussion, both in his novels and in his differently-factual writings. His *A New Voyage Round the World by a Course Never Sailed Before* (1725; in fact 1724),[3] a work set in 1713–17, used a maritime account in effect in the service of colonialization, with Defoe pressing for the establishment of a colony on the tip of South America, which would have given an entry into the Pacific as well as a base in the South Atlantic south of St. Helena. He made an ironical introduction of the relationship between action and presentation:

> It has for some ages been thought so wonderful a thing to sail the tour or circle of the globe, that when a man has done this mighty feat, he presently thinks it deserves to be recorded, like Sir Francis Drake's. So, as soon as men have acted the sailor, they come ashore and write books of their voyage, not only to make a great noise of what they have done themselves, but, pretending to show the way to others to come after them, they set up for teachers and chart-makers to posterity.

Defoe's book drew on recently published travel accounts, and also on the hope of making profit from Spain's Pacific empire—and in doing so

2 P. Gauci, *The Politics of Trade: The Overseas Merchant in State and Society, 1660–1720* (Oxford, 2001).

3 J. Jack, "*A New Voyage Round the World*; Defoe's *Roman à Thèse*," in *Huntington Library Quarterly*, 24 (1961): pp. 322–36.

taking benefit away from France, who was seen even when they were allies as a foe competing for the Spanish trade. English interest in the Pacific was causing French and Spanish diplomatic alarm even before the "Glorious Revolution."[4] George Ridpath, a Whig journalist who had fled abroad when tried for libel, notes in 1713 that "some people promise themselves mountains of gold from the South Sea,"[5] the term used for the Pacific.

Some of Defoe's *New Voyage* read like a pamphlet, notably the section, "An Observation concerning the Sail and Climate of the Continent of America, south of the River de la Plata, and how suitable to the genius, the constitution, and the manner of living of Englishmen, and consequently of an English colony." For readers at home, the *Atlas Maritimus et Commercialis* (1728) would have further explained the significance of this area. The latter was a project in which Defoe was very heavily involved,[6] one that reflected his continued energy even as he neared the close of his life.

Defoe's engagement with the opportunities of the trans-Atlantic world was also seen in his treatment of British developments, this contributing to a more general repurposing of the empire as Protestant, commercial, wide-ranging, maritime, and free.[7] This was notably true of his pamphlets, but was also seen in other works by Defoe, particularly in the *Tour*. There, cities were ranked in large part with reference to how far they helped the nation's commercial interests, rather than historic designations as cathedral sees or county centers. For Defoe, Liverpool—which was neither—was more consequential than St. David's or Oakham. Defoe saw trade as the key to urban improvement, as in the discussion of Dumfries:

> as it almost everywhere appears, where trade increases, people must and will increase; that is, they flock to the place by the necessary consequences of the trade, and, in return, where the

4 Barillon to Jean-Baptiste, Marquis de Seignelay, Master of the Marine, 5 Jan. 5 Feb. 1688, AN. AM. Archives Etrangères, B1 758; Barillon to Charles, Marquis de Croissy, Foreign Minister, 8 Jan. 1688, AE. CP. Ang. 165 f. 33.f

5 Ridpath to Count Bothmer, Hanoverian minister, 27 Dec. 1713, HL. HM. 44710.

6 P. Rogers, *Defoe's Tour and Early Modern Britain* (Cambridge, 2022), pp. 250–76.

7 D. Armitage, *The Ideological Origins of the British Empire* (Cambridge, 2000).

> people increase, the trade will increase, because the necessary consumption of provisions, cloths, furniture, etc necessarily increases, and with them the trade.[8]

In contrast, Kirkcudbright is depicted as having the *opportunities* for trade, but no trade, which is attributed to poverty and the resulting lack of effort. Defoe's analysis of the failure of enterprise extends to the gentry who "will not turn their hands to business or improvement," and view trade as incompatible with gentry status. So too with Ayr, but not—in contrast—with Irvine. Scotland is presented as having much to gain from British colonial trade, and Glasgow is seen as having considerable potential, not least in being less exposed to privateering than trade from London.

Settlement in the colonies was also seen as a particular opportunity for Britain, the colonies, and those sent there, as indeed would be even more true during the century. Defoe refers to the varied types of settlement. Aside from that funded by the settler, there was indentured servitude (for seven years or other terms) as a means to finance emigration, and in contrast to that forcible transportation. Over the longer term, there was a shift from indentured servitude to both transportation and slavery as a means to provide unpaid labor. Defoe observes:

> … servants, and these they have in greater plenty, and upon better terms than the English; without the scandalous art of kidnapping, making drunk, wheedling, betraying, and the like; the poor people offering themselves fast enough, and thinking it their advantage to go; as indeed it is, to those who go with sober resolutions, namely to serve out their times, and then become diligent planters for themselves; and this would be a much wiser course in England than to turn thieves, and worse, and then be sent over by force, and as a pretence of mercy to save them from the gallows. This may be given as a reason, and, I believe, is the only reason why so many more of the Scots servants, which go over to Virginia, settle and thrive there, than of the English, which is so certainly true, that if it does on for many years more,

8 *Tour*, 12.

> Virginia may be rather called a Scots, than an English plantation.[9]

In *Colonel Jack*, in a passage that could have come from a pamphlet, Defoe presents Virginia as having much to offer, not least in terms of how settlers could benefit in the end:

> That in Virginia, the meanest, and most despicable creature after his time of servitude is expired, if he will but apply himself with diligence and industry to the business of the country, is sure (life and health supposed) both of living well and growing rich.

In his *Essay upon Projects* (1697), Defoe makes reference to a particular instance of gaining wealth in the Americas: "Bless up! that folks should go three thousand miles to angle in the open sea for pieces of eight! Why they would have made ballads of it."[10]

This relates to a character straight out of fiction. Born in modern-Maine and fatherless at six, William Phips (1651–95) grew up in poverty and had no formal schooling. Training as a carpenter and marriage to a widow helped him gain the relevant means to found a shipyard in 1675, and in the 1680s he began treasure hunting from Spanish shipwrecks in the Caribbean, eventually finding a fortune in 1687. In 1689, Phips played a role in the overthrow of James II's allies in Massachusetts and, knighted and made Major-General and Governor of Massachusetts, he later became a command in attacks on French Canada.

Defoe's overly optimistic account of servitude in the British colonies helped substantiate his emphasis on spiritual regeneration. This account was in keeping with a wider tendency in news stories and criminal biographies to present returned convicts. Such a presentation did not capture the degree of harsher exploitation that transportation more generally involved.[11]

9 *Tour*, 12.

10 Defoe, *An Essay from Projects* (London, 1697), p 15.

11 G. Morgan and P. Rushton, *Eighteenth-Century Criminal Transportation. The Formation of the Criminal Atlantic* (Basingstoke, 2004).

In America, the situation was more difficult economically than often suggested in Britain. There was also a gap in the intensity of spiritual regeneration between early Dissenter Proselytization and the later energy of the "Great Awakening."[12] In his discussion of transportation, Defoe captures a rapidly changing situation, with the Transportation Act (1718) allowing transportation as a penalty for a wide range of non-capital crimes. Acts from 1720 extended the crimes for which transportation could be a penalty. Prior to 1718, transportation had been used as part of the pardoning process in the case of capital punishment, serving to dispose of prisoners after the Monmouth rising in 1685, and in 1716 for 639 Jacobite prisoners.

Far less attractively, Britain was also the leading state in the Atlantic slave trade, while many of the colonies it developed incorporated slavery, for example Virginia and Maryland, as mentioned in *Colonel Jack*. Defoe did not really engage with colonies in areas where slavery was of slight consequence, although Moll Flanders might offer an optimistic account of emigration to Virginia but without mentioning slaves: "how with carrying over but two or three hundred pounds value in English goods, with some servants and tools, a man of application would presently lay a foundation for a family, and in a very few years be certain to raise an estate."

London, Defoe's major stamping ground, played a major role in the slave trade, not least through its capital, as the length of voyages required considerable investment. The Company of Royal Adventurers Trading into Africa, chartered in 1660 and reformed as the Royal African Company in 1672, was more successful in this cruel trade, and London dominated Britain's slave trade until the 1710s when it was superseded by Bristol, which in turn was to be superseded by Liverpool. The regulatory framework that had maintained London's control was dismantled in 1698 by the Ten Per Cent Act (named because the merchants had to pay a 10 percent duty to maintain the Company's forts). As a result, the African trade was freed from the control of the Royal African Company whose position had been undermined after the Glorious Revolution, which led to a decline in government support. The Ten Per Cent Act legalized the position of private traders, and made shifts in the relative position of ports far easier, helping secure the rise of Bristol at the expense of London.

12 D. Todd, *Defoe's America* (Cambridge, 2010).

There was no comparable liberalization in the structure of the East India trade, and the continued legal and practical dominance by the East India Company encouraged illicit trade as well as piracy. This is presented by Defoe in *Captain Singleton*.[13] Earlier in *The Villainy of Stock-Jobbers Detected* (1701), he had attacked the rift between the two rival English East India Companies then in existence. Defoe's focus is not on the consequences for India, though he implies these were beneficial to it. This was a matter that is now highly contentious but it was not so in Britain at the time. His concern is on the results for England, especially greater imports from India, which, it was frequently argued, hit industry and employment:

> many parts of that trade are certainly beneficial to the English trade in general; but to carry it on to such a magnitude as is palpably destructive to the English manufactures, and impoverishing to the nation by exporting such quantities of bullion in specie, must certainly make it a public nuisance, a burden to trade, and a damage to the nation.[14]

Trade with India involved lobbying and was contentious in British commercial politics to a degree not seen at all with the slave trade. Access to the markets of Spanish America, including for slaves, was a major goal that was not contentious. From the modern perspective, Defoe's "colonial" writings understandably are scrutinized largely in terms of racism and slavery. In practice, far more than racism was involved in contemporary British use of the language of slavery, and it is necessary to try to recover this wider dimension.[15] This language was widely used to denote any form of oppression—whether political, religious, or social. It was particularly applied against both Catholicism and France. Thus, the *British Journal* of 2 May 1724, in an attack on the Catholic clergy's use of penance, describes it as

13 S. Ahmed, *The Stillbirth of Capital: Enlightenment Writing and Colonial India* (Stanford, 2012), pp. 54–64.

14 Defoe, *Villainy of Stock-Jobbers Detected*, pp. 6, 18–19.

15 D. Carey, "Reading Contrapuntally: *Robinson Crusoe*, Slavery, and Postcolonial Theory," in Carey and L. Festa (eds.), *The Postcolonial Enlightenment: Eighteenth-Century Colonialism and Postcolonial Theory* (Oxford, 2009).

"servitude ... such is the witchcraft of superstition, that men are slaves by their own consent." *Reasons Against a Standing Army* (1717) claims that "to know whether a people are free or slaves; it is necessary only to ask whether there is an army kept amongst them."[16] Defoe used the language. In a series of pamphlets appearing in early 1713, he writes of slavery as the consequence of a Jacobite takeover. Slavery was also a dangerous and demeaning psychological condition, that of servitude to the emotions and to irrational drives—or, rather, drives that are irrational in the minds of those who enjoy reason and therefore have mastery over themselves.

As far as the specifics of racism and slavery are concerned, there are also contradictory indicators. Crusoe is enslaved when his merchantman is captured by Moroccan privateers: "At this surprising change of my circumstances from a merchant to a miserable slave, I was perfectly overwhelmed." Indeed, a large number of English people were enslaved in North Africa during the century. Feeling "that now the hand of Heaven had overtaken me," Crusoe spends over two years as a slave. Escaping southward by stealing a boat, Crusoe, who has made £300 on a £40 investment on a previous Guinea trading trip, is frightened of the West African "savages," the threat of which he compares to wild beasts. Yet, having overawed them by shooting dead a "mighty creature," a "most curious leopard," Crusoe is able to trade with "the negroes," an instance of the establishment of status won by the use of force.

Rapidly changing his status, as Crusoe does in the first section of the book and as do so many of Defoe's characters, Crusoe then becomes a Brazilian plantation owner. In this capacity, he offers an account of opportunities for Britain: "my goods being all English manufactures, such as cloath, stuffs, bays, and things particularly valuable and desirable in the country, I found means to sell them to a very great advantage."

Crusoe had become a transplant in the New World, but the very opening of the novel reveals him as such in Britain, and provides information on how he had become English. The account prefigures that which George I might have made as he came to Britain from Hanover, the dominant power near Bremen:

16 Anon., *Reasons Against a Standing Army* (London, 1717), p. 14.

> I was born in the year 1632, in the city of York, of a good family, though not of that country, my father being a foreigner of Bremen [Germany], who settled first at Hull. He got a good estate by merchandise, and leaving off his trade lived afterward at York, from whence he had married my mother, whose relations were named Robinson, a very good family in that country, and from whom I was called Robinson Kreutznaer; but by the usual corruption of words in England, we are now called, nay, we call our selves and write our name, Crusoe, and so my companions always called me.

As English, Crusoe sees slavery as a condition not of race but instead of circumstances, a view that was to be taken by critics of industrialization. Indeed, his father warns him at the outset about avoiding a poverty that is presented in terms of slavery: "sold to the life of slavery for daily bread."

Captain Singleton also experiences slavery. In the opening pages of the book, he is kidnapped and sold as a child, and goes to sea only to be captured as the ship returned from fishing near Newfoundland by Algerine pirates in about 1695. The kidnapping, near Islington, was of Singleton aged about two, and as a result of this "hellish trade" he was sold "to a beggar woman that wanted a pretty little child to set out her case" and then to a gypsy woman who was eventually hanged as a criminal.

The speculative geography of *Robinson Crusoe* corresponds with practices of utopian writing, as also seen in Haywood's *Memoirs of a Certain Island, Adjacent to the Kingdom of Utopia* (1724–5). Drawing also on an established pattern of describing the consequences of shipwrecks and the nature of discovery, *Robinson Crusoe* also entails, and possibly deliberately so, the idea of a life and society that could exist outside the constraints and ideology of inheritance, not least among them all those problems of being a second son. Although Crusoe is shown more generally as using gift-giving as part of a *sociability* that is not that of economic individualism[17]—the island, nevertheless, is the republic of a solitary. Yet, far from this being some sort of Whig dream and obviously referring to recent

17 As argued in R. Braverman, *Plots and Counterplots: Sexual Politics and the Body Politic in English Literature 1660–1730* (Cambridge, 1994).

British politics,[18] there was in Crusoe a monarch at once absolute, utopian, moral, and a clear fiction.

On the island, in effect one exiled as a punishment for sin, Crusoe is a hard-working solitary for years, providing the basis for Defoe's version of a Puritan spiritual autobiography, and then to his surprise with the finding of, and by, Friday, he becomes a master. Initially, he sees the latter role in conventional terms:

> I fancied myself able to manage one, nay two or three savages, if I had them, so as to make them entirely slaves to me, to do whatever I should direct them, and to prevent their being able at any time to do me any hurt. It was a great while that I pleased myself with this affair.

In the event, Friday is saved from the prospect of death by Crusoe's direct intervention, which leads to his killing a "savage." Although Defoe is careful in this context not to present Crusoe as being a redeemer, he very much depicts him as a religious teacher, not least in moving Friday clearly away from cannibalism.[19] Crusoe is the Dissenter in a utopia where there is no clergy. Indeed, in a key, almost ironical, instance of the universal message of Christianity, one that is specifically used to criticize Roman Catholicism, Defoe explains to Friday that Christ has been sent "to redeem us," a universal point, but then criticizes the native worship of Benamuckee:

> By this I observed that there is priestcraft even amongst the most blinded ignorant pagans in the world; and the policy of making a secret religion, in order to preserve the veneration of the people to the clergy, is not only to be found in the Roman, but perhaps among all religions in the world, even among the most brutish and barbarous savages.

Slavery is not merely mentioned in *Robinson Crusoe*, although with its setting largely outside England, this remains the novel in which it is discussed or

18 D. Yu, "Sociality and Good-Faith Economy in Daniel Defoe's *Robinson Crusoe*," in *Eighteenth-Century Fiction* 30 (2017–18): pp. 153–173.

19 C. Flynn, *The Body in Swift and Defoe* (Cambridge, 1990).

referred to at greatest length. The concern in several of the novels with criminal behavior, for which transportation to British colonies was a penalty, ensured that slavery was also considered in that context, and therefore not in one that involved racial issues. Moll Flanders discusses with her arrested highwayman husband his willingness to be hanged rather than submit to transportation:

> I blamed him on two accounts; first, because if he was transported, there might be an hundred ways for him that was a gentleman, and a bold enterprising man, to find his way back again.... [H]e had a kind of horror upon his mind at his being sent over to the plantations, as Romans sent condemned slaves to work in the mines ... as likely to repent sincerely in the last fortnight of his life, under the pressures and agonies of a jail and the condemned hole, as he would ever be in the woods and wildernesses of America.

Far less attention is devoted by Defoe to the "Negro man-servant" whom Moll and her husband buy in Virginia, which is, with the "English woman-servant" who is bought, "things absolutely necessary for all people that pretended to settle in that country."

Mortified at having robbed a poor old woman in London, Colonel Jack refers to how, as a consequence, she in effect "was a slave at near three-score," slavery being a result of poverty. This indeed is a key moment in his redemption. Jack subsequently is inveigled into a ship bound for Virginia and thus sold by the captain into servitude. This leads to a moral reflection about enslavement: "... I was brought into this miserable condition of a slave by some strange directing power, as a punishment for the wickedness of my younger years."

In turn, Jack becomes a slave-overseer for his owner and manages the slaves with "kindness and courtesy," thus improving their attitudes. This enables Defoe to offer an account of government from the perspective of the plantation. In what is an implicit critique of the Hobbesian approach, mercy rather than fear is seen as a key element, Jack seeks:

> "to try whether as Negroes have all the other faculties of reasonable creatures, they had not also some sense of kindness,

> some principles of natural generosity, which in short, is the foundation of gratitude; for gratitude is the product of generous principles.

The language used, however, would not meet modern views. Shown mercy, Mouchat thanks Jack, crying "like a child that had been corrected," and Jack tells him:

> you see the white men can show mercy: Now you must tell all the Negroes what has been reported of them; that they regard nothing but the whip; that if they are used gently, they are the worse, not the better; and that this is the reason, why the white man shows them no mercy; and convince them that they would be much better treated, and used kindlier if they would show themselves as grateful, for kind usage, as humble after torment, and see if you can work on them.

Mouchat promises accordingly. This dependence scarcely accords with modern assumptions, nor, indeed, to the extent of creolization in parts of the Americas,[20] but was crucially important to the situation in the British colonies.

Although it was not a Dissenter colony as were those in New England, Defoe was particularly interested in Virginia and had a number of sources on this colony, including probably a 1693 report in the Royal Society's *Philosophical Transactions*.[21] As he correctly pointed out, the Chesapeake plantations were less "cruel and barbarous" than those in the West Indies, which in part was due to the less physically onerous character of tobacco cultivation compared to those of sugar and rice, but also reflected differences in care. This contrast, indeed, translated into better life-expectancy. Defoe underlines the point, for the section is written as if for a pamphlet, although looked at differently his pamphlets conversely included elements of novel-writing:

20 L.M. Rupert, *Creolization and Contraband: Curaçao in the Early Modern Atlantic World* (Athens, Georgia, 2012).

21 I. Vickers, "A Source for Moll Flanders's Experience in Virginia," in *British Journal for Eighteenth-Century Studies* 8 (1985): pp. 191–4.

> I have dwelt the longer upon it, that if possible posterity might be persuaded to try gentler methods with those miserable creatures, and to use them with humanity; assuring them, that if they did so, adding the common prudence that every particular case, would direct them to for itself, the Negroes would do their work faithfully, and cheerfully.... [I]n our plantation, they were used like men, in the other like dogs.

However, bar the idea of salvation through Christ being open to all, it may be doubted how many readers would have agreed, "How much is the life of a slave in Virginia, to be preferred to that of the most prosperous thief in the world."

Crusoe was not the only one in Defoe's novels to pursue wealth in distant waters. In contrast to the mundane reality (although not when the novel was set) of a Carolina ship taking rice to the Chesapeake in *Moll Flanders*, Colonel Jack assembles in New England and New York a cargo of British cloth and linen that he intends to sell in the Caribbean where, indeed, he sells it to Spanish merchants in Cuba. This leads him to dream of profit:

> I that had a door open, as I thought to immense treasure, that had found the way to have a stream of the golden rivers of Mexico flow into my plantation of Virginia.... I dreamed of nothing but millions and hundreds of thousands.

In the event, Spanish frigates intervene and he loses his ship and all his cargo, as would indeed have been the case had one acted.

War with Spain in 1718–20 saw a marked upsurge in press reports of privateering, as did confrontation with Sweden.[22] Defoe's readers would have expected to read of privateers. At the same time, allies could also take British merchantmen, as did the French, allied against Spain in 1718–20, in 1719 with a Bristol ship, the *Amazon*, on the West African coast.[23] Yet,

22 *Whitehall Evening Post*, 18, 22, 27 Nov., *Post Boy*, 20 Nov., *St James's Evening Post*, 27 Nov. 1718.

23 James Craggs, Secretary of State for the Southern Department, to Stair, envoy in Paris, 26 Feb. 1719, NAS. GD. 135/141/19A.

through diplomacy, force, intimidation, and law, the government sought to control, if not end, piracy and privateering, and, in doing so to reinterpret past actions within a system and practice based on notions of law, right, and sovereignty, overcoming earlier breaches of that order.[24] Defoe's early maritime interests, and his later commitment to national commercial strength, meant an involvement in this process, often dramatized in his novels by the fate of fictional characters.

Unlike Smollett later, Defoe had never himself visited the transoceanic world. Indeed, Defoe's engagement with it was in part through novels and other writing, as well as trade, a matter of planning improvement, both that of Britain and also of the indentured servants who were sent there—the majority of British immigrants coming to America. To Defoe, they could become better individually and also capable of creating value, in short, of the moral capitalism that was so important to his prospectus. The use of capitalism in this context was, and is, intended to suggest the value and values involved in moral growth. More specifically, Defoe—who had invested in indentures in a cargo he sent to America in 1688—was also making sense of the Transportation Act of 1718 in terms of explaining potential. In discussing this, the pliability of human nature in the face of discipline and admonition, a merciful control comes to the fore, and (for there is no but) Defoe gives this a religious characteristic.

Published on 25 April 1719, and part of a more general literature of traveller narrative accounts,[25] *Robinson Crusoe* is written against the background of the developing conflict with Spain, whose fleet had been attacked and heavily defeated off Sicily the previous August, the most spectacular victory since that in 1588 against the Spanish Armada. This war was invested with the ceremonial of publicity. The 27 December 1718 report from Malling in Kent, published in the *St James's Evening Post* on the 30th as a demonstration of support, reports:

> This afternoon the bailiff of this town, attended by a number of loyal gentlemen, mounted on horseback with their swords

24 M. Norton, "Temporality, Isolation and Violence in the Early Modern English Maritime World," in *Eighteenth-Century Studies* 48 (2014): p. 38.

25 A. Blaim, *Robinson Crusoe and His Doubles: The English Robinsonade of the Eighteenth Century* (Frankfurt, 2016).

> drawn, read His Majesty's declaration of war against Spain, and afterwards proceeded to the Crown Tavern, where a noble bowl of punch was provided to His Majesty's health, success to the war and the present ministers.

Defoe's sequel, *The Farther Adventures of Robinson Crusoe* (1719), an exploitation-work, never had the same attention. In it, Crusoe revisits his island and travels to Madagascar, South-East Asia, China, returning to London via Siberia and Archangel. The third book was *Serious Reflections During the Life and Surprising Adventures of Robinson Crusoe: With his Vision of the Angelick World* (1720), in which, as in the *Farther Adventures*, the conflict with Spain surprisingly does not play a role.

Like *Farther Adventures*, *Captain Singleton* (1720), a piracy narrative, exceeds the span of British politics, as Singleton travels extraordinarily widely, including across Africa as well as round the Indian Ocean. The novel shows Defoe's ability to construct accounts of the outer world, as well as engage with what was readily known—notably about Madagascar-based piracy. Defoe himself may have written *A General History of the Robberies and Murders of the Most Notorious Pyrates* (1724), a commercially-successful work, although this attribution has been contested.[26] The assumptions of *Captain Singleton* were well-established, notably in terms of the value of European reason and weaponry. As so often occurs with Defoe, the protagonist moves from sin to improvement, in this case in particular turning his back on piracy and suicide, the latter representing the "Devil's Notion." The world depicted is differently imaginative to that in *Robinson Crusoe*, and the adventure dynamic unfolds in a markedly contrasting fashion—that of rapid movement—but the two novels each demonstrate Defoe's ability to write with great energy.

26 A. Bialuschewski, *Daniel Defoe, Nathaniel Mist, and the "General History of the Pyrates," Papers of the Bibliographical Society of America* 98 (2004): pp. 21–38.

12. Conclusions

On 30 May 1723, the *Weekly Courant* of Nottingham carried a London report of five days earlier:

> For several nights last week, a bird was heard to sing in the Dissenters Burying Ground in Bunhill Fields; it began at 11, and continued its song for most of the night. This drew a great concourse of people that way; and some of the old women would needs have it the spirit of a female child that was found there a few days before, supposed to have been murdered. On Thursday it ceased its note, and the old women in the neighbourhood being assembled, according to custom, were puzzled to assign a cause for the loss of their feathered songster, one of more age and gravity than the rest, declared she thought he had absented on account of Mr Layer being to be hanged next day.

Christopher Layer, a Jacobite, was executed at Tyburn on 17 May for his role in the Atterbury Plot. In a very different context to the newspaper report, there is an engagement with the ability of birds to think in Defoe's *Tour*, with the added thoughtful discussion, under Southwold, of bird migration. This is as part of a more general interest on the part of Defoe in resemblances between humans and animals.[1] As later with Sir Arthur Conan Doyle's strong interest in Spiritualism, the contradictions of Defoe's lifetime are not such that they should be reduced to some simplistic account, whether or not pertaining to modernization.

While his extensive poetry, which was important to his oeuvre in 1701–

1 S.H. Gregg, "Swallows and Hounds: Defoe's Thinking Animals," in *Digital Defoe: Studies in Defoe and His Contemporaries* 5 (2013).

6,[2] does not put personality to the fore but instead offered essays in verse—for the descriptive immediacy in Defoe's novels is usually that of personality and plot, and not of setting. The latter, even in London, is generally etched with economy and, in contrast, only really offered at great length in *Robinson Crusoe.* And only then this occurs in order to provide a counterpart to the protagonist when there is no other character, and so as to describe the challenge of what could be a real utopia, in the sense of a land that makes redemption possible. Crusoe's island was also part of Defoe's careful use of fiction to offer an apparent fact and, in doing so, as in *A New Voyage round the World,* to suggest further truths, as of an hitherto unknown southern continent.[3]

Yet, whatever the setting, there was a major role for contingency in Defoe's novels. The rapid shifts in fate for Defoe's characters matched at an exaggerated rate the contingencies that affect his own life and that of the country. George Bubb MP, a rising politician and envoy in Madrid, comments on the execution of Jacobites:

> a little common sense with a good deal of vigour and resolution goes a great way in the world; and without the two last, all schemes of public and private life are merely imaginary and never can be reduced into practice with a good grace.[4]

Contingencies could be linked, as seen for example by Defoe, who generally underplays recent history in his *Tour,* but nevertheless, includes a discussion of Monmouth's total failure in 1685 when he tried to mount a surprise attack at Sedgemoor:

> had he not, either by way of prevention, and accordingly marched out of the town in the dead of the night to attack

2 J.P. Hunter, "Defoe and poetic tradition," in J. Richetti (ed.), *The Cambridge Companion to Daniel Defoe* (Cambridge, 2008), pp. 216–36; A. Mueller, *A Critical Study of Daniel Defoe's Verse. Recovering the Neglected Corpus of his Poetic Work* (Lewiston, 2010).

3 M. Lincoln, "Tales of Wonder 1650–1750," in *British Journal for Eighteenth-Century Studies* 27 (2004): pp. 227–30.

4 Bubb to Stair, 30 Mar. 1716, NAS. GD. 135/141/6.

> them, and had he not, either by the treachery, or mistake of his guides, been brought to an unpassable ditch, where he could not get over, in the interval of which, the King's troops took the alarm, by the firing a pistol among the Duke's men, whether, also, by accident, or treachery, was not known; I say, had not those accidents, and his own fate, conspired to his defeat, he had certainly cut the Lord Feversham's army all to pieces; but by these circumstances, he was brought to a battle on unequal terms, and defeated.[5]

There is no evidence to support such a sense of certainty, but it captures Defoe's attempt, alongside the inherent interest of the exploration,[6] to add drama to his *Tour* and also contributes to the resulting national account.

At the same time, for all categories of Defoe's writing, there is a sense of contingencies being not a matter of chance and occasion of drama, but also reflecting the moral economy of a divinely-ordained world. This was one in which all were tested and their responses, particularly in terms of acceptance, fortitude, and redemption, play a key role. Pressing against the constraints involved Defoe as writer—and, very differently, some of his characters—in contradiction, not least between the 'should be', the 'am,' and the (self-)delusion. There is, however, no formulaic approach to what were often improvised responses, as self-interest was pursued in the case of grasping opportunities.

Due to divine purpose, contingency plays out in a context of a true fixedness and fairness, a context framed by Providence. This theme was likewise central in national identity, with Defoe presenting a far more general stance, and was to be enacted in Handel's oratorios as he compared England with Old Testament Israel. Indeed, nationalism was the product, history, and record of struggle—collective and individual—as well as its defence. Defoe provides particular accounts of this struggle, both in foreign seas and lands, and at home.

5 *Tour*, 4. Feversham was the Royal Commander.

6 E. Peraldo, "Narrative Cartography in the Eighteenth Century: Defoe's Exploration of Great Britain in *The Tour*," in J. Tivers and T. Rakić (eds.), *Narratives of Travels and Tourism* (Aldershot, 2012), pp. 97–108.

This struggle had a moral character that is difficult to capture today. There was struggle against vice, both international and domestic, political and religious. This theme linked moralists who had very different political prospectuses, and also captured the moral obligations of statehood. Liberty and religion seemed to be dependent upon the moral calibre of the people, and this calibre was threatened by the subversion encouraged by poor governance. Each achievement was no more than a stage upon the road, as nationhood had to be defended, and not least of all if the country wished to be ensured the support of Providence.

This defensiveness accorded with the belief that Anglo-Saxon liberties had been overthrown by the Norman Conquest, an approach clearly taken by Defoe—for example, in his account of the New Forest in Hampshire, one given greater thrust by being immediately located after the continuity represented by the discussion of Stonehenge and nearby prehistoric barrows:

> This waste and wild part of the country was, as some record, laid open, and waste for a forest, and for game, by that violent tyrant William the Conqueror, and for which purpose he unpeopled the country, pulled down the houses, and which was worse, the churches of several parishes or towns, and abundance of villages, turning the poor people out of their habitations and possessions, and laying all open for his deer.[7]

To Defoe, improving the New Forest might be presented as righting an historical wrong.

A patriotic sense of national uniqueness can be seen in Defoe's work. At the same time, and linked to this, there is a utopian character that echoes a seventeenth-century interest in often radical change, an interest that was particularly prominent in the 1650s and the 1690s and associated in part with Dissenters, and by their critics. The political resonances of Defoe's work could be complex because the previous sentence might suggest a Whiggishness on his part, but there was also a "Country" dimension to his views. This, moreover, as Harley eventually did in his career, looked to a

7 *Tour*, 3.

particular type of Toryism. This element led in the *Tour* to Defoe's depiction of an opposition to the financial interest that would have done credit to Swift, who was far more conventional in the depiction of Tory social themes than writers expressing "Country" themes. Having attacked stock-speculation and implausibly argued that it helped draw "many thousands of families" to live in London, and therefore made the city disproportionately large, Defoe offers a prospectus:

> … if peace continues, and the public affairs continue in honest and upright management, there is a time coming, at least the nation hopes for it, when the public debts being reduced and paid off, the funds or taxes on which they are established, may cease, and so fifty or sixty millions of the stocks, which are now the solid bottom of the South Sea Company, East India Company, Bank [of England] etc will cease, and be no more … by which the reason of this conflux of people being removed, they will … return again to their country seats … this overgrown city … in time, 'tis to be hoped, all our taxes may cease, and the ordinary revenue may, as it always used to do, again supply the ordinary expense of the government.[8]

This, of course, has never happened. Defoe's subsequent comments on the now, in his eyes, benign relationship between Court and City [of London] were optimistic. At any event, the idea of the future could reflect a commitment to forthcoming improvement that, in practice, was largely lacking in the politics of Whig government in the 1720s, or, indeed, even viable. Under Walpole, there was a reaction by government against the policies and attitudes of the Stanhope-Sunderland ministry. In practice, Defoe settled over finance for a functionality, at least in this case, which matched Walpole's objectives and a transactional approach to government. Indeed, there was a contrast between "King William's time" when there was a financial crisis for the government that Defoe viewed with concern, and the present situation, one in which the financial interest that Defoe had shortly prior castigated in the *Tour*, nevertheless emerges with much praise:

8 *Tour*, 5.

> By this great article of public credit, all the king's business is done with cheerfulness, provisions are now brought to victual the fleets without difficulty, and at reasonable rates. The several yards where the ships are built and fitted out, are currently paid: the magazines of military and naval stores kept full: in a word, by this very article of public credit, of which the Parliament is the foundation (and the city, are the architectures or builders) all those great things are now done with ease, which, in the former reigns, went on heavily, and were brought about with the utmost difficulty.[9]

There is subsequent praise for the Bank of England. Consistency is not always to the fore for Defoe, but that is not surprising; first, given the very different directions of the period, rather than one clear pulse of supposedly Whiggish modernization; and, secondly, given the contrasting tendencies of the latter and the kaleidoscopic impact of divisions and events.

So also in the next letter of the *Tour* in which there is an account of Tring, where Henry Guy (1631–1710), the Secretary of the Treasury, was interested in enclosure, although for aesthetic not economic reasons. Defoe is even-handed, or, if anything, he sympathized with the poor as he would not have done, at least to the same extent, had agricultural improvement been the leading goal of the enclosure:

> There was an eminent contest here between Mr Guy, and the poor of the parish, about his enclosing part of the common to make him a park; Mr Guy presuming upon his power, set up his pales [fences], and took in a large parcel of open land, called Wigginton-Common; the cottagers and farmers opposed it, by their complaints a great while; but finding he went on with his work, and resolved to do it, they rose upon him, pulled down his banks, and forced up his pales, and carried away the wood, or set it on a heap and burnt it; and this they did several times, till he was obliged to desist. After some time, he began again, offering to treat with the people, and to give them any equivalent

9 *Tour*, 5.

> for it. But that not being satisfactory, they mobbed him again. How they accommodated it at last, I know not: I mention this as an instance of the popular claim in England; which we call right of commonage, which the poor take to be as much their property, as a rich man's land is his own.[10]

Defoe was keen in this and other instances on the idea of liberty as a particularly British, more specifically English, characteristic: "a nation who have the greatest privileges, and enjoy the most liberty of any people in the world."[11] This claim, which obviously, and typically, ignores slaves, also reflects the aftermath of the "Glorious Revolution" that permitted a new context and perspective for the judgment of events, trends, and risks. In contrast, Defoe was not particularly interested in medieval struggles against royal authority. There is a clear parallel with the focus in the *Tour*, in which he writes:

> My business is not the situation or a mere geographical description of it; I have nothing to do with the longitude of places, the antiquities of towns, corporation buildings, charters etc., but to give you a view of the whole in its present state, as also of the commerce, curiosities and customs, according to my title.[12]

The emphasis is very much on towns—and, if there are none "of note,"[13] this means that an area is of scant interest. Defoe deliberately avoids visiting Hadrian's Wall, as "antiquity" is not his "business" in the *Tour*. More generally, this affects his treatment of Northumberland,[14] and also his concern with offering what in effect is a map of Britain,[15] which presents the past and offers a prospectus for the future.

Yet, one of Defoe's strengths is his ability to reflect on what he is doing,

10 *Tour*, 6.
11 *Tour*, introduction to volume 3.
12 *Tour*, 8.
13 *Tour*, 9.
14 *Tour*, 9.
15 C. Parkes, "'A true survey of the ground': Defoe's Tour and the rise of thematic cartography," in *Philological Quarterly* 74 (1995).

and that helps provide the authorial voice that links Defoe as writer of fact to the more generally developing style of the novelist. As an instance of an inherently contrarian character that extends to the many voices of the author as describer,[16] letter nine of the *Tour*—that regarding the North-East of England—in effect closes with a rejection of the content and tone set hitherto, one indeed that contrasted with what is seen hitherto in that very chapter:

> I cannot but say, that since I entered upon the view of these northern counties, I have many times repented that I so early resolved to decline the delightful view of antiquity, here being so great and so surprising a variety, and every day more and more discovered; and abundance since the tour which the learned Mr Cambden made this way, for as the trophies, the buildings, the religious as well as military remains, as well of the Britains [sic], as of the Romans, Saxons, and Normans, are but, as we may say, like wounds hastily healed up, the callous spread over them being removed, they appear presently; and though the earth, which naturally eats into the strongest stones, metals, or whatever substance, simple or compound, is or can be by art or nature prepared to endure it, has defaced the surface, the figures and inscriptions upon most of these things, yet ... the venerable face of antiquity has some thing so pleasing, so surprising, so satisfactory in it, especially to those who have with any attention read the histories of passed ages, that I know nothing renders travelling more pleasant and more agreeable. But I have condemned myself (unhappily) to silence upon this head.

Defoe then said he would remedy this on a future tour, and while he certainly had time to produce another fictional one, he was not to do so, and no later writer offered his combination of energy and vision.

With Defoe, alongside the details of change in the present came a sense

16 E.A. James, *Daniel Defoe's Many Voices: A Rhetorical Study of Prose Style and Literary Method* (Amsterdam, 1972); R.J. Merrett, *Daniel Defoe: Contrarian* (Toronto, 2013).

of a transformation from the Romans and the significant "noble undertakings" they had made. Defoe's reflection was one in which living standards were part of the proposition, more especially with the social background to the liberal capitalism and parliamentary sanction, represented by turnpikes. This was a contrast not only with the Romans, but also with authoritarian empires of Defoe's present time:

> But now the case is altered, labour is dear, wages high, no man works for bread and water now; our labourers do not work in the road, and drink in the brook; so that as rich as we are; it would exhaust the whole nation to build the edifices, the causeways … which the Romans built with very little expense.[17]

As a result, Britain, Defoe argued, needed new responses, and it was those that he offered. This was notably so both in histories of the recently achieved, such as *The History of the Union* (1709), and in his journalism.[18] New responses included his fictional accounts of potential through change—collective and individual—and of how to achieve it. The latter includes how to resist malign counters, from Jacobitism and stockjobbing, to diabolical elements, the sin of despair, and the unwillingness to seek to improve. This was a total future framed as an offer and it was one that Defoe embraced with new literary forms, ranging from the newspaper to the novel.

17 *Tour*, appendix to volume 2.

18 E. Peraldo, *Daniel Defoe et l'ecriture de l'histoire* (Paris, 2010).

Index